BREATH

IN

THE

DARK

Dy:

BREATH IN THE DARK

A Childhood Lost

JANE HERSEY

Matador
9 Priory Business Park,
Wistow Road, Kibworth Beauchamp,
Leicestershire. LE8 0RX
Tel: (+44) 116 279 2299
Fax: (+44) 116 279 2277
Email: books@troubador.co.uk
Web: www.troubador.co.uk/matador

ISBN 978 1780881 652

British Library Cataloguing in Publication Data.
A catalogue record for this book is available from the British Library.

Typeset in 11.5pt Minion Pro by Troubador Publishing Ltd, Leicester, UK
Printed and bound in the UK by TJ International, Padstow, Cornwall

Matador is an imprint of Troubador Publishing Ltd

In memory of my dearest mother Annie Levene

PREFACE

My only expectation in life was to hear my mother breathe. Hence, the title *Breath in the Dark*. This story is told through the voice and thoughts of a traumatised, socially isolated child enduring the stresses and strains of day-to-day life under difficult circumstances. My only sense of self was gained from my body smell and the body smell and behaviour of my mother.

Currently there are approximately 175,000 child carers in the UK known to the authorities. No figures exist for the number of children who do not make themselves known for fear of being parted from their families. These children are usually caring for a lone parent who is suffering; emotional, drug and alcohol related problems, living in poverty. They often lack educational opportunities, are unsupported emotionally and are stressed. In adulthood they are likely to be unemployable and may not have the ability to form and maintain constructive relationships.

CHAPTER 1

Manchester 1959

It was a dark, damp, misty night, inside the bedroom as well as across the city. Please don't let the lights outside that had frightened me and brought me running to the window be fire.

Naked except for an old sodden dress, turning away from the window I shuffled in the dark back to the bed, sniffing and looking around. My heart pounding, my breathing heavy: I was so sure it was the smell of fire. The bedroom, free from any comforting wallpaper and carpets, seemed for the moment to be back to normal.

Settling down on the bed, stroking the plump, still body, watching my mother's face just to make sure she was still breathing, as a six year old, that was all I wanted. Not toys or chocolates or comforts; just to know my mother was still alive was enough.

The urine soaked bed sagging in the middle seemed so comforting now that the panic was over. Pulling the coat that was the only source of warmth over us, I clung onto my world. "*Gehen shloffen meine kinder*, go to sleep my child." She closed her eyes again. I was sucked into the well of the bed, engulfed by her huge breasts and stomach keeping me warm. The night passed slowly, and brought in its wake the cold reality of day. Awakening slowly, I felt hungry and cold, but there was warmth in the smiling face that said, "My little one, what would I do without you?" The panic of the night had disappeared, as it had so many times before. Stretching wearily and pleased to see the daylight, I climbed off the bed.

As I walked towards the bedroom door, panic and fear set in once again. What would be behind the door of the old dilapidated Victorian house? Monsters, ghosts or howling, shrieking faces waiting to bite me and tear me to shreds, my shivering little body could sense them. "*Shama Yisroel Adoinoi Elowhaynoo.*" I shouted these words perhaps three or four times before gently easing the door open. The more times it was repeated, the more likelihood of the monsters shrivelling up and going away, they couldn't survive the sound of the precious Hebrew words.

Now that was out of the way, just double checking that none had survived to creep in and get my mother, the main thing was to go and prepare the fire in the living-room. I crept along the landing, pulling at the bits of broken linoleum with which I would make the fire, making sure there would be enough for another day, then down the stairs with a terrible sense of dread hanging over me, still saying "*Shama Yisroel.*" It was very dark going down the stairs, but the *Shama* would keep any harm away. My mother had taught me the prayer on one of the few occasions when she could open her eyes and face the world. She had been taught it as a child by her Jewish parents, both of whom were now dead.

Approaching the living-room and standing on tiptoe, I tried to reach up to touch the *Mezuzah* on the door, it was so exciting. As soon as the fire was ready, I pushed the couch close up to it, and ran back upstairs to try to coax my mother out of bed.

The damp was not so noticeable now, there was a warm

glow, the melting linoleum was burning blue and orange, there were more pieces in the corner to keep it alight. I sat and began to watch the melting droplets.

"Come downstairs, Mummy. The fire's really nice for you. Try to come downstairs, I'll take care of you."

Jumping up, I ran out of the room and up the stairs into the bedroom. I began touching her arm to wake her up. It was an effort to pull her out of the sunken bed. She sat on the side of the mattress and wrapped the coat around herself for warmth, still wearing the dress she had slept in and lived in for as long as I could remember. Looking dishevelled and lost, she followed me downstairs. I knew she was doing it for my sake.

Lying in her place on the couch, she said, "Let me *shloff*, Hikey, be a good girl," then fell asleep again. I picked up two or three pieces of linoleum and put them on the fire. I began to look around the room. Perhaps I could find some sweets or something, so long as it was food. There was nothing, so I took my place on the floor beside the couch. Today was Sunday, so there was little chance of finding anything. Perhaps there was something, maybe in the bedroom a penny might have dropped out when we had covered ourselves with my mother's coat. She was asleep, now I could go and have a look.

I opened the living-room door with the same ritual, closing it quickly behind me to make sure I didn't let too much heat escape from the room. It was very precious, so I tried to retain it for as long as possible, then I went up the stairs, where it was still very dark, holding the banister rail, reciting the *Shama* over and over again, not giving those horrible monsters a chance to spring out of either of the doors to get me. Into the bedroom, checking over my shoulder, all the time looking around, even under the bed, there was only the mattress reaching to the floor. On my knees I searched about the room, feeling under the ripped linoleum. There was nothing. My mother was still asleep as I quickly returned to the living-room. I was praying that she would not wake up, wanting and needing to be fed, praying that she would not feel the hunger in her sleep.

Once again sitting beside the couch, feeling the heat of the fire, my eyes fixed on the little black droplets falling over the grate. I listened to each breath my mother took, petrified even at that tender age that her breathing would stop. The hours were passing by, it began to get dark outside. I stayed at her side for the rest of the day, watching the fire, listening, protecting her from all the monsters and ghosts in the house, praying for the morning to come.

My mother awoke, desperately wanting a cigarette, begging me to find one. I looked in every nook and cranny, at last finding a cigarette end. She watched my every move. "*Gott sei dank,* thank God, don't lose it, Hikey." It was getting dark now, the fire was dimming for lack of material. I lit the cigarette until it glowed red. I heard her say, "Watch my little one," and saw her making patterns in the darkness, it was something she did that always made us laugh. Then she fell asleep again. The darkness closed in, and my ears became like radar in the pitch blackness. I listened for all those monsters, willing them to stay away, begging them to leave us in peace. I even looked up the chimney, just to make sure there were no monsters' legs edging down, trying to get in.

Keeping very quiet, so that if a fire broke out I would be able to hear the crackling wood, I kept smelling for smoke: how would I get her out of the house? I was trying hard to plan it all out. If I kept sniffing, I would smell the fire as soon as it started. I mustn't allow myself to fall asleep, just in case. It was getting colder and damper, the hunger and stench were like familiar friends to me. Planning an evacuation in my mind until I knew it by heart, would keep me awake.

Daylight came very slowly, the darkness lingering on. Stretching out on the floor, I began shaking my mother's arm, trying to waken her. "Come on, Mummy, wake up. The Post Office will be open soon. Come on Mummy."

Today was Monday. Today we would have food. I could go to the doctor's surgery to try to get him to give my mother some tablets that would bring her back to life, perhaps for a day. Pulling her arm, I helped her to sit up on the couch, straightening the dress she had slept in, helping her to put on the coat that had served as a blanket during the night.

"Get my handbag Hikey, make sure my National Assistance book is in it."

We didn't have to walk down to the National Assistance offices to get the money any more now that they had sent us a book, we just had to take it to the Post Office.

"I'll carry your bag, Mummy," I said, when we were ready to go, running to the front door. Walking out of the house into the daylight, I was jumping up and down, swinging the bag about, happy as could be because my mummy was taking me out. I loved it. It was still very cold and drizzly outside. I didn't care. I was playing hide-and-seek in her coat, tripping over her feet and laughing.

We walked up Johnson Street to the Post Office at the top. This area of Manchester, just off Cheetham Hill Road, was very run down. It was part of what was then the Jewish Community. Inside the Post Office we joined the queue of people waiting for money. I asked about the old woman in front of us with black numbers printed on her arm. My mother told me that she had been in the concentration camps, that her expression was always one of anguish. She always carried a pair of baby's bootees with her. She wasn't alone, I was told: there were others. I stood closer to my mother and watched very carefully as the book was handed over the counter, checked, and then passed back with the money. My mother placed it in her bag. It would take away the panic and hunger for a while.

"The Levys had burning *shmattes* put through their letter box, and Halpern the butcher. Fascist *momzers*," I overheard an old lady say. My heart was pounding so fast I gasped for air.

Outside the Post Office, my mother gave me some money.

"I'm going home, Hikey. Will you get the shopping?"

"Yes Mum." I walked towards the nearest delicatessen, the shopping list imprinted on my mind… chopped liver, chopped herring, bagels, and much more.

At last the bags were full of food, now for some cigarettes. If she woke in the night crying for one, I wouldn't have to panic. Then on the way home a bottle of 'pop'. Walking home as fast as possible, swinging the bags to and fro and singing to myself, I felt very excited as I anticipated the taste of the food.

The house drew nearer, the front door was in sight. It was good to be home, especially with all the food. My mother was lying on the couch, hands outstretched, waiting for the chopped liver. Ripping the paper, she scrabbled the liver out with her fingers. We were both grabbing at the food, oblivious to everything else, not stopping until we were so full that it was hard to move. These were moments to savour, and would become rare in the course of the week.

Monday was also the day to try to get some 'Purple Hearts' from the doctor's surgery. The name was familiar to me: they somehow breathed life into my mother, they had become part of my life as well. Any amount would do. If I went home without them, there would be crying and shouting, followed by more sleeping and silence, more misery. As I left the house and walked down to the surgery, my heart was thumping: "Please doctor," I pleaded to myself, the agony almost unbearable.

At the surgery, the receptionist handed me a small piece of card with a number on it. "Take a seat. You will be called later."

The waiting was terrible, time was passing so slowly. Eventually, my number was called out: "The doctor will see you now."

I walked down the corridor to the doctor's room at the end.

"Come in!"

"Please Doctor, can I have some Purple Hearts for my Mum, Mrs Levene?" I asked, standing at the open door.

Without lifting his head, he replied, "No."

My heart started thumping harder than before. I knew his mother could have all the tablets she wanted, without even asking, and that made me feel very sad. "When I grow up, I'm going to be a doctor, then I won't have to ask anybody for them," I told myself.

Arriving home, I found my mum lying surrounded by piles of half eaten food, snoring away contentedly. My place was sitting on the floor beside her, playing with the leftover food, pretending to be a shopkeeper, protecting it as if it were buried treasure, wanting the scraps to last forever.

Later in the day my mother was still asleep. I took some money out of her bag, and set off to buy some coal bricks. The coal yard was a long way down Rochdale Road, but it was possible to buy broken bricks there a lot cheaper than anywhere else.

Everything would feel warm now, there would be heat and somewhere to cook for the next few days. Back home, I placed all the broken bricks in the corner near the fire, making sure none was lost or wasted. Taking the small scraps first, I put them on the fire. It was now ready to cook on. It was almost dark now, so it was time to make us some savaloys before the night set in. There was one pan in the house, it stayed in the living-room with us, and doubled as a toilet.

We lived downstairs for the next few days. By Thursday, everything was gone: no money, no heat or food, only panic and fear to get by on.

The months passed and my mother's stays in bed were more prolonged, her sleep deeper. I dared not try to wake her as she would lash out uncontrollably. "Let me *shloff*, don't breathe near me, please get away," she would shout, crying and gasping for breath, convinced that she was dying and begging for someone to help her. "Get off the bed, sit on the floor and don't move."

It felt hard and cold on the floor. I sat rigid, ears pricked just in case she stopped breathing.

"Hikey, go to the doctor's," she pleaded. "I need some tablets."

"I'll go now, Mum. Don't worry."

I set off on my way, my heart was thumping. If only he would give her some of the little purple tablets that enabled her to wake up and be nice. Most of the time the answer was,

"No," but there was always hope, as I sat in the doctor's surgery, moving from chair to chair, getting nearer the doctor's room. Maybe this time he would say, "Yes." Perhaps I could run home with them clutched in my hands, knowing they would make my mother be nice to me. Again, the answer was, "No."

"Please, Doctor, she can't breathe and keeps saying she's going to die."

"Take this prescription home to her. These tablets should help."

To me, they became as precious as the Purple Hearts. I always tried to make sure there were some in the house, even these became rare, and the panic of seeing her wake up so distressed was intolerable.

Life didn't change from one week to the next. Leaving the house to go shopping became more of an ordeal, having to hold on to walls to keep my balance. Having to stamp my feet on the ground to make my heart start beating again, not wanting to die and leave her alone, all these fears were now part of my life. I should be going to school now, and was afraid to be seen on the streets in case I was forced to leave her alone in the house.

Time passed. One morning there was a dreaded knock at the front door, we never had any visitors. It didn't even occur to me that my mum had a family. I felt very sorry for all the other children I saw, assuming that all relatives died before babies were born. The knocking continued. It was a signal to be quiet and huddle together, looking at each other, keeping still.

"Keep very quiet, Hikey. It must be from the school. They mustn't hear us." It meant panic:

"They want to take me away, Mum. We won't open the door." It couldn't be anyone else.

"They're not taking me, even for a day."

"Shush," she said, pulling me towards her on the bed. "Be quiet."

My memories of school were almost non-existent, only the children's faces remained in my mind. Why couldn't they all understand that my mother would die without me?

"Mum, I'm not going to school, ever. I love you."

The knocking stopped, she let me stay in bed with her for the rest of the day. She slept all the time. I tried not to move in case it woke her up. Everything felt safe again.

I awoke the following morning hearing footsteps coming towards the front door. The knocking was here again. I didn't like it. It was frightening. "Mummy." I was crying, shaking her, feeling terrified. We both knew I would have to go and see who it was. Creeping out of the bedroom, I was praying "*Shama Yisroel,*" knowing there was something evil outside the front door, hoping the *Shama* would make it disappear.

"See if you can see who it is out of the bedroom window."

I tiptoed into the bedroom and looked out of the window. I was too small to see anyone immediately below.

"I can't see, Mummy."

I crept out of the bedroom, shaking and very frightened. Descending the stairs, I could see a dark shadow peering through the frosted glass on the front door. Standing on tiptoe, on a wooden box I tried to reach the catch, barely able to grip it. I could hardly see because something inside my head was banging away with the terrible fear that there was one of the dreaded monsters outside.

I gave up the struggle to open the door, turned around and ran back up the stairs. I jumped on to the bed and hid under the coat.

"Someone's coming Mum, what if it's a monster?" The front door creaked open we clung onto each other, listening to the footsteps in the hall downstairs. My heart was thumping. The footsteps became louder, coming up the stairs and along the landing. "Don't turn into a monster, please," I was pleading, peeping out from under the coat. The bedroom door opened. I could see a skirt, the legs were human. "Thank God," I whispered.

"Mrs Levene, I would like you to come downstairs. I would like to talk to you."

My head was reeling.

"Please go away," I whispered. "Don't come back." The woman's voice was insistent, trying to keep my mother's attention. She started telling my mother that she was to go into hospital and I was to go into a children's home. It would be the same one that my brothers were in.

That seemed to jog my memory. My only recollection of my brothers was of us all being in bed with my mother for days on end because there was no food or heat. It all felt too much. I just wanted somebody to shut the woman up, and make her leave my mum alone. She belonged with me, not in hospital. My body was shaking. I pulled the coat off me and stood up on the bed, tripping over my mother. I jumped to the floor, flew down the stairs, managed to open the front door and ran down the street, crying that my mother would die without me. I ran and ran, to get help.

"Stop!" said a voice behind me. I felt my body jolt. A man had stopped me. He took me back up the road to the woman, who was walking to meet me.

"Come on, you must come home with me." She was telling me that an ambulance would call in a few days time to collect my mother, on the same day I would be taken to the children's home.

My mother was still in bed. "Don't worry, Hikey. We'll be alright. Get into bed with me." We both fell asleep.

A few days passed, and the same woman came back for me. I begged to be able to stay until the ambulance had taken my mum away, needing to make sure that they didn't make a mistake and forget to come for her, not being able to bear the thought of her being alone. They let me wait for the ambulance. It felt overpowering as I watched them take her away.

"Goodbye, Mummy. God bless, I'll see you in the morning. I love you." I couldn't stop crying.

"I love you too, Hikey." The ambulance doors closed, and she was driven into the distance.

"Please don't die. Please come back." The tears flooded down my face, as I repeated the words; the car door opened and I got in. Something wanted to make me shout, "Dad, help us." I knew I must have had a father, but didn't know if I was different and there had never been one, not knowing or being able to understand.

My mind went blank, at the same time something inside me was screaming. Who am I? What am I? Who do I belong to now? Who will get food for my mum? What about her breathing tablets? Will they just put her to bed and forget about her? I sobbed.

CHAPTER 2

The journey to the children's home passed very quickly. On the way I asked, "Can I write to my Mummy? Can I do it when we get there, please?"

When we arrived, I was shaking, feeling sick and dizzy not knowing who to cling to.

"Come on, dear. This is where you'll live for a while. Don't worry, you'll soon settle in."

"I want to be sick, my tummy hurts, I want my Mummy." The car had stopped, now my arm was being tugged.

"Mind your head," said the lady, who had been sitting next to me in the car. "Come on, dear!"

We were in the countryside, the home was very big. My eyes and nose were streaming, the tears were uncontrollable. Wiping my eyes so that I could see what was happening, I cried, "I haven't got any paper. Will you give me some so that I can write to my Mum?"

Another lady, wearing a white coat, had walked to the car. She was plump, like my mummy, I kept thinking perhaps if I stare at her face for long enough, she will look like her, as well.

"Your name is Jane, is it?" She asked me in broken English. Instantly I knew that I didn't belong here, not even for a single minute. It was a home for sickly Jewish children. It was my mother who was sickly, not me. I should be taking care of her in hospital.

"You must come with me. My name is Mrs Lichenstein," said the very large woman, pulling me by the arm. "Will you come now?"

We walked towards the huge house. My heart and head felt heavy. I almost tripped over the pet dog. I knew that its mummy needed to be looked after too. I bent down to hug it.

"Stop that now, girl! You must come with me to the bathroom." She grabbed my arm.

"I want my Mummy."

We approached the bathroom, walking through a small room with lots of lights, then to a huge room full of baths, big white ones everywhere. It was all so cold and unreal! All I wanted was just to be sitting near the fire at home with my mummy making sure she was still breathing.

"Come on child!" Mrs Lichenstein was pulling my dress over my head. I lived and slept in the dress, it was like a second skin. "This will have to go in the bin. It smells! We will find you another one."

The bath was filling, and the air was getting hot and steamy. Mrs Lichenstein helped me get into the bath. I just wanted to grab her breasts. I tried hard, she pushed me away.

"Sit down, so I can wash you." She started scrubbing me. My body was shaking, she carried on scrubbing hard. Pulling my head back, she rubbed at my scalp till even the little lice were shaken to death. The brown lather of the Derbac soap falling everywhere, I imagined I could hear the little lice screaming for help. She dragged a metal fine-toothed comb through my hair, discarding all the little bodies in the bin.

"All this hair will have to come off." It felt as if I were having my identity washed off me, my protective film was being destroyed. I desperately wanted to shrivel up and die. Mrs Lichenstein pulled at my arm once again.

"Come on, Jane, we will dry you now." She gave me a dressing gown to put on.

"My name's not Jane, it's Hikey. My Mum will tell you. Let me have my dress back, please," my sobs were getting louder.

"No, we will find you a new dress, a clean one. Come with me." Still pulling my arm, Mrs Lichenstein led me down the corridor towards some stairs. We went up the stairs, and came to a small room. It was full of shelves. "Here let me see if this fits." There were knickers and vests, dresses and cardigans, which she kept holding against my body.

"This will do."

"My Mum won't know me with this on," I told her, pulling away, "I don't want it."

"Put this on, now!"

The clothes felt horrible against my body. I just wanted to pull everything off, and put my own dress on. I knew that was mine, these clothes weren't. Everything smelt the same, like disinfectant. It was the smell of death to me. Nothing smelt real. This place was for nice children, and I couldn't feel part of it. I knew it was false, they were pretending to be nice and clean. I desperately wanted things I knew and loved near me.

"Please send me home," I begged, crying. My lips were bleeding, they were permanently deeply cracked in the middle. It was so painful to cry, but I couldn't prevent myself. Mrs Lichenstein took my hand and led me to the kitchen. Again, the room was huge. My reaction was to cling on to this strange sounding woman. Looking up, I could see that she was making a drink for me.

"This will build you up, just like me." It was raw egg and milk mixed together.

"Your mother will be pleased if you drink this all up." She handed me the glass. "Let go of my dress. Come on, Jane."

"No. My name's Hikey. My Mum will tell you."

"Come on, Jane, and let go of my dress."

"I want to go home to my Mum. Please let me see her."

"Be a good girl. I'll show you where the slide is for the children to play on."

I didn't want to play with them. "I'm staying with you," I told her.

Pulling my arm, she said, "I'm getting very impatient and angry, now. Come on child, or you will have nothing to eat. You will have to go to bed." Her skirt felt so secure, that holding on to it was all that mattered, I couldn't let go.

She grabbed my arm once again. "Come on, now!" she shouted, and led me hurriedly down the corridor and up a flight of stairs. We were heading for the dormitory. I wanted to open the door of each room I passed to see if my mother was waiting for me.

Mrs Lichenstein was very strong, and pulled me with great force so that I couldn't stop to try the door handles. Eventually, we reached the dormitory.

"You will have the egg and milk drink each day. The one I just made, you will have later."

We were standing by a large fire door.

"This is where you will *shloff* with the other children." My heart sank. There were lots of beds all lined up, lots of clean sheets, no coat to cover me and protect me from monsters, no pans to wee in. I couldn't take it all in, and felt exhausted.

"Here are some pyjamas. Put them on, and get into bed."

"*Shama Yisroel*," I said. Taking the pillowcase off the pillow, I placed it over my body. Somehow, that would protect my mother, I had to make sure it didn't drop off, or she might die.

Mrs Lichenstein walked over to the window and closed the curtains. "*Shloffen*," she said, and closed the door behind her. My eyes closed and I fell asleep.

All of a sudden, I could smell fire. My eyes opened. It must have been the middle of the night. I could hear the noise of crackling wood, everything looked orange.

"There's a fire. Help me. We're all going to die." My bed and pyjamas were soaking wet. I was glad because it would stop the fire burning into me. Still crying and secure under the bed, I could see legs and feet running around.

The dormitory door opened, and a voice shouted, "Get into bed, children! Get off the floor, girl!" The nurse sounded very angry, my heart was banging, and I couldn't move.

"Come on girl, get off the floor and be quiet!" She pulled me from under the bed.

"Your bed's soaking wet. We will have to get you a bed change. First you must get washed." There was a small bathroom just off the dormitory. "I'll run the bath, and tell you when to get in."

After the bath, she gave me some clean pyjamas to put on.

"We don't like children that wet themselves. You must make your bed now. I will show you how. You have to make hospital corners. Now get in. You must remember how to make your bed properly. Now go to sleep, like the other children."

I got into bed making sure once more that the pillowcase was over my body. I was shaking and felt panic-stricken. The door was a safer place to be. I could get out quickly if there was a fire. I got out of bed and lay down on the floor. It felt much better here, and I soon found myself feeling drowsy.

"Jane, get off the floor!" Still half asleep, I was being pulled to my bed. "And you will stay there this time, do you hear? You are disturbing all the other children." The nurse left the room. As soon as it was safe I made my way to the door again. It felt so comfortable here, and I soon fell asleep. Again, the nurse came in and took me back to my bed. Each time she did, I would wait and go back to the door as soon as she had left the room.

Eventually the morning arrived, and the nurse turned off the orange dimmer lights that had shone like burning timbers. Night time had always meant panic and fear. I was pleased when daylight arrived.

"Come on, children, make your beds. Has anybody wet themselves? If you have, you know what to do." I didn't want her to see that it had happened to me again.

"Wash and dress for breakfast, children!" she shouted. I wouldn't walk down the stairs with them. They were different.

We were all taken into the dining room. I was shown to my place. On the table, between the knife and fork, was the glass full of raw egg and milk; there were bits floating about in it. First we had to say prayers. They were in Hebrew. Mrs Lichenstein was standing in the corner of the room. When the prayers had finished, she came over. "Drink this up." As I looked round at her, my arm caught the glass, it smashed on the floor. All I could feel was panic. They were trying to make me like the other children. I wanted the food they were eating to take home for my mother. If only I could have the knives and forks, cups and plates to take home for her. Nobody else in the world mattered. If only we had these nice things at home, I could make nice meals for her, sit her at the table, feed her and take care of her. I ran out of the dining room, crying and worrying about her. I would only eat if they gave her back to me.

The nurse followed me and, very angrily, shouted at me:

"You must be good. Go and get dressed with the other children ready to go for a walk in the forest." I just wanted to sit somewhere, listening out to see if my mum was here. The forest had lots of wood in it, and could set on fire easily. I could smell the wood burning and hear the crackling. Running back to the house I shouted, "The forest is on fire. You must get everyone out, quick."

"Sit on the chair," the nurse told me. "There isn't a fire. What is the matter with you?"

"If I burn to death my Mum will be on her own." I was gasping for breath because the air wasn't making my heart work. I stood up, banging my foot on the floor to make it better. "I'm alright now. Please can I write a letter to my Mum?" These feelings were with me all the time. I couldn't understand how the children at the home kept their hearts beating. Trying to remember how to start my heart was hard, and trying to hold on to reality was even harder. I knew what my reality was, and it wasn't theirs.

Then one day the news arrived that my mother was to be sent home soon. Because I was grieving so much and because I was a girl it was decided that it would be better for me to go home as there was no-one else to look after her. The nurse told me that my mum needed to be looked after, but I already knew that.

The evening before I was sent home was so exciting. The

nurse gave me a bag and some clothes to take with me. I was left on my own in the dormitory to pack my things. The bathroom door was open, there was a shelf with bath mats and bath towels.

It would be so nice, I thought to myself, if we had some at home.

When the packing was done, I rushed into the bathroom, and took one of each, stuffing them into the bag quickly. They would make my mother's life more comfortable and the house more colourful. I desperately wanted nice things for her. I had almost completed packing, making sure that the bath mat and towel could not be seen, when the nurse came in, and noticed that the bag was swollen out of all proportion. She was staring but I carried on, not caring. There was some string. I wrapped the bag all over with it, making sure that she couldn't look inside. She was still watching, staring at this cocoon-like object.

"Please don't take my bag away, it's for my Mummy," I whispered to myself. I would soon be back where I belonged, with my mummy. I felt more maternal and more determined than ever to look after her and care for her, having no idea that our roles had been reversed.

CHAPTER 3

I had no idea why my mother had gone into hospital. She was home now, that was all that mattered. My large bundle was in the living-room. It was very hard to open. I tugged and pulled at it until it started to come undone.

"Look Mummy, I've brought you a present," pulling out the bath mat. "Look, Mum." I took it over to the couch, where she was lying in her usual place. It was so exciting.

She stroked my hair. "What would I do without my Hikey?"

I laid the bath mat gently down on the floor, placing it very carefully in front of the fireplace. I stood back and felt very pleased with myself. It looked so much more homely now. I pulled at the bag once again, placing the towel over the back of the couch. They looked so colourful.

We had been told that we could go to the Jewish Board of Guardians on a Sunday morning. They would be open to hand out second-hand clothes and we would also get a food parcel at *Pesach* time (the Passover). Life was feeling much better now.

Lying on the couch in front of the fire, mum was smiling at me. "I need to *shloff* now. I love you, Hikey." The room was so cosy. I was home and nothing would ever take me away again.

Before long, the towel had been used to wipe blood off her legs. I didn't know what it was, or why it was there. From time to time, she would rip off a small piece of towel and place it between her legs, leaving it for days, without being fully awake, doing it almost semi-consciously.

It seemed to take so long for Sunday to come. It couldn't come fast enough. At last it was Sunday morning. The Jewish Board of Guardians was further down Cheetham Hill Road, towards town. My mother told me it was called Frankenburg House. Setting off down the road, I didn't know what to expect. It was nice to be full of anticipation, imagining and daydreaming about what delights were awaiting me.

I soon arrived. It was a corner house, Frankenburg stood out in large letters over the door. Walking through the front door, I saw there were lots of people standing in the hall, waiting patiently. "You may all wait outside the room at the top of the stairs," we were told. "The door will be open soon." It felt very exciting as we all walked up the stairs.

At the top of the stairs, a man unlocked the door to the room. There were tables piled high with old coats, shoes and boxes of dresses on the floor. Looking around, I saw in the corner boxes of cracked plates, broken cups and dented pans. I noticed an old pair of brass candlesticks. I managed to get my hands on them, pulling them to my chest. I smiled to myself. My mum had told me about *Shabbas* candlesticks and that all Jewish families had them. They were now placed firmly under my arm, and nobody was going to take them away from me.

I turned and walked over to the table piled high with old jackets and coats. Pushing my way through all the legs and bodies, I could almost reach one of the tables. There were two jackets hanging off the table, I would have them. I couldn't carry more than two. Looking around to see if there was anything else, I noticed a box with women's underwear in it.

Rummaging through, still holding on to my belongings, I managed to pull out a huge bra, it felt very soft, "That's for my Mum," I told the lady next to me.

As I left the room and walked down the stairs, it was very hard to keep hold of everything. I was feeling very pleased with myself, wishing for the next Sunday to arrive when they would open the doors again.

Once out of the building, I parcelled up my belongings properly on the street outside. There was a second-hand shop at the bottom of Cheetham Hill Road. My mother had taken me there with her once or twice when she had something to sell. It would be nice if I had lots of coats so I could get lots of money for her.

The shop was in sight now. I opened the door pushing my way in. The whole place was piled high with old clothes. Perhaps the shopkeeper would give me half-a-crown.

"Please," I asked the woman behind the counter, "can you give me some money, maybe half-a-crown, for these jackets?"

"I can give you tuppence for them."

"That will do," I answered, dropping the jackets on the floor. The candlesticks were still tucked under my arm and the bra was around my neck. Taking the money before she changed her mind, I made my way to the nearest delicatessen to buy some pickled cucumbers.

Arriving home bursting with excitement, I pushed the door open.

"Mum, look at what I've got." The candlesticks were my favourite.

"Look Mummy, these are for you," I told her, placing them on the mantelpiece. Sitting beside her on the floor, I tried desperately to wake her.

"Let me *shloff*. Be a good girl, be quiet."

It was all too much. I couldn't stop arranging the candlesticks on the mantelpiece. The bath mat was still in front of the fire. The room seemed so much more comfortable now. It was Monday tomorrow. Perhaps the doctor would give me some Purple Hearts. We stayed downstairs that night, it was impossible for me to sleep. I wanted my mum to put on the bra and to notice the candlesticks. There were so many things to tell her about.

The following morning arrived. She was still asleep on the couch, the paper from the pickled cucumbers under her stomach. I longed to be there instead.

"Mummy, I'm going to the doctors. I'll be back soon."

On the way to the surgery I was daydreaming about the doctor giving me a prescription for her. She was so nice when she had her tablets.

I walked into the surgery, collected my number from the receptionist, and took my seat. The wait made me very anxious and I was gasping for breath. I had to stand up just in case my heart stopped. It was easier to start it going again if I stood up. All the numbers were being called out, at last it was my turn. I walked through to the doctor's room, praying hard. Suddenly he shouted, "Please hurry!"

"I'm sorry, Doctor," I said in apology for being so slow.

"Please can I have some Purple Hearts for my Mum, Mrs Levene? And some tablets to help her breathe?"

He started to write out a prescription. Looking at the piece of paper, I saw that he had written eight on it. I grabbed it and ran as quickly as I could to the chemist's shop, then home. It had seemed such a long time since I had been able to run through the front door and shout, "Mummy, I've got them."

She was still on the couch in the living-room. Bending down beside her I said, "Mummy, look. I've got the tablets. Come on, take two. I'll get you some water." I placed the cup of water in her hand, holding her head so that she could swallow the tablets. It was just a question of time now until they took effect.

After what seemed to be ages, she sat up. I had been so afraid that it would never happen again.

"Come here, Hikey." She cuddled me. "You must go to school tomorrow."

"Will you be alright, Mum, if I leave you?"

"Yes, Hikey, will you come with me to see Doris? We'll go later on when I feel a bit better. It's been so long since I've seen her."

I knew that Doris was her sister, but couldn't remember having ever seen her. "We'll go later, Hikey."

It was evening now, and my mother decided that she felt well enough to make the journey. "Come on, Hikey." She opened the front door for me, and we set off walking. "It's not far, we should be there soon."

At the top of the street, we stopped to admire a garden. There were lots of shrubs with flowers all over them. "We'll take some of these flowers for Doris." Just as we had managed to pull some flowers off the overhanging shrub, the front door opened. "Shoo, or I'll call the police! Off you go!" said a plump woman. She was very angry.

"Don't worry, Mum. I'll buy you some when I grow up," I told her, reassuringly.

We were almost at my Auntie Doris's house and my mum was getting very excited. "I hope she's at home. You knock on the door, Hikey."

The door opened. My Auntie Doris stood there, looking very displeased. "What do *you* want, Annie?"

"Can we come in for a while?"

We were taken into the house. I knew we weren't welcome. Once inside, I had to sit on a chair and be quiet. There was no warmth in the visit, and we soon left.

"Why is she so miserable, Mum?" She didn't answer, and we made our way home. My mother was crying. I felt very sorry for her, and very angry with my Auntie Doris.

On the way home, mum wanted to sit down. "I can't go any further. I'm going to wee myself." She squeezed my hand, trying to stop herself, but the water just dripped out.

Suddenly, two youths appeared out of an entry. My mother pulled me to her. "They're blackshirts." We both stood still, hoping they would walk past.

"Are you a dirty Jew?" One of them asked my mother. She didn't answer.

"Dirty Jews, go home," they kept saying. We stayed very still wanting them to go away. They seemed to be walking past us then one of them turned to my mother and pushed her. She fell to the ground.

"Mummy, are you alright?" She looked as if she were dead.

I couldn't help her up, she was too big. "Mummy, are you alright? Please answer me." She started to move and pulling her arm, I managed to get her off the ground.

"What are blackshirts, Mum? Why did they do that?"

"It's alright, Hikey. Don't worry about it."

"If I see them again, I'll hit them," I told her. She was holding my hand now.

"Come on, we'll go home."

We were at the top of Johnson Street now, almost home.

We heard the sound of breaking glass. My mother pulled me to one side to protect me. As we walked round the corner, we saw two boys running off into the distance. The bubblegum machine outside the Post Office had been smashed, all the bubblegum was falling out onto the pavement. My mother rushed up to the machine: holding her dress under it, she managed to save most of the contents.

"We'll take these." We walked to the bottom of the street without losing any of them. "At least we will have something to eat for the rest of the week."

The following day arrived and I was to go to school.

"Come on, Hikey, I'll take you. Here's some bubbly gum to take with you." She had six more tablets left. In terms of her being awake that was a day and a half.

"I'm ready now, Mum. Are we going?"

She left me in the school playground. I was suddenly surrounded.

"That's the Jewish girl," one of the children said.

"Are you any relation to the man who killed Jesus Christ?" was the first question.

"No. How old is he?" I asked, not being able to remember if we knew someone of that name. "I'm sure my Mum wouldn't have done it, but I'll ask her when I get home."

The next question put to me was easier. "Is cabbage kosher?" asked a little boy.

"Why do Jews smell of Salami?" The questions seemed to be never ending, I was glad when the lady rang the bell for us to go into school.

The day was spent wishing for school to end so I could rush home and see my mother awake, panicking in case she needed me. I constantly gasped for air; it was difficult to breathe.

At last it was home time. I rushed home as fast as I could, through the back door into the house. The smell of saveloys cooking greeted me. The pan was on the fire, bubbling away, the little pink saveloys bouncing about. My mother was sitting by the side of the pan, making sure it didn't spill over. We ate them with pickled cucumbers. There were four more tablets for tomorrow. Days like these were to savour and look forward to.

My visits to the Jewish Board of Guardians were also to be cherished. Making the journey in all weathers, there was always the hope that they would be open. It was the most wonderful feeling in the world to see the doors opened, and even better to see the door to the upstairs room being unlocked. Standing in that room, I couldn't fix my eyes on one object. I darted about, looking everywhere, especially in the boxes that were kept near the corner. Sometimes, there were pretty plates and cups. That they were mostly cracked didn't matter.

Occasionally, we would be told that the office downstairs would be open if we needed any money, perhaps sixpence or a shilling. That meant I could go to the delicatessen for a smoked salmon skin or bits of pickled meat that had fallen from the slicing machine: they were always a lot cheaper. It was nice to be able to stand in the shop, waiting in the queue, knowing that I could ask for food and pay for it, instead of just walking past, trying not to get caught in the aroma that lingered outside. If there was no money being handed out, the old jackets always came in handy. They didn't have much worth, but a few jackets always managed to fetch a few pence.

It was almost Passover. A few weeks beforehand I was handed a food voucher. It was to be taken to the local kosher butcher and delicatessen Halpern's and Halbershtad's. At Passover, all the food had to be free from flour (*chometz*), had to be specially produced and had to carry a special seal of approval (a *hechsher*). Before that happened, all the *chometz* in the house had to be thrown away, all the usual pots and pans had to be put away, and special utensils used because of the festival. Of course, the traditions of the festival had no meaning to us, the excitement of the food was all that mattered.

The voucher had written on it the amount we could spend and it was to be left till the week before Passover before it was taken to the shops. I took the order to the delicatessen, and was told that it would be delivered before the weekend. From there, my next stop was the doctor's surgery. I felt so good. If only the doctor would give me some tablets. Life would be wonderful.

Once again, I found myself in the surgery, hoping and praying. My number was in my hand, all that was left was for me to wait. I watched person after person hand in their number and head towards the doctor's little room. If only he will give me some, I kept saying to myself. Finally, my number was shouted out, and I made my way down the corridor.

"Please, Doctor, can I have some tablets for my Mum?" I was practising the words as I stood outside his room and knocked on the door. "Please, Doctor," I was repeating to myself.

"Come in!" the doctor shouted, in his usual loud voice.

"Please, Doctor, can I have some Purple Hearts for my Mum?" I smiled at him, and crossed my fingers behind my back.

"No," was the reply.

Walking back home, I was imagining what the food parcel

would look like. It was the end of the week now and we hadn't eaten for days. I wondered how I could set the food out on plates. We had no table, but it would be a nice party for us both. Everything would be nice. On the order for the delicatessen I had asked for some white *Shabbas* candles to put in the candlesticks on the mantelpiece. That would make everything complete.

My mother was still on the couch, asleep. "Please wake up," I wished under my breath. I longed for her to wake up so that I could tell her that tomorrow the food was going to arrive. She stayed on the couch all night, asleep the whole time, and I took my place beside her on the floor.

When the morning arrived, I pulled back the blackout shutters and sat by the window from the crack of dawn, listening for a car, watching, willing the arrival of the food. I waited for what seemed hours. Perhaps they're not coming, perhaps they've taken it to the wrong house, I kept thinking. It was mid-afternoon when I heard a car door slam outside. I rushed to the window. There was a little van with the back doors open, a young man wearing a *Yamulkeh* was pulling a box out of it. I still wasn't sure, and waited until he started to come up the path before I ran to the door to open it. Struggling hard to reach the catch, I could clearly see the outline of the box through the glass. The door opened and the young man placed the box on the floor just inside the door. "There's another one," he told me. It was too much for me to take in. While he was getting the other box I dragged the one in the hall through to the living-room, and placed it near to the couch. He placed the second box in the hall, and shouted, "Have a good *Yom Tov*!"

"Thank you. Goodbye!" I shouted after him.

Both the boxes were now in place next to the couch. It was hard to stop looking in them. Taking each item one at a time, I managed to place them all over the living-room floor. The first box had lots of *Matzos* in it. I noticed the two white candles. They were wrapped in newspaper, and were almost thrown away.

"Mummy, look what we've got. Come on, Mum, wake up." I tried to shake her gently. "Look, Mum, I've got you some candles." Placing them in the candlesticks, I tried to wake her.

"Mum, please wake up." She started to open her eyes. "Look Mum."

"What's in the boxes?"

"All sorts of food." She was pulling at the boxes wearily.

"Look, I've put everything here on the floor. There's savaloys, salamis, olives, pickled cucumbers. I'll put the food on plates to make a nice party."

But she couldn't wait. She ate and ate, not chewing, or looking at the food, just swallowing and gulping, frenziedly eating what was in her hands and watching what I was taking off the floor at the same time, making sure she was missing nothing.

It wasn't what I had planned for her. It wasn't a party. It wasn't laid out on the plates I had brought for her. We weren't eating it together, enjoying it. I watched, not knowing what to do to keep her awake. I didn't know how to make her want to live. I was almost seven now, and I knew I wasn't enough.

I desperately wanted to fill the place of the people who were missing from her life: I was trying to be mother, father and husband to her. If only I could be all these people, I was thinking to myself.

A few weeks later we were visited by the social worker

who told us that because we were living in a slum clearance area we had been allocated a brand new flat in a high-rise block. She said that the Jewish Benevolent Society would deliver some second-hand furniture for us.

CHAPTER 4

On the day of the move my mother took some Purple Hearts she had been prescribed. We left the house with only the brass *Shabbas* candlesticks and my mother's handbag.

My mother had the letter with the details.

"32 Bracknell Court. It's down Blackley New Road." I clung onto her coat not knowing what to expect. The bus passed a large building, "That's King David the Jewish school, you'll be going there. You're going to the Open Air School first, for a few months, till they have a place for you." My heart started pounding. The bus stopped and we had to walk up a hill to get to the flats. My mother was gasping for breath. "My *boche*, my belly, my back. I need to sit down for a while." We sat on the wall and I squeezed her hand. "I'll look after you Mummy." She smiled at me.

We arrived at the block of flats. "We're on the sixth floor." I looked up. I could smell fire. How could we escape if a fire broke out? How would I get her out of bed or off the couch if I heard the sound of burning wood?

We entered the main door and headed towards the lift. My heart was pounding as the lift door opened. What would we do if we got stuck in it, I wondered? I smiled at her, not wanting her to know how anxious I felt.

Mum opened the front door and we rushed into the flat. The two bedrooms had two beds each. Our bedroom had a sideboard, my brothers' bedroom had a wardrobe. My brothers were away at Delamere. My only memory of them was being huddled together in bed with my mother, in the old house. We would stay in bed for days and play 'I spy', wishing the days away until there was money for food.

"Hikey, come in here, this is the bathroom." I looked through the door. There was a bath, toilet and sink. Then we went into the living-room: it had an old easy chair, a couch and an old sideboard.

"Look, Hikey, we've got an electric fire." She headed towards the small kitchen.

"Look, a stainless steel sink, and a gas cooker. We're the first family to move into the flats. Look at it all, isn't it lovely?"

She sat down on the chair.

"I'm *oitskimatted*, Hikey. I need to go to bed."

"OK, Mum. I'll come with you. I'm *oitskimatted* too"

The following day I awoke thinking about all the things I could buy to make the flat nice for my mother when I started work. My mother told me the address of our new doctor.

"I'm going to get you some tablets, Mum." I stroked her arm. As soon as I left the flat I could hardly breathe, praying she wouldn't die while I was gone.

I didn't go in the lift in case it got stuck. I ran through the door to the stairs and ran all the way down in case there were monsters following me. I thought I could smell fire.

Once out of the building I walked to the bottom of Riverdale Road. I saw a bus stop. I didn't have any money for the bus. I went across to ask where Victoria Avenue was. I was told how to get there, and started walking down Blackley New Road. I was trying hard to breathe, and had to walk near the wall as I was so sure that I would faint. On my way down the long road I saw a bus. On its front was Victoria Avenue. I saw it go all the way up the road and turn right. The buses came about every 25 minutes. I kept looking, following them. I was now on Middleton Road, and noticed a chemist shop. I knew where I could get the prescription made up.

Before long I was at the bottom of the Avenue. All I had to do now was look for the number of the surgery. It was quite a long walk. At last I found the building. It looked huge, totally different from the other surgery. I felt I would be laughed at as soon as I entered the front door. I was afraid they wouldn't let me in. I walked in, relieved that I had found it, mentally begging the doctor to give me some tablets. The medical cards were taken from me. I was told to sit down. There weren't as many people or chairs in the room as there were in the other surgery. I didn't have a card with my number on, and was afraid I would be overlooked.

I waited and waited, then I was told that the doctor would see me. I wanted to run to him and cry that my lips were hurting me and bleeding, that my mummy wasn't well, but I didn't. I asked him if she could have some Purple Hearts. I saw one of his hands move towards his pen and the other towards his prescription pad. I couldn't believe it. He told me he was giving me a prescription for Duraphet tablets: they were almost the same thing. He looked at my lips. As he touched them I was in agony. They were very badly split. He told me he would give me a prescription for a cream called Hydroderm.

He told me to rub it gently over the cracks. I thanked the doctor and left the surgery. I couldn't help but cry. It had taken me such a long time to walk to the surgery; having to stop every now and then and stamp my foot on the ground to start my heart going, had slowed me down. I wanted to start the long trek home so I could get out of the cold and show my mother what I had for her.

I remembered where the chemist was. It was on the way home, I couldn't miss it. Eventually, I reached the shop and stood with the prescription in my hand, desperately waiting for him to take it off me. When it was my turn, I passed it up to him, and saw him walk off. It seemed such a long time. I was looking all around. There were bars of nice smelling soaps, talcum powders and little bath cubes. I was wishing I had the money to buy some to take home to my mother. The chemist came back, and handed me a bag. Holding it with both hands, I started to walk home. The shop was around the corner from Blackley New Road. After a twenty minute walk I was at the front door to the flats.

I ran towards the lift. I could hardly wait to get up to the flat so that I could give my mother the tablets.

"Mum, look what I've got. Please wake up." I gave her a glass of water and helped her to sit up. She managed to swallow the tablets, and fell asleep again. I was sitting on the floor beside her, still holding the white bag. I took out the cream and piled it on my lips. They felt so much better now, and I fell asleep. Later on, my mother was shaking me. "You must go to school. I'll take you." We got the bus to the Open Air School. It was mid-morning. I sobbed when my mother left. The teacher told me to follow her down the corridor. The classrooms had large doors which opened up onto the playground. After we had something to eat and a short period outside we were put to bed and could sleep for a long time.

It was too difficult to leave my mother alone, I couldn't breathe at the thought of leaving the flat or going to school. A letter arrived from King David School to say a place was available. I went to the doctor and he gave me some tablets that made her wake up.

"Come on, Hikey, we must go for your school uniform. We'll go soon when I feel better." We both fell asleep for a while, as we waited for the tablets to take effect.

"Hikey, get my bag and we'll go." She put on her coat and we left the flat. It felt wonderful to leave with her, holding her hand. We walked to the Post Office at the top of Cheetham Hill Road.

"Look, that's the school," my mother pointed out. It made me feel ill when she said that, knowing I would have to leave her on her own. She had only four tablets left, and I felt frightened for her.

We waited in the Post Office for our money. "Come on, Hikey, I don't feel so well. Let's get into town as soon as we can."

"OK, Mum. Don't worry."

We walked across the road to the bus stop. While we were waiting for the bus my mother noticed a television shop.

"Would you like a TV?" Taking my hand she led me to the shop. We looked in the window. There were lots of television sets with little Red Indians on them. "Let's go in." My mother chose a sixpence in the slot model.

"Would you like a little Red Indian to sit on top of the TV?" The assistant asked me.

"Yes, please."

We went back to the bus stop, and waited for the bus. I was standing with my arms around my mother, playing in her coat. She was hugging me. Her legs were wet and she was standing in a small puddle. I looked at her, her cheeks blushing bright red. I didn't know what was causing her to wet herself so often.

"The bus is here, Hikey," she said, taking my hand so we could board it. I could see that she wasn't well.

At last, we were in the town centre. Looking round at all the big shops I couldn't wait till it was time for me to start working.

I was thinking to myself, if only it were possible to buy some of these nice things for her.

"Come on, Hikey, this is our stop," she said, pointing to the big store we were going to. She was still feeling ill, and we went straight to the uniform department. She handed the voucher to the assistant. It read: *one pullover, one skirt, one blouse and one tie.*

It was very exciting getting new clothes. I watched carefully as they were folded and all wrapped up in brown paper. When the package was ready, the assistant handed it over to me and smiled. "Thank you," we both said at the same time.

As we walked down the stairs, we came to the Women's clothing department. Everything smelt brand new. I couldn't help wanting to look around, praying that one day I would be able to buy her all these things.

"Don't worry, Mummy. When I grow up and start work, I'll buy you everything."

"It's alright, Hikey, as long as we're together, you, me, Jeffery and David, that's all I want."

She put her arms around me, and led me out of the store. We headed straight for the bus stop. By now she was feeling very poorly. "If the bus doesn't come soon, I'll have to sit on the pavement." As she said that, I noticed wee dribbling down her leg again. I was very pleased when the bus pulled up. We boarded the bus, sitting as near to the front as possible. She looked dreadful. I wanted to ask somebody to help her.

She sat, half asleep. All I could do was hold her hand. As the bus drove onto Cheetham Hill Road, she took the money out of her purse, and asked me to do the shopping.

"I'll have to go home, Hikey." The bus was getting nearer to the shops now. Making sure I had hold of the money, I started to make my way off the bus.

"See you later, Mum," I shouted as the bus stopped, afraid to leave her.

I didn't waste any time doing the shopping, and soon headed towards the bus stop. It had been such an exciting day that I almost missed my stop; new clothes, a television, and my mother still had some more tablets left. If only she could have them all the time, everything would be different.

The flats were in sight. Gathering all my bags together, I got ready to get off the bus. "Hurry up, bus," I whispered to myself, wanting to make sure she was alright. The bus stopped. As soon as I looked up at the window, I saw my mother was there, smiling and waving. I ran and ran, just wanting to be with her. As I approached the main door of the flats, she was pressing the buzzer to open the door for me. I wanted to be with my mother as soon as possible. I ran into the lift and pushed the button.

I should have gone up the stairs. If the flats catch fire I won't be able to get her out alive, I thought to myself. I could feel my heart stopping. I banged my foot hard on the floor: it worked, my heart started again. "I'll never get in the lift again. Please let me get home to see my Mother," I repeated these words while I stamped my feet. My mother had left the door open, pushing it with my shoulder, I managed to get all the bags inside.

"I'm home, Mum. I've got all the food."

She was sitting on the couch. I ran up to her and hugged her, so pleased that she was awake. It was wonderful to have her company. I sat on the floor beside her and emptied all the food out onto the floor. We were both glad to eat. We stayed on the couch and fell asleep for a while. Later in the day, she awoke.

"Hikey, wake up," she whispered in my ear. "Come on, Hikey, I want to talk to you. You must go to school tomorrow. Go and try your uniform on, and we'll see what it looks like."

Half asleep, I tried to open my eyes. I didn't want to get off the couch. There were such long periods when I could not get near her, when I couldn't rest my head on her warm body.

"Can I stay here with you, Mum?" I said, wanting to stay wrapped around her forever. After about half-an-hour, she persuaded me to put on my uniform.

The skirt was first, it was huge. It hung round my ankles, all the grey pleats were flowing everywhere. I had to hold it up to stop it from falling down: now for the blouse and tie.

"You do look smart."

The jumper was next. It was purple with yellow stripes round the V-neck. It was almost the same length as the skirt. The sleeves seemed to go on forever.

"Don't worry, Hikey, you'll soon grow into it."

The school was at the top of Cheetham Hill Road. My mother had pointed it out to me.

"Will you be alright, Mum, when I go to school?"

"Don't worry, Hikey, I want you to go."

That evening, we were both getting excited about the

television, which was to arrive at the end of the week.

Everything was ready now. My uniform had been laid over the chair, ready for tomorrow. We were both looking at the corner that would be the home for the television. It was getting dark now. We both got into my mother's bed, holding onto each other. Nothing could harm us now. There was no need for the *Shama*.

The morning arrived. My mother was still asleep. Trying not to wake her, I managed to take two tablets out of her bag.

"Come on, Mum, here's your tablets and a cup of water." She started to wake up. "Mum, take these." I held the cup of water to her mouth so she could swallow them. She fell asleep. I waited for her to come round.

Taking the uniform off the chair item by item, I dressed myself. My stomach was churning. I was hoping she would be alright while I was at school.

"Hikey, are you ready? I'll walk to the school with you."

I walked through to the bedroom. She was sitting on the bed. It felt so good to see her awake and sitting up.

"Pass me my bag. I'll comb your hair," she said. She took her coat off the bed and put it on, and we left the flat. She walked with me as far as she could. I was almost at the school, and found the path to the playground.

"Go straight home, Mum. I'll see you later," I shouted, trying to make sure that she went home.

The day dragged. Nothing registered, nothing sank into my mind. The events of the day were dwarfed by the anxiety to get home to her. At last, the final bell rang, and I was on my way home, running as fast as possible to get back to her.

"Open the door, Mum." She was waiting to greet me at the flat door. She kissed and hugged me.

"Look," she said. Some boxes of things had been delivered from the Jewish Benevolent Society for when my brothers, Jeffery and David, came home; some extra bedding, plates and cutlery.

"Look, Hikey, in the kitchen." The Benevolent Society had also brought us a kitchen table, with a tablecloth. My mother had two tablets left: she was keeping them for tomorrow, so I could go to school. Again the next day dragged, the anxiety to get home overwhelming.

School ended, I ran home as fast as possible, praying she would be standing at the window, waiting for me. As I approached the flat, I looked up at the kitchen window. This time there was nothing, no waving no smiling. I ran up the hill, panicking, praying desperately for her to be alright.

I pressed the button at the main doors to the flat. There was no reply. My eyes were filling, my head throbbing, waiting for someone to open the door for me. It wasn't long before a young woman came out of the door. Pushing my way past her, I ran to the lift and pressed the button for the first floor. I ran up the remainder of the stairs, making sure there was nothing strange following me. My heart pounding, constantly smelling for fire, at last I was at the sixth floor. Struggling to get the key in the front door, my heart sinking, I was almost too afraid to go through to the living-room in case she was dead. Running through, I saw that she was lying on the couch, fast asleep. The tablets had worn off. I shook her.

"Let me *shloff*. Get away," she groaned.

Sitting on the floor beside her, wanting her to come back to life, I stayed rigid, watching her mouth to make sure she was still breathing, wanting to hold her hand, but knowing if she woke up, she would want food.

I noticed the television set. It must have arrived this morning. The small sixpence in the slot meter was on the side, an arrow pointing to where the money should go. There was no electricity. I sat watching the Little Red Arrow Indian. He was sitting on top of the television, smiling at me.

We both stayed in the living-room all night, my mother on the couch, covered with her coat, me beside her, on the floor.

"I'm not going to school. I'm not going to leave you," I was telling her, even though she was still asleep.

My mother awoke early. It was almost daylight and very cold. She wanted food, chocolate and pop, but there was no money.

"Find me a pencil and a piece of paper." There was a pencil on the sideboard. I had been given it in school. The only paper was the brown paper in which my uniform had been wrapped. She started to write a short note. It read, *Please can you lend me a shilling till Monday morning?*

"Take it to Mrs Rifkin." She lived in the next block of flats.

"If she can't, try anybody," my mother shouted after me.

It was impossible to get money. Nobody had any. On my walk home, I was praying she would be asleep again, so that she wouldn't ask for anything. She was asleep and didn't wake for the rest of the day. Tomorrow is Sunday, I thought. The Benevolent Society is open in the morning. Perhaps they will give me some money. In the middle of the night, she woke up screaming for food. I couldn't do anything. I could only try to make her understand that there was no money, and the only chance of any help was the Jewish Benevolent Society, first thing in the morning.

The rooms in the flat had taken on a familiar stench now.

The atmosphere was damp and bleak. My mind was numb to the outside world.

The cold and hunger was to stay in my mind, as a natural course of events. Sometimes my mind would wander to a small thread of cotton hanging off my uniform, or a scrap of paper lying on the floor: they both tasted equally as nice. I liked wandering into the kitchen, pretending to be a housewife, pretending I was cooking a meal, pretending I was a person, not knowing what that involved. If only we had some food or money. If only it was possible to magic a nice meal, I could wake my mother and give it to her.

The morning arrived. I waited for a few hours, then made my way to the Benevolent Society. "Mum," I had said before I left, "I'm going now." She didn't budge. I left, hoping she would be alright.

My mother had explained where the Benevolent Society was, and after a long walk, I managed to find it. It was in a very large Victorian house with a huge driveway. I walked through the front door. It seemed very cold and empty, like the children's home. There was a reception area in one of the rooms.

"Please can I have some money for Mrs Levene?"

"If you wait in the room opposite. You will be seen later."

The room was full of people sitting, waiting patiently, like the Board of Guardians. Eventually, my name was called, and I was directed to a larger room. The door was very big. There was a hazy smell of cigar smoke coming out of it. Pushing it open, I noticed three men sitting at a large table. The room was full of smoke.

"Please, can I have some money for my Mum, Mrs Levene?" I begged, looking round, hoping one of them would say, "Yes."

"Has your mother received her National Assistance?"

"Yes, but it's all gone. We have no food or electricity."

It was impossible for me to look at them. Please. The word kept repeating in my mind. I was too afraid to look in case the answer was, "No."

"Here's sixpence," said one of the men. He gave it to me and wrote the amount in his book.

Once outside, I headed in the direction of the nearest delicatessen. It felt good to have the money in my hand. Walking home with food, no matter how little, was wonderful.

The days didn't change from one week to the next. There was still the excitement on a Monday morning, getting the National Assistance money, then going to the delicatessen to buy food, trying to make sure that nobody from school would see me.

CHAPTER 5

The sun shone through the window. It was mid-morning, the curtains were too narrow to cover the window and stop the sun's rays. Lying on my bed, curled up tightly so that it was possible to get all my body under the coat, I pulled my jumper over my face, trying to keep the sun out of my eyes. I desperately wanted to fall asleep again. My mother was still asleep in the next bed. The two had been pushed together so that it was possible for me to feel the slightest vibration that told me she was still alive. The coat that covered her body was almost on the floor, her dress had ridden up, exposing all of her legs. I wanted to cover her and keep her warm, but I didn't. If she woke up, she would want food and all the usual things.

From the bedroom, it was possible to hear the lift if it stopped at our floor. My heart would jump for fear it was the School Board or someone to take my mother away. Suddenly, there were footsteps. The lift must have stopped, the noise woke me again. I held my breath, hoping that whoever it was would go to another flat. There was knocking on the door. Please don't wake her up, I was thinking to myself. The knocking continued. "Annie, it's me, Minnie Shelefski!"

My mother grabbed my arm and wouldn't let me move. Eventually, the knocking stopped. "It's my friend from school. I can't let her in here." She had tears in her eyes, and fell asleep again. I ran to the kitchen window to see if Minnie was at the bus stop. There she was, walking down the hill. Crossing the road, she waited for the bus, a slight woman with black, wavy hair. I knew it was her, and wished she would come back to see my mother. I was so relieved it wasn't someone to take my mother away. Nobody would make me go to school.

My mother's breathing was getting worse, most of the time she just seemed to be lonely and desperate, bingeing when possible. But she was alive; that was all that mattered to me.

She mostly stayed on the couch. I was more than happy to stay by her side day and night. It was important for me to know that she was still breathing. The nights were the worst, when she would wake, not knowing where she was, thinking that I was her enemy, imagining that I was trying to take her away, hitting out at me, pushing me away, at least, she was still breathing.

Over the past few months, the doctor had written only one prescription for Duraphet tablets. It was getting much harder to get even a few. Perhaps he would let me have some. I waited on the couch for a few hours, my coat over me to keep me warm. I could hear the children coming home from school. That meant the evening surgery would soon be open.

My mother was still asleep. I stood near the bedroom door and started reciting the *Shama*. That would keep her from harm. Without disturbing her, I left the flat. On my walk to the surgery, I was imagining all the nice things it would be possible to buy if I were old enough to work. It kept my mind off the terrible cold and intense hunger. By the time I arrived at the surgery, it had started to rain. Walking into the large, warm building, I wanted to run upstairs and find a bed, or curl up on the floor, but the tablets were the most important thing.

"Take a seat," the receptionist told me. There were only three or four people before me. I hoped that my heart wouldn't need starting while there were people about. At last, it was my turn.

"The doctor will see you now." Those words always sent my heart racing. I entered the doctor's room.

"Sit down. I won't keep you a minute." He seemed to take such a long time to finish his paperwork. At last, he looked up at me.

"Can I have some Duraphet tablets for my Mum? Mrs Levene?"

"No," was the answer, without hesitation. "I'll give you some Hydroderm cream for your lips. They're still badly cracked. You should dress warmer, and wear socks," he said, looking at my feet. Picking up the prescription, I left, and started to make my way home.

The chemist shop was in sight. I hoped that he would make a mistake and give me Duraphet tablets instead of the cream. The shop was empty. I handed the prescription to the chemist.

"I don't want this cream. Can I have some Duraphet?" He looked at me. "Please can I have some tablets for my Mother? She needs them," I was begging him. "Please can I have some?"

"Alright, but just this once." He walked through to the back room. After a few minutes, he reappeared holding a small white box. "There are four tablets in the box." He handed it to me.

"Thank you very much." I looked up at him, expecting to wake up and find it was all a dream.

It didn't take me long to run home. As soon as my foot was inside the front door, I shouted, "Mum, Mum, we've got some. Wake up quickly." I was shaking her, trying to explain what had happened at the chemist. "Come on Mum, I'll get you some water."

She swallowed all four tablets together. I sat on the floor, frightened, not knowing what they would do to her.

"Mummy," I cried, pulling her arm almost out of its socket and shaking her hard.

"Let me *shloff*," she shouted, hitting out at me. "Go away."

"Don't close your eyes, Mummy." I was panicking, not knowing what to do.

I ran to the next door flat. The lady there was usually friendly whenever she saw me, but there was no reply. I went back inside. There was no room to sit beside her on the couch. I sat over her, shaking her and pushing her eyelids open, slapping and hitting her, trying to stop her from falling asleep. Eventually, her eyes opened.

"I'm going to get the doctor for you, Mum." She was gasping for breath.

"Get me some breathers." They were little pink and white tablets that helped her breathe properly. I couldn't find any, anywhere. She was panicking, gasping for breath.

"Don't worry, Mum, I'm going to get the doctor. I won't be long." There was no money for the bus, so I ran as quickly as possible to the surgery. I begged the receptionist to send the doctor to the flat to see my mother.

"She can't breathe. Please tell me the doctor will come and see her?" The receptionist told me he would call at the end of his surgery.

"Can I have some breathing tablets now?" She told me to go home and wait for the doctor.

When I arrived back home, my mother was still asleep.

"Come on, Mum, the doctor's coming soon."

She held my hand, and told me she loved me. "Don't worry, Hikey, I'll be better soon," she murmured. We just sat, waiting for the doctor. There was a knock on the front door. We looked at each other.

"It must be the doctor. I'll go and see."

He walked through into the hall and I led him to my mother. His face went blank. "This place is filthy. Can't you clean it up? It's disgraceful!" I could see him looking at the bareness, he held his nose, looking round slowly, taking everything in. I knew that he blamed me.

"Can't you clean this mess up?" My eyes filled with tears, I ran into the bedroom. I didn't want my mother to see me crying.

I stayed there while the doctor was seeing to her. Wiping my eyes, I went back into the living-room.

"You'll have to go to hospital," he was telling my mother. She asked him if he would get in touch with the Jewish Benevolent Society to make arrangements for me. The thought of her being in hospital made me feel sick. I didn't know what to do. The doctor went, leaving a prescription for some breathing tablets. I sat with my mother. She looked at me.

"Don't worry, Hikey, I'll be better when I come out. I'm going to sleep for a while." She was holding my hand; I didn't want her to let go of it. "When I'm better, you can play outside," she told me, and fell asleep.

I didn't move from her side. It must have been the middle of the night when she opened her eyes, and told me to go to bed.

"No, I'll stay here with you." She begged me to go but it was impossible for me to leave her. I sat beside the living-room door, where she couldn't see me, all night.

When the morning came, I took the prescription for her breathing tablets to the chemist. After I had arrived home with them, there was a knock on the door. I didn't answer it.

"My name is Miss Sassoon, from the Jewish Benevolent Society," a voice shouted. "Are you there, Mrs Levene?"

I opened the door. "You must be Jane." I found it hard not to cry. It felt too much to hear an adult mention my name in a kind way. She came through the door and followed me in.

"My Mum's in here, asleep."

She carefully placed her briefcase on the sideboard, trying to find a clean spot. She looked round for somewhere to sit, deciding to remain standing.

"Shouldn't you be at school?" I ignored her, not even trying to explain how I felt. It was clear enough to me. As long as my mother needed me, I would be there.

Miss Sassoon had a notepad in her hand. "Do you get a food parcel from the soup kitchen?"

"Yes," I wanted her to know how helpful it was, "and sometimes on a Sunday morning, I can get sixpence, and at *Pesach* time we have food vouchers."

She turned to my mother. "Mrs Levene, Jeffery and David will be home for *Pesach*, probably for good."

My mother was half asleep. She smiled. "Thank you, Miss Sassoon." She fell asleep again.

"When your mother goes into hospital, you will go into the Sarah Laski Children's Home on Crumpsall Lane. It isn't too far from the hospital, and you will be able to visit at the weekend." That made me feel very happy, the thought that my mother wouldn't be too far away.

"You must go to school from the Sarah Laski Home. Your

mother will get a letter from the hospital saying when she will be admitted, and I will get in touch with the Home."

"Thank you, Miss Sassoon." I followed her to the front door.

I waited for the letter to arrive, each day listening out for the postman. It arrived three days after Miss Sassoon's visit.

My mother was to go into hospital the next day. An ambulance would call in the morning. She would have to take a nightdress, dressing gown and slippers.

"Mum, I'll put the letter in your bag, so you'll know where it is." She was still asleep, and couldn't hear me. I put the letter in her bag. Perhaps this time, the doctors would make her better. Every word in the letter meant so much to me, the name of the person who sent it, the name of the hospital. They were all going to look after her, and make her better.

I spent the night wishing I could get her some slippers and a nightdress, but there was nothing I could do. She woke up in the early hours of the morning.

"Hikey! I need tablets. Is there anything to eat?" She was in bed, my heart sank. I was standing near the living-room door, not wanting to go into the bedroom.

"Go to sleep, Mum. I'll see what I can do." My head was resting on the door. I was tired, and didn't know what to do.

"Hikey, go to the shops. I need some chocolate and pop."

Please go to sleep, I was praying very hard.

"Hikey, where are you?"

"I'm here, Mum, looking for some money. Go to sleep, Mum."

"Hikey, go to the shops. I need some chocolate and crisps."

"Go to sleep Mum." I held my breath, desperately wanting her to go to sleep. I stayed where I was, near the door. She fell asleep again. It was such a relief. I crept into my bed, and stayed absolutely still, so as not to wake her.

"Goodnight, God bless, I love you," I said under my breath.

In the morning, I stayed in bed until it was light. My mother was still sleeping. I left her until the ambulance arrived and the phone buzzed.

"We won't be long," I told the ambulance man.

I ran into the bedroom. "Come on, Mum, the ambulance is here. I'll help you on with your coat. You'd better get up, quick." She turned towards me, I helped her to sit up.

"Come on, Mum. They're waiting. Put your arm in the sleeve." I pulled her dress down, and straightened it.

"Your breathers are in your bag, Mum, with the letter from the hospital and your National Assistance book."

We left the flat, and waited for the lift to arrive.

"Don't worry, Mum, I'll visit you tonight. Miss Sassoon told me how to get to the hospital." She put her arms round me, and held me tight.

The driver helped her into the back of the ambulance.

"I'm not going till my Mum's alright." He smiled at me.

"See you later. Love you, Mum." The doors closed, and she was driven off. Miss Sassoon had told me to go straight to the Home from school.

My heart sank as I approached the school. The lessons had already started. I was afraid that they wouldn't let me in. The lessons had no meaning for me. All I could think of was my mother, worrying in case she couldn't find her breathing tablets, feeling she would be lost without me. The final bell rang. I made my way to the Home.

What if they don't know I'm coming? The thoughts were churning round and round in my head. What if they send me home? What if they've all gone out? Walking along the road, holding onto the walls, I desperately wanted to run into the houses. Perhaps someone would let me stay.

The Home was a short walk from the school, it was in sight. Please open the door, I begged silently. I started running as fast as possible, into the driveway and up the steps. I found myself banging on the door, frightened in case they weren't expecting me. The door opened.

"You must be Jane Levene. I'm Matron. Come on in." She took me into her office and started writing on a piece of paper.

"Do you have any clothes with you?"

"No."

"We'll get you cleaned up." She handed me over to her assistant.

"Come on, Jane. I'll run a bath for you. Is your mum in hospital?"

"Yes. She's going to get better," I told her, looking round, trying to see what there was for me to take home for her.

The Home wasn't as big as Delamere, the one I had been to before. As we walked up the stairs towards the bathroom, I couldn't stop looking to see if there were any nice things for my mother. As she started to fill the bath, I was watching to see where the towels were kept.

"Get in the bath, Jane." She started scrubbing me, and checking through my hair. "Keep your head still," but I couldn't. It just kept turning everywhere, looking and remembering where things were kept.

I didn't like anyone touching me or washing me. Somehow, it made the pain of being parted from my mother worse. I could feel the pain coming from my innermost depths and travelling to the end of each hair on my body. I didn't like it here. If only I could be back at home, was my only thought. I didn't want to be scrubbed and rubbed. That made it worse. I wanted to be curled up nice and warm.

"I'm going to see my Mum tonight." The nurse looked at me. "When I grow up, I'm going to take her on holiday and buy her nice clothes and carpets." She was still scrubbing away.

"I'm going to get a good job, so I can look after her and get her nice clothes."

"Well, perhaps you should get dressed first."

"Can I have a carrier bag and some string when it's time for me to go home?"

"Come on, get dried. We'll see." She helped me out of the bath. "It's almost teatime."

"I'm going to see my Mother tonight." She was drying me.

"You can't go in the dark, by yourself!"

The house seemed so cold and lonely. I didn't know what to do with myself. The pain of separation from my mother was overwhelming.

"I want my Mum," I cried. "I promised to visit her. She'll think I don't love her. I want my Mum. Please let me go."

She took me downstairs to the Matron's office. "You will have to wait till the weekend," the Matron told me. "Go and play with the other children. Tea will be ready soon."

The nurse took me to the playroom. There were other children playing. There were lots of cupboards, and toys strewn all over the floor.

"Play here. Tea will be ready soon." She closed the door behind her, and left me standing. I found a corner, pushing all the toys away. They were keeping me away from my mother. I wanted to curl up and sleep for ever.

I didn't like the children in the room. I wasn't one of them and just wanted to stay away from them. My head felt very heavy and my eyes wanted to close.

"Please can I go to bed?"

"No," replied the Matron. "You must eat your tea with all the other children."

When the meal was over, we had to clear away the pots and wash up. I was so hungry. How could the other children leave any food? I couldn't understand it. There were three kitchens one for meat, one for milk and one for glass. It was my job to clear the plates into the milk kitchen. My eyes couldn't leave the sight of the leftover food. I wanted it all.

"I'll wash up," I said, stuffing as much food as possible into my mouth. It felt good, the taste, the feel, I had to rush in case I was seen. Now my stomach was full, everything seemed alright.

"Go and play with the other children," the Matron told me.

"No," was my reply.

I wanted to be wrapped up warm. The desire for sleep was so strong. I followed the other children to the playroom. There was my corner. The urge to curl up was too much. Wrapping my arms around myself, I fell asleep.

"Come on Jane. It isn't time to sleep," a voice woke me up. The nurse was shaking me. "Wake up, play with the other children!" she insisted, lifting me by the arm. The desperation to sleep overcame me. My eyes closed, and nothing could open them.

The following morning, I awoke. My first thoughts were, my mum, she'll think I don't love her. I promised to visit her.

My school uniform was waiting at the side of the bed, along with a pair of socks, a pair of knickers and a vest.

"Come on, Jane, put this underwear on. Get dressed, get yourself washed, and go downstairs for your breakfast!"

The table was already set. There were boxes of cornflakes on the table, white jugs full of hot milk. I felt bewildered, thinking about my mum. It made me feel breathless as if my heart had stopped. I knew I didn't have enough air in my body. There wasn't enough to keep me alive. I stamped my foot on the floor to get my heart going.

"What are you doing?" asked the Matron.

"I'm starting my heart up." I was surprised that she hadn't seen the other children do it, wondering how they started their hearts beating.

As I was walking out of the dining room, I noticed a pile of material in the corner. Looking closely, I saw that they were pieces of curtain material with cardboard stuck at the top.

"What are these?" I asked the Matron.

"They're swatches of curtain material."

"Please can I have some to sew up?"

"We'll see when you get back from school."

As I left the Home to make my way to school, all I could think about were the pieces of material. I felt very excited. If they were sewn together, they would make nice cushions to put on the couch. They would make the flat look nice for my mother. All day at school, I was hoping the Matron would let me have them. "I'll not tell Mum, so it'll be a nice surprise."

The day dragged. I longed to get back to the Home so I could ask the Matron for the pieces of material. I ran all the way back, in case someone else wanted them. I ran into the Matron's office.

"Please can I have the curtain material?" Before I could say any more, the answer was, "Yes."

"Thank you, Matron."

"What are you going to make?"

"Cushions for my Mum for when she goes home."

"I'll go and get you a needle and cotton."

It took me hours and hours to sew all the pieces together; by the time the weekend arrived, I had made four cushions. I took them and put them under my bed, ready to take home.

At the weekend, the Matron called me into her office, to tell me that I could visit my mother.

The morning dragged until it was time to leave the Home and make my way to the hospital. It wasn't far, and was easy to find. I was bursting to tell my mother about the cushions, but I was determined to keep it to myself. They were to be a surprise. Walking down the corridor, looking for the ward number, I was telling myself not to say anything about the cushions.

At last, I found the ward. The doors were already open. She was sitting up in bed, smiling and talking. For a moment, I looked around. Was that really my mother? Or was it someone who looked like her? My feet were glued to the floor.

"Hikey, come on." It was my mother. I ran to her, and hugged her.

"I've got something to tell you, Hikey," she whispered in my ear. Her breath was warm on my face. "I'm better. I don't need the tablets anymore." I couldn't believe my ears. I couldn't stop crying. "I'm going to find a job, and I'll take care of you," she whispered.

It was the happiest moment of my life. She stopped hugging me, and started showing me off to all the women around her. "I don't know what I'd do without her," she told them.

"I'm coming home tomorrow so come straight home from school. I'll be waiting for you."

Visiting time was soon over. The nurse came in to usher all the visitors out of the ward.

"See you tomorrow, Mum. Love you," I said, hugging her as hard as possible.

"See you tomorrow, Hikey. Be a good girl."

As soon as I arrived back at the Home, I made my way to the Matron's office. "Please can I have some string?" The Matron handed it over to me.

"My Mum's coming out of hospital tomorrow, so I can go straight home from school."

"Yes, I know."

"Should I leave my vest and knickers when I go?"

"No, you can keep them."

"Can I have a carrier bag to put my cushions in, please, Matron?"

"Yes. Have this one."

"My Mum's better," I told her, leaving the room.

All the children were playing in the playroom. I made my way to the bedroom. I pushed open the door to the bathroom, quickly taking some towels and a bath mat. My heart was pounding, praying that nobody would see me. I ran into the bedroom, and pushed them all under the mattress.

I shut the bedroom door. Listening out for footsteps, I quickly put one of the cushions in the bag, then a towel, then another cushion, and the last towel and bath mat. Please don't anyone come upstairs, I was praying to myself. I managed to squash everything down in the bag, and started wrapping the string around it, as fast as I possibly could. Then I heard footsteps outside the door.

"Jane, where are you?"

"I'm in the bedroom packing, ready to go home."

She picked the two remaining cushions off the floor. I looked up at her. "I'm going to tie them together."

"What's that?" She looked at my bag.

"My cushions, I'm packing them," I answered, terrified that she would want to see them. By this time, the bag was well and truly wrapped, not even the most patient person would have attempted to take a look inside.

"You can pick these things up tomorrow on your way home from school. They will be in Matron's office."

That night, for once in my life, I went to bed in a happy frame of mind. There was nothing to be frightened of. My mother wasn't going to die. If my heart stopped, I knew how to start it up again. Everything was going to be alright. I couldn't wait to show her the presents I had for her.

CHAPTER 6

I awoke early, running downstairs to make sure the nurse hadn't opened my bag and taken the towels out. Very quietly, I opened the door a little. The bag was in the corner. It hadn't been touched.

"Thank you, Matron, for not taking them off me," I whispered. The nurse was behind me. "Jane, go and get dressed. Breakfast is almost ready."

It was time to leave for school. Before I left, I checked once more that my package was alright. The day in school dragged. My mind was so full: the cushions would make the flat look so nice.

At last, the final bell rang. I made my way back to the Home. I went straight to the Matron's office.

"Please, can I have my bag?" I begged.

"Yes, take it. Here, Jane, here's tuppence for the bus fare home."

"Thank you." I headed for the bus stop at the top of the road. My bag was by my side. It was safe now, no-one could take it off me. It took a long time for the bus to arrive. Waiting in the shelter, I couldn't keep still, I was so excited. I was jumping and skipping. "Please hurry, bus." I whispered to myself.

A bus appeared in the distance. It was hard to see the number. When it came close I saw that it was my bus. I sat near the window, pressing my nose against it, with my package on my knee, making sure it couldn't get lost. I was afraid my heart would need starting up, that always made people stare at me.

As the bus turned on to Blackley New Road, it was hard to think straight. Is mum going to be in the flat? Perhaps she's had to stay in hospital? Had the doctor made a mistake? I couldn't believe that she was going to be at home. It was almost my stop. I made sure that both my hands were holding the package tightly.

The bus pulled up with a jolt, almost throwing me off but I didn't care, I was too excited. Looking up at the kitchen window, I saw that my mother was there. She was looking for me, smiling and waving. I waved back as hard as I could, running to the front door. It was in sight. I pressed the button to our flat. "Mum, Mum," I was saying through the intercom. She pressed the button, and I pushed the door open. Waiting for the lift, I was jumping up and down. It was all too good to be true. The lift arrived and I pulled the doors, helping them to open quickly. I tried to reach the button for the sixth floor, it was impossible. I pressed the button for the first floor instead. I left the lift at the first floor, and ran up the stairs.

"You won't get me, monsters, my Mum's here," I was saying out loud, to let them know.

At last, I reached the sixth floor. I pushed the door to the landing, and rushed to the flat. The door was already open, there was a smell of cooking as I walked into the hall. It was all too much.

"Mummy, Mum. Where are you?" She was in the living-room, standing near the window. "Mummy," I clamped my arms round her. "Are you alright, Mum?"

"Yes, Hikey. I'm cooking you some tea."

"Mum, look, I've made some presents for you." I let go of her and started pulling at the string. "Look, Mum," I beckoned her as I pulled the cushions out, placing them on the couch, "I made them for you."

"They're lovely, Hikey."

"Look, Mum, I've got some towels and a bath mat!"

She took my hand and led me to the kitchen. There was a plate of chopped and fried fish, a plate of *gefilte* fish and a jar of *chrane*. It was like a dream. I just stood in awe, watching her spooning the *chrane*, surrounding myself with the newly made cushions.

"Mummy."

"What Hikey?"

"When I grow up, I'm going to buy carpets and lots of nice things for you."

"I know."

She walked through to the living-room, carrying the plates of fish, and sat on the couch with me.

"You're not going to sleep, are you, Mum?" She hugged me. She felt so warm and loving. I wanted to curl up on her lap and never move. Thank God, I thought, all those *Shamas* must have worked.

"Look, Mum," I whispered, pointing to my bag. Getting off the couch, I managed to pull out the bath mat and the towels. The bath mat was placed under the electric fire that was fixed on the wall. Then I took the towels and placed them over the bath.

Too excited to stay in one place, and smelling the rest of the food in the kitchen, I had to take another look, to make sure it wasn't a dream. Picking up a bagel, I walked back into the living-room.

"Come here, Hikey, come and sit down," my mother laughed. She took the bagel off me, and put her arms round my waist. "Sit down," she looked at me, "I'm taking you to town tomorrow. Would you like me to take you for something to eat?"

"Yes, please!"

"Down by the side of Frankenburg House, there's a sewing factory. Perhaps they need a machinist. We'll go there first."

She was getting tired. It was early evening, she told me she would have to sleep. I was so afraid she wouldn't wake up again.

"Where are you going to sleep Mum?"

"We'll both go to bed soon. Don't worry, Hikey, things will be different now."

I couldn't tell her how frightened I was.

The morning arrived. I found myself standing by her bed, watching her, wondering if she was going to wake up. She opened her eyes. "I'll get up soon. Go back to bed for a while."

It took her a long time to come round: eventually she did.

"Here's some money, Hikey. Go to the shop and get some chocolate and cigarettes."

When I returned, she was up and ready. "Get my bag, Hikey, and we'll go."

"When I grow up, I'll buy you a new dress and coat, and some stockings and underwear and nice shoes."

"I know, Hikey." She took my hand. "You don't have to keep telling me, I know you will."

We left the flat and walked towards the bus stop. There was a bus just at the top of the road. It felt so wonderful to be with her. My mother helped me on to the bus, and we sat near the window at the front. We were sharing the chocolate. It felt so good not to have to worry about getting tablets from the doctor to help her breathe and wake up. The bus was almost at Frankenburg House.

"Come on, this is our stop." She held my hand.

We walked down the street at the side of Frankenburg House until we arrived at the factory. My mother was taken into a small room. I waited for her. She soon came out.

"Hikey, I'm going to start work next week!"

We were both very happy. We left the factory and walked back up the road towards the bus stop. I could hear that she was getting breathless and she was sweating badly. There was something wrong, she was trying hard not to show it.

"Hikey, do you mind if we go straight home?"

"No, Mum, of course I don't."

We crossed the road, to get the bus home. At last it arrived.

"Come on, Hikey, let's go home." We boarded the bus. She gave me the rest of the money she had in her bag and squeezed my hand.

"Will you get the shopping? You know what to get."

"Of course I will. Don't worry. You go home."

The bus stopped near Levy's delicatessen, halfway up Cheetham Hill Road: that was my first stop. When all the shopping was finished, I just had enough money for my bus fare. I made my way to Upper Park Road to catch the 145 bus home. I sat at the back of the bus, so that when it turned onto the road near the flats, I would be able to see if my mother was at the window. I looked up, and she was there.

I got off the bus, put my bags down on the pavement and waved to her. "Love you," I mimed, I knew she couldn't hear me, but it didn't matter.

She knew how much that meant to me, to see her waving and smiling.

The flat door was already open when I arrived home.

"Mum, are you alright?" I shouted down the hall.

"Yes, Hikey, come on."

She was sitting on the couch. I emptied all the food out of the bags, and sat beside her. She ate most of the food very quickly and uncontrollably, but I knew that she was much better than she had been in the past.

We spent the day sitting on the couch. She told me that she wanted me to start going to school properly.

"On Sunday I'm going to the Benevolent Society to try and get you some shoes for school."

I was still at the junior school. The Hebrew lessons were my favourite. It was hard to learn anything. I had missed so much time at school. My mother wanted me to be able to speak Hebrew and go to the synagogue on a Saturday morning. It would make her very happy.

Monday was a more important day for both of us. I spent the night wondering if my mother was going to start crying for the breathing tablets, begging me to try to get some Duraphet tablets. I was too frightened to think about all the nice things we were going to do together, in case it was all a dream.

She slept all night, only moving to pull the coat over her feet to keep them warm. The morning arrived, and she was still asleep.

I panicked. "Mum, Mum," I whispered, shaking her, "it's time to get up, Mummy please." I was afraid of the reaction I would get.

She turned round in her bed so that she was facing me.

"Don't worry, I'll get up in a minute."

"We'll have to walk, there's no money left."

She started to get out of bed, then came over to me and helped me out of bed, lifting my skirt to make sure I had my knickers on, straightening my pullover. It felt so good just to stand near her, feeling her pulling and tugging at me. She put her coat on and picked up her handbag, making sure the National Assistance book and the voucher for my school shoes were in it.

"Come on, Hikey," she said, taking my hand and smiling,

"We'd better get going." Before we reached the front door, she took an old handkerchief out of her bag and licked it. "Come here." She held my face, wiping it clean.

Very slowly, we walked to the top of Cheetham Hill Road. My mother found it very difficult and we had to stop a lot so that she could rest. When we arrived at the school, I was afraid to leave her on her own, but she insisted that she was alright.

"Don't worry, Hikey. Meet me outside the factory after school, and we'll get your shoes. Go on, you go to school now, I'll see you later." She kissed me, and I waited until she had crossed the road to the Post Office and was standing in the queue waiting for it to open.

As I walked into the playground, my stomach was churning. I didn't really want to leave my mother, and yet there was an intense feeling of excitement that she was able to go to work. In school, I couldn't concentrate. My mind was so accustomed to worrying about her, that I couldn't adjust. It was difficult for me to breathe. I was constantly feeling my pulse to make sure the blood was still circulating around my body. The Hebrew lesson began and I tried very hard to keep my mind on the work, knowing how happy my mother would be if I could speak the language. It seemed almost impossible to concentrate.

When school was over, I walked down to the factory to meet my mother. When I arrived she wasn't quite ready. I waited for her. She was in a big room. There were two rows of machines. She was sitting at one of the machines, busy sewing a small anorak. She lifted her head and turned round. She put her arm round my waist and pulled me towards her.

"This is my Hikey," she told everyone, and kissed me on the cheek. I felt very embarrassed, and also very pleased. She showed me the anoraks she had made. "I'll make one for you in a few weeks' time. Come on, Hikey, we'll go now." She put on her coat and took my hand. I still wasn't sure if it was all a dream, it felt so good. We walked to the shop to get the shoes then made our way home. The week passed very quickly: by Friday morning we were getting very excited about her wages.

School finished early for the Sabbath. I don't remember much about the day, except wanting desperately to go and meet my mother. It didn't take me long to walk down to the factory. When I arrived she had already finished.

"Look, Hikey," she showed off her wage packet, "We'll go to the shops on Cheetham Hill Road to do the shopping."

We went in and out of all the delicatessens, into the fish shop, then to the hardware shop to buy a *hackmesher* to chop the fish.

"Come on, Hikey, we'll get the bus home."

We carried all the bags to the bus stop on Upper Park Road.

"Wait here for me, I've forgotten something." I waited at

the bus stop, surrounded by all the bags, still not sure if I was about to wake up out of a dream. My mother was gone only a few minutes. As she came back, the bus pulled up, and we were both pleased to be going home. We sat at the front of the bus, so it would be easier to get off.

"I've bought you a present, but you're not having it till we get home."

I smiled at her. "Alright, Mum." I put my arms round her waist.

As we got off the bus, she was sweating very badly and complained that she felt weak. It frightened me. I began to worry in case she was doing too much. It was a terrible effort for her to walk to the flats, and it took us a long time.

At last, we were home. I took all the bags to the living-room. My mother went straight to the couch, and sat down.

"Look in the bag to see what I bought for you." She was gasping for breath.

On top of one of the bags was a box. It had a pair of imitation glass high heeled shoes in. They were called 'playshoes.' I loved them.

My mother went into the kitchen with the food, and started to cook some potato *latkes* and chopped and fried fish. I was walking round the flat with my playshoes on, they were clicking on the bare floor. Suddenly she said, "Hikey," very drawn out. I stopped near the kitchen, and knew that the noise was getting on her nerves. We looked at each other and laughed.

"Sorry, Mum."

"It's alright," she told me, hugging me and laughing, "next week I'll take you to the pictures. There's a lovely film on called *The Jolson Story*. You'll like it."

The following week, we went to the pictures. It was a wonderful experience, and I was too excited to notice that her health was beginning to fail again.

By the end of the week, she had given in her notice at the factory.

CHAPTER 7

My mother decided to contact another sewing factory that was advertising for outworkers. She felt more able to work from home as she was finding it harder to leave the flat. Over the next few weeks, she made all the arrangements and the machine and material were delivered. She felt more at ease working like this, and managed to do a little at a time.

Miss Sassoon called at the flat, to tell us that Jeffery would be coming home in a few weeks' time, and David would be home in a few months. My mother was very pleased about that. It made her even more determined to work. The next day a bedside table and some blankets were delivered from the Jewish Benevolent Society. They were for Jeffery's room. I made the bed ready for his homecoming. My mother managed to carry on for a few more weeks, machining at home. She was finding it harder but managed a small amount, and was much better than she had been in the past.

One day, I arrived home from school to find her sitting at the sewing machine. She was slumped over it, crying, holding a tiny anorak. She had been to the shops, and spent the last of her money on food, and eaten everything. She gave me the anorak and told me to try to sell it for a few shillings. After I had knocked on many doors, a lady gave me a shilling for it. When I arrived home she made me hide the money from her: Jeffery was coming home tomorrow, it was for some food for him.

"Hikey, go to the shop before it closes, and get me a large

cornflakes box." I managed to get to the shop just before it closed. The shopkeeper let me choose one from a pile of boxes in the corner. I held on to it very carefully with one hand and walked home holding the wall with the other, wishing the air would go into my lungs without me having to stand still and gasp for it.

When I got home, my mother told me that she wanted to make a doll's house for me: "It's your birthday soon." She sat on the couch and started making it. It was getting dark. I sat watching her for hours, cutting out the windows and drawing bricks onto the box. When she had almost finished the doll's house, she put it to one side and started telling me about my father. He had wanted her to go to Israel with him, and to have us adopted here: "He didn't like children." When she wouldn't agree to having us adopted, he had left her.

I knew very little about my mother's family. She was never well enough to talk about them and they never visited us. She told me that she had a brother. I had never seen him. He lived in London. She had a sister who had married out of the religion. I had never seen her either. My mother had never told me any of these things before. I had just assumed that there was no-one else. "My parents were lovely people. You're named after my mother, she would have loved you if she were still alive." She started crying, wishing that her parents were alive and wishing her sister, Doris, would visit.

"Don't cry, Mum. You've got me. I'll take care of you and Jeff's coming home tomorrow."

"I know, but sometimes I really wish I had a grown-up to talk to."

My ears closed to what she was saying. It hurt me, even though I understood what she meant. She started talking about my father again. He had left after each child was born.

Then she started telling me about the war, when she and her sisters would practise speaking German. If the Germans invaded, they would change their names to Anita Garabosh and Dorita Garabosh. She laughed about it, telling me that it had been very frightening to imagine they could have been caught by the Germans.

Then she started talking about my father again. She had met him when they were both working in a sewing factory. She also told me about another man called Ben. He had wanted to marry her. He was a businessman from out of town, but she fell in love with my father, and they got married. As well as the factory work, she was a dressmaker, doing some work from home. Any money she earned, my father gambled away. He sold all the furniture in Johnson Street for money to gamble with.

When David was born, he left for good. He left her with no money. She had no shoes for Jeffery when he was little, and put rags on his feet. My father would come and show her the shoes he had handmade to order for himself. Then, one day she walked with us to the Bridgewater Canal because she wanted to jump in and take us with her, but she didn't when she thought about us. She talked for hours and hours. She made me promise to go to the synagogue on *Yom Kippur* to say prayers for her mother and father.

She stayed awake all night, frightened that she wouldn't be able to support us now Jeff was coming home. She desperately wanted to be able to continue sewing. The following morning I didn't want to go to school and leave her, but she insisted, so I went.

My next recollection is of some months later. I was sitting

beside the couch watching her, remembering the few months we had had together, remembering how warm and soft she felt. I longed to sink my head into her breasts and feel her arms around me.

She had stopped working, and was sleeping more and more. Jeffery came home from school. I sat still, knowing what was going to happen.

"What's for tea, Mum?" Jeffery asked. My heart started racing as he walked up the hall. "What's for tea, Mum?" He could see that she was asleep. He went through to the kitchen to see if by some magic he could find what he wanted. He came out of the kitchen and slammed the door.

"Can't you get up? Get off the couch!" he screamed, pulling and shaking her. She didn't move, and I stayed beside her. He went through to his bedroom, crying, and started kicking and punching the door until it had a huge hole in it. Suddenly, there was a crash. The door was lying on the floor. Jeffery walked round, banging and kicking anything he could. My mother hardly moved. "Don't worry, Mum, he loves you," I was whispering to her, but she was fast asleep.

After a few hours, Jeffery came into the living-room. "Is there anything to eat?"

"No."

He had found some comics in the refuse hopper and had brought them home. Jeffery sat on the chair reading them. I looked at the pictures for hours. It was getting dark and there was no gas or electricity. Jeffery went to bed to try to keep warm. I wanted so much to be able to get food for him, and take care of him, but I couldn't. I stayed beside my mother all night to protect her and make sure she didn't stop breathing.

The morning arrived. Jeffery got up to go to school. "Why can't she do something? Why can't you do something? Why can't she wash my clothes, or cook something?" He got very angry, and started ripping the old armchair.

"I'm going to get the food parcel this afternoon," I said.

He left the flat and banged the door behind him. I went into his bedroom to try to tidy up, hoping it would make him happy. The wardrobe was broken, and the door was hanging off. It was hard to make it look nice, but I tried. The rest of the day was spent beside my mother. She woke up in the afternoon, wanting food, hitting out at me. "Don't worry. I'm going for the food parcel soon." She fell asleep again. I waited until I could see children getting off the bus from school. I knew it was time for me to go.

"Mum, I'm going now," I whispered, shaking her arm, "I won't be long." She just nodded. I made my way to the soup kitchens, by the side of the Benevolent Society.

When I arrived, I looked for the box with 'Levene' written on it. It was on the top shelf. I tried hard not to drop anything. The box contained two small loaves, one jar of bramble seedless jam, one packet of kosher margarine, a small pack of sugar, six small eggs and one packet of tea leaves.

I thought I would go to meet Jeffery from school. School had finished about half-an-hour before; sometimes he stayed behind with his friends. The school was only round the corner and he was still in the playground with some other boys.

"Jeff," I shouted: he ran off. I started walking home, and after a while caught up with him. He was on his own.

"Jeff, wait for me. Look, I've got the food."

"Go away, you've got bad breath. You're not my sister. Don't tell anyone you are and don't let anyone see the food parcel, or you've had it!" He didn't want his friends to know we lived on charity.

I followed him home, carrying my box, smelling the freshly baked bread. It was driving me mad! When I arrived home, Jeffery had put some of the comics in the bathroom, to use as toilet paper. He was very upset because my mother was still asleep.

"We'll save these comics for later. We didn't read them properly!" he shouted from his bedroom. The comics were strewn all over his room. I made us all some jam sandwiches.

The following morning, Saturday, Jeffery stayed in bed. He wouldn't chance going out in case any of his friends saw him in his school uniform. I could hear him. He was in his bedroom, pretending to play the drums with his fingers. He loved drumming and would spend hours at it. Later on, he came out of his bedroom and went into the kitchen.

"There's no bread left, Jeff," I whispered, following him in. There was only some jam and margarine left, we ate that. We left the eggs until there was some money to put in the gas meter. Tomorrow, I could go the Benevolent Society. If they were open, I might be able to get some money.

My mother started to wake up. "Is there anything to eat?"

I hated having to say no, "But I'll go to the Benevolent Society tomorrow, Mum, and try and get something."

"Go and try to borrow some money from someone, get some chocolate," but I didn't know where to go. Jeffery didn't like me doing that, in case his friends found out. She fell asleep again; I stayed by her side.

In the middle of the afternoon, Jeffery came out of his bedroom. He walked up and down the hall, looking very angry. I was wondering what he was going to do.

"Can't you tidy up?" he screamed in my ear. "You're both the same, useless. Mum, get up!" he shouted again, pulling at her arm, but she didn't budge. After a while, he went back to his bedroom. "Don't you dare follow me, you stay out of my room!" He stayed there till the following morning; I stayed in the living-room. All night I sat wishing the morning would arrive, praying my mother wouldn't wake up begging for things I couldn't give her. At last, the morning arrived and it was almost time for me to go.

"Are you coming, Jeff?"

"No," was the reply. I wanted him to come with me. I was very frightened of walking on my own in case I couldn't breathe.

The Benevolent Society was in sight now. I found myself praying out loud for a shilling or two. My turn came to go into the big room. I could feel myself shaking and fighting back the tears.

"Please can I have a shilling for Mrs Levene?" I begged.

"Hasn't your mother had her National Assistance?" I was asked by the man smoking a cigar.

"Yes." I started to cry.

"Where is it?"

"We haven't got anything left."

He reached to the tin on the table, and took out a sixpence.

"What does your mother do with the money?" he asked, writing in his book.

I didn't answer. The money was in my hand: that was all that mattered.

As soon as I left, I headed towards the nearest delicatessen, and bought some chopped liver and a few bagels, then I made my way home as quickly as possible. Jeffery was looking out of his bedroom window. I held up the small bag so that he could see I had something. I opened the front door to our flat.

"Mum, I've got your favourite, chopped liver! Come on, Jeffery." He was still in his bedroom. My mother took the bag off me, and started eating the chopped liver with her fingers. Jeffery got very angry, "You're disgusting! Why can't you get up and eat?"

We had a bagel each. He was still shouting at her. She told us she needed Duraphet tablets, and fell asleep again. Jeffery was still shouting at her, I couldn't understand why he didn't feel the same way as I did. All I wanted was just to see her alive and breathing. It didn't matter to me that she couldn't do anything. I didn't want to be parted from her.

On Monday morning, Jeffery was very upset that he hadn't been able to clean his clothes. He wanted my mother to be able to do it. He left the flat, banging the door behind him. I found the National Assistance book, and went to the Post Office. When I came home with the shopping, I tried to hide some food from Jeffery.

My mother was still on the couch, and had opened her eyes. I emptied the food on the floor near the couch for her. I couldn't stop her from eating, bingeing madly, just stuffing as much food down her throat as possible. I had seen it so many times before. All I could do was to sit and watch, knowing there was nothing I could do.

When Jeffery arrived home from school, she was still asleep, surrounded by half eaten food which she wouldn't let me take away. Jeffery stood looking at her. "Please try to get up, please," he begged her.

She woke up and opened her eyes. "Let me *shloff*, or I'll kill you," she shouted, pushing him away.

The following day, when Jeffery had left for school, my mother begged me to go to the doctor; "I need some tablets. You must get me some." She was trying to grab my arm. I left so I could be in time for the morning surgery, hoping desperately that the doctor would give me a prescription.

It was soon my turn to see the doctor. I found myself sitting on the chair at the side of his desk. I looked at him.

"Please can I have some Duraphet tablets for my Mum, Mrs Levene?"

Without hesitation, he reached for his pen and wrote out the prescription. I felt so relieved. "Can you give her some breathing tablets as well?" He looked at me. "The pink and white ones that help her breathe."

He added them on, handing the prescription to me.

"Thank you very much, Doctor," I said, and left, heading towards the chemist shop. I pushed open the door, and went straight to the counter and waited for the chemist. As he walked from the back of the shop, he looked at me.

"Hello, I haven't seen you for a long time."

"My Mum went into hospital, and she was much better for a while,"

He looked puzzled. "Did she have electric shock treatment?"

"I don't know," I replied, not understanding what he meant. He handed me the tablets, and I made my way home.

My mother was still asleep when I arrived. "Mum, wake up. I've got some Duraphet and breathers." I was shaking her.

"Come on, Mum. Look, I've got the tablets. I'll go and get you some water." She took two Duraphet, there were four left for tomorrow. All I had to do now was to wait for her to come round.

Later in the afternoon, she felt well enough to get off the couch. We had some money left, and she sent me to the shop for food. She wanted to make a nice meal for Jeffery. When I came back with some fish, she had already put the last of the money in the gas and electricity meters. "I'll make some chopped and fried fish." I couldn't wait for Jeffery to come home. I wanted him to be pleased with my mother.

He arrived home from school, and could smell the cooking.

"Jeffery," my mother shouted. "Here's some chopped and fried fish." He walked through into the kitchen. I could see how pleased he was, but he was very unhappy that she was taking the tablets.

"Tomorrow, I'm going to the Benevolent Society," my mother told us. It would be *Pesach* in a few weeks' time and she wanted to try to get some food vouchers. She was given vouchers for the butcher, fishmonger and delicatessen.

All her Duraphet tablets were gone. She would wake up crying for them, as well as the breathing tablets and food. Sometimes, she didn't know who we were. Jeffery would get very upset, we didn't know what to do. We would look all over the flat, hoping we could find a few pence to buy some chocolate.

The following week, I went to the doctor, hoping to get more tablets for her. His answer was, "No." He gave me a prescription for cream for my lips. I told him I didn't feel very well, and he added a tonic to the prescription.

Walking towards the chemist, I was trying to find the courage to ask him to change my prescription for Duraphet tablets, not knowing what his reply would be. When I asked him, he said he would change the prescription, and gave me four Duraphet instead of the cream and tonic. I saved them for *Pesach*. I was determined not to give them to her until the day we had the food delivered. I wanted her to be able to cook for us.

My mother had the vouchers: the day came when we could exchange them for food. That morning I went through all the motions of going to the doctor. When I arrived home, I told her that the doctor had given me a prescription. I gave her two of the tablets, and waited for her to wake up.

Later in the day, we walked to the top of Blackley New Road, and collected some of the shopping. There was fish, chicken, cheese and about three bags full of food. The man at the delicatessen said they would deliver the rest in about two hours' time.

We took the bags home, and put them in the living-room. My mother had to sit down for a while to recover. Soon, there was a knock on the door, and we had two boxes of food delivered from the delicatessen. My mother had fallen asleep. I pulled all the boxes to the side of the couch so she could see them as soon as she woke up.

When at last she started to wake up I said, "Look, Mum, we've got salami, and saveloys, and lots of boxes of *Matzos*."

"I'll make chicken soup and gefilte fish." I was kneeling, looking in the boxes. I moved over to her, and sank my head into her tummy, and we hugged each other.

"Will you be able to cook anything tonight for Jeffery's tea?"

"Yes, and you can both help."

Jeffery arrived home from school. As soon as I heard the front door open, I ran down the hall, "Jeff, come on. Look what we've got."

We went into the living-room, and were looking through the boxes, eating some of the cheese. My mother was in the kitchen, cooking. "Will you wash up, Hikey?" The sink was full of dirty pots. She was making chicken soup. She took all the innards out of the chicken. She kept the small eggs to put in the soup, leaving the rest on the side.

"Let's play butchers," Jeff said, "What would you like madam?"

"Half a pound of lamb's liver."

"That will be one and six," he said, wrapping the chicken innards in some paper, and laughing. We played for ages. My mother cooked as much food as she could. There were plenty of *Matzos* and I hid a few boxes for when the food ran out. We could have egg and salt water or *Matzo* with jam.

It was the school holidays. Jeffery wasn't to go back to school until the next week. My mother was sleeping all the time. I mostly stayed by her side, afraid to leave her. Sometimes, Jeffery and I would go to try and borrow a little money from people in the houses that surrounded the flats.

One day, on the way back, we stumbled on a rubbish tip, across the road from the flats. Looking around, we found a small fish tank, and filled it with tadpoles from the nearby pond. Jeffery told me that they were his pets. Just as we were about to leave, he found two tins of bottle green gloss paint: we decided to decorate the flat for our mother.

When we arrived home, Jeffery left the paint in the hall, placed the fish tank on the balcony, and filled it with water.

"Don't go near them. They're mine."

Then we started painting. We were very excited, and couldn't wait to get it finished. There was only one brush, so we took it in turns. We started on the white paintwork around the door frames, then we did the small windows above the doors. We carried on until the paint ran out. We were very pleased with ourselves and thought we had done a good job.

Later on, my mother woke up. "What's that smell?"

I ran to her. "Mum, we've decorated for you. It looks lovely now."

"You've painted the windows?"

"Don't you like it, Mum?" I said, crying, "Aren't you pleased with it? We did it for you."

She gave me a hug, and started to sleep again. "Let me *shloff* now, Hikey,"

She slept for the rest of the day, waking up every few hours, begging for her breathing tablets, feeling very thirsty. She seemed to be getting worse, and we didn't know what to do.

It was the middle of the night, I was still beside her, in the living-room. She woke up, crying that she couldn't breathe, I had given her all the breathing tablets; there were none left.

"Help me get up," she asked, tugging at my skirt and holding my hand. She wanted to go to bed. I helped her to get off the couch. Her coat fell to the floor. She was soaking wet from head to foot. The sweat was pouring off her body.

"Get me a drink, quick." She drank two or three cups of water, and was still begging for more. At last, I managed to help her to the bedroom. "I need more water," she was shouting.

I had to open all the windows so that she could feel a little breeze. Sitting on the floor beside her, I was praying that she would fall asleep, just for a while. She finally managed to fall asleep. I could see, even in the dark, how much she was sweating. She kept sticking her tongue out, I didn't know what to do.

She woke up again when it was almost light. She pulled my shoulder. I turned round. "I need some water, quickly." She was hardly able to open her mouth. When she had drunk the water, she asked me to look for a tablet. "Look everywhere," she begged me.

I looked around, and went back into the bedroom to tell her that there were none anywhere. She was lying still. I slapped her thinking that she was going to die, her eyes seemed to be rolling in her head.

I rushed into Jeffery's room, pulling him out of bed.

"Quick, Jeffery, come on, there's something wrong with Mum." We both went to look at her.

"Go to the hospital," she was whispering.

We ran out of the flat and holding hands ran all the way to Crumpsall Hospital. We ran so quickly, it was hard to keep upright on our feet. We reached the hospital, and ran inside.

"Please send the doctor to my Mum," I was telling the nurse. We were both begging for a doctor. The nurse took us to the reception area, and asked us for some details.

"She's very poorly."

"Go home, the doctor will come soon."

When we arrived back at the flat, the doctor was already there, waiting at the door. He went through to the bedroom. I couldn't look at her, in case she was dead. "*Shama Yisroel*," I was repeating. "Please don't die, Mum."

The doctor came out of the bedroom. "She'll have to go into hospital straight away," he told us. "Is your father here?"

"No," we replied.

"Who looks after you?" I didn't understand what he meant.

"The last time she went to Crumpsall Hospital, I went into

the Sarah Laski Home," I told him. He wrote it down, and told us an ambulance would call as soon as he could arrange it.

After the ambulance had taken my mother to the hospital, Jeffery and I made our way to the Sarah Laski Home. He told me I could hold his hand and he held it all the way there. As soon as we reached the front door, he told me not to tell anyone I was his sister.

"You're smelly! I don't like girls!"

The Matron opened the door. She was expecting us. We were both taken to get washed and given a change of clothing. I asked the Matron if she could ring the hospital to make sure my mother was being looked after.

All the time, I was looking around for things to take home for her.

At lunchtime, I wanted to sit next to Jeffery at the table. I wanted to stay with him all the time, but he wouldn't let me.

"Go away," he said.

I never seemed to get enough food. I got into the habit of making sure the clearing up was left to me, so that I could finish off as much of the leftovers as possible. On the first day Jeffery went out to play with some of the other children. They were playing on the swings and slides.

"She's not my sister," he told one of the other children, and ran off with them. I didn't like any of them, and was pleased to be on my own. We had to stay outside. When I tried to go back into the house, I wasn't allowed in. "You must stay out and play with the other children," the nurses told me. All I wanted was to curl up and hold myself to keep warm, to sleep as much as possible.

At the weekend, I was told that I could go to visit my

mother. Sometimes at mealtimes, the larder door was left open. The larder was near the kitchen, and was full of fruit and biscuits and all kinds of other food. I kept peeping in, and slipping inside at the first opportunity. I quickly took some oranges and a packet of biscuits. "I'll take these for my Mum," I whispered. I managed to hide them under my coat.

Just before I left for the hospital, the Matron called me into her office. She gave me a thrupenny piece. "This is your spending money." I felt very excited, knowing that I had some money to buy some chocolate for my mother. I had the oranges and biscuits as well.

I walked down to the hospital. Opposite the main gate, I noticed a small shop. I crossed the road, and bought my mother a bar of chocolate. It was so exciting to have all these things for her. The number of the ward was written on the back of my hand. I walked along the corridors until at last I saw the number at the bottom of a flight of stairs. Checking that all the oranges and chocolate were still under my arm, I made my way to the ward. My stomach was churning and my heart was pounding. I couldn't wait to see her. I missed her so much.

The ward door was closed and the little round windows were too high for me to see through. When the nurse opened the door, I couldn't hold back the tears. I could see my mother, sitting up in bed. "Please be well, Mum. Please be better."

"Hikey!" I ran to her, and put my arms round her. All the oranges and biscuits fell on the floor.

"Look what I've got for you, Mum," I told her, picking them up off the floor, and putting them on her bedside cabinet.

Suddenly, a doctor was standing beside me. "Don't you know she mustn't eat things like this?"

I was sobbing, not knowing what was wrong, not understanding why he was shouting.

"She doesn't know," my mother told him. I was still crying so much that I felt as if my head would burst. My mother pulled me to her.

"It's alright, Hikey. The doctor's only trying to help."

"Your mother's diabetic. She mustn't eat sweet things if you want her to get better."

I stayed on my mum's bed, just holding her, not understanding what was being said. "I'm sorry, Mum," I told her, wiping my eyes.

"I'm coming home next week." She held me till visiting time was over.

The following week came and the Matron called Jeffery and me into her office. "Your mother's going home tomorrow. You will be able to go home before teatime."

We were both very excited. I had managed to get some small tubs of kosher powdered jelly, called 'Snowcem.' I had them hidden, ready to take home. I had also managed to get a tea towel and a hand towel to take home for her. The Matron had given me a long scarf. When I went to bed I placed it over my body. I was sure, somehow, that it would protect my mother so I made sure I didn't lose it.

The following day, we got ready to go home. It was late afternoon when the Matron told us we could go. We ran together as fast as possible to get back home to her. Jeffery had a key to the front door, so we let ourselves in.

"Mum!" I mumbled, afraid she wouldn't be there, "Mum."

She was sitting on the couch, holding a piece of paper.

"What's that, Mum?"

"It's a diet sheet. I can only eat what's on it."

I read the diet sheet: *one ounce of butter, one slice of bread* it went on. Reading it, my heart sank.

"Hikey, I have to take one of these insulin tablets every morning, or I'll go into a coma." I was getting very frightened, trying to take it all in. "I must have a meal within half-an-hour of the tablets, or I will go into a coma," she was telling me. "I have to take the tablets at six o'clock in the morning." It was all too much, and my mind seemed to go blank.

I put my mother's insulin tablets in the kitchen, so I would know where they were, and tried to stick the diet sheet on the wall. It fell off: I put it in a drawer to keep it safe. The National Assistance money hadn't been collected because she had been in hospital; I looked for the book, putting it to one side. I could cash it first thing in the morning. My mother was asleep on the couch; all I could do was to wait for the morning to come.

We had no clock, so when morning came, I looked out of the window to see if there were people walking about or buses running. It was the only way to get an idea of what time it was. I reached for the bottle of insulin tablets on the shelf, taking one out. I held it very tightly, knowing how important it was, and filled a cup with water.

"Mum," I whispered, shaking her arm, "Here, take the tablet." I knew that once she had taken it, she had to have some food quickly. There was only half-an-hour in which to find her something; I searched everywhere. There was nothing. I took her coat off her, and looked through the pockets. She had two of the biscuits in it that I had taken to the hospital.

Thank God! The words were going through my mind.

"Mum, come on. Eat one, Mum, eat the biscuits. They should do. It's almost time for me to go to the Post Office. I'll get something proper then."

She closed her eyes again, I was afraid to leave her. It was getting lighter now. I looked out of the window to see children going to school. Picking up the National Assistance book, I left the flat without waking her, hoping she would be alright.

The Post Office was open. All the shopping was quickly done. It didn't take me long to get home. The first thing I did was to get the diet sheet. I took it through to the living-room and read it again. My mother was awake now. "Where's the shopping?" It was in the hall. "Go and get it."

"Mum," I said, still holding the diet sheet as she binged on the food desperately. "You'll die, Mum."

"I'll be fine, Hikey. Don't worry," she said, stuffing the food into her mouth between each word.

My mum's going to die. The words were echoing through my mind. "Please come home, Jeff," I was praying. I took the diet sheet into the kitchen, putting it in the drawer, along with the insulin tablets and the breathing tablets. I'll read it again later, so I know it by heart, I was telling myself.

My mother was asleep again, the rest of the food still beside her. I sat near the couch, looking at her face, not knowing what to expect. There was a knock on the front door. I stayed still, hoping that whoever it was would go away. My mother didn't wake up.

"Mrs Levene, it's the School Board!" A voice came down the hall. "Open the door!" I walked down the hall and opened the front door. A man holding a briefcase was standing there.

"My Mum's asleep. She's just come out of hospital."

"What's your name?"

"Jane Levene," I told him, frightened he was going to take me away.

"Why aren't you in school?"

"My Mum's not been well. I'll go tomorrow."

"Fine, make sure you do," he said, leaving.

Closing the door, I leaned against the wall. "Thank God he didn't take me away."

"Mum, the School Board man has been." She woke up.

"Mum, the man from the School Board's been." She didn't take much notice, and asked me to try to get some Duraphet tablets.

Jeffery had just arrived home. My mother shouted to him.

"Jeffery, go to the doctor's. Get me some Duraphet." She gave him five shillings. "If the doctor won't give you a prescription, see if the chemist will sell you some." She knew the chemist had changed my prescription for Duraphet tablets, and hoped he would sell her some.

When Jeffery arrived home later, the doctor had refused to give him a prescription for Duraphet tablets. He told the chemist he was Annie Levene's son, from 32 Bracknell Court, and that he had five shillings. He asked the chemist if he could let him have some Duraphet. The chemist gave him four tablets in return for the money.

My mother took two of the tablets and later in the evening she started to wake up a little. Before she woke up I managed to hide some food for the morning. Jeffery had taken some food into his bedroom, and stayed there. He hated it when she took the tablets, and would get very angry when she asked him to go to the doctor. At last, she was awake and sitting up. I wanted her to read the diet sheet to see what she could eat. She wouldn't even look at it. She couldn't stay awake for very long, even with the tablets.

Jeffery was still in his bedroom. I was hoping he would come into the living-room, but he didn't. It was very hard for me to sleep, in case my mother went into a coma, or it went past the time for her insulin. The night dragged. When I could see the sky starting to get lighter, I waited a while then took an insulin tablet from the bottle in the drawer.

"Come on, Mum, you've got to take your tablet." I reached to fill the cup with water. She was still asleep. "Mum, you've got to take your tablet." She woke up and swallowed it.

"I'll get you something to eat." The food was still in the bags on the living-room floor. There wasn't much left. First, I looked at the diet sheet, to get an idea of what she could have: all that was left was some cooked chicken and chopped liver; she ate them. I managed to hide a few small tins of spaghetti where no-one could find them, for her after her insulin.

Jeffery woke up early and looked for something to eat. There were some bits of food left. I couldn't let him have the spaghetti, even though I wanted to.

My mother woke up and wanted her Duraphet tablets. They were the last two. I gave them to her along with a breathing tablet.

"Go to school, Hikey. I'll be alright."

I helped her into bed, and left some water on the floor for her, and a few bits of food.

"I'm frightened to leave you." She begged me to go. I made sure that the front door key was in my pocket, and left for school.

Nothing mattered in school, nothing sank in. I noticed that the children gave me some funny looks, but I didn't care. I just wanted the time to pass till the bell rang. When it did, all I could remember was running and running, banging my feet to keep my heart going, and praying my mother would be still alive.

At last, I reached the last corner before the flats. The doors to the stairs were open, I ran up them as fast as possible, looking behind me now and again, just to make sure nothing was following me. As I put the key in the lock, my heart was pounding, my whole body was pulsating and shaking.

"Mum," I shouted. There was no answer. "Mum, I'm home." She was lying on the bed. She's in a coma. What do I do? The words were thumping around in my head. I slapped her face and pulled her tongue out of her mouth, so she wouldn't choke. I kept pulling her tongue and smacking her face.

Her eyes opened and she grabbed my hair. "What are you doing? Why are you waking me up?"

She was hitting me and pulling at my clothes, but she was alright. That was all that mattered.

CHAPTER 8

Jeffery was about to leave for school. He was looking around the flat, hoping to find a piece of chocolate or a toffee. He was very hungry, there was nothing and would be nothing until Friday and the food parcel. I knew he would get a dinner at school. I was hoping he could get a double portion so he wouldn't feel hungry later.

"See you later, Jeffery." I wanted my mother to wake up and see him off, but she didn't. I couldn't give him the last tin of spaghetti, that was for tomorrow morning, after the insulin tablet. My mother was asleep, I watched her very carefully. She had experienced a few comas up to now, it was very frightening. I made sure that there was always some sugar available. If she got too bad, Jeffery and I would run to get the doctor. It was impossible for me to take my eyes off her mouth, watching it move or open, putting my hand against it to make sure there was breath coming out. She woke up wanting food, Duraphet and breathing tablets; there was nothing left. "Please go to sleep," I was praying, wishing Friday would come as quickly as possible.

There was a loud knock on the door. "It's the School Board," I whispered. It must be. "They want to take me away," I said to my mother, "I'm not going to open the door." She was asleep. I stayed in the living-room with her, ignoring the knocking.

"Annie. Open the door, will you?"

I shook her and her eyes opened. "Mum, there's someone at the door."

Again he shouted. "Open the door."

"Quickly, it's your father," she pushed me towards the hall.

As I walked down the hall, he was still shouting, "Open this door, now!" I opened the door, he pushed past me. I recognised the face from the old doctor's surgery. I had seen him a few times waiting to see the doctor. Thank God, I thought to myself. He's brought some food for my mum. Perhaps he's going to take me to the ice cream van and buy me an ice cream. Perhaps he wants to collect me from school like the other fathers.

He was standing over the couch, talking to my mother. He seemed as tall as a mountain. I looked up at him as he walked into the kitchen. "Can't you tidy the place? It's filthy." He looked at me. I felt frightened. "I'm going to lie down for an hour. Don't disturb me or I'll smack you," He walked into the bedroom.

My mother was asleep, and I stayed beside her. Later on I crept to the bedroom door, not understanding why my father was asleep. He should be helping my mother, doing something, talking to her. She needed him. I knew that. He turned and looked at me. My hands were shaking. "Go and make me a cup of tea and make sure the cup's clean."

I went into the kitchen, standing there, looking around. I had never made a cup of tea. No-one had ever asked me. We had tea leaves, we got a packet each week as part of the food parcel, but I never used them. The sugar was for mum, in case she went into a coma. I couldn't give him any of that. I put some tea leaves in a cup, filling it with cold water. I tiptoed back to the bedroom, past my mother. She was fast asleep. I wanted him to sit on the couch with her and tell her he would take her out for a treat. My father lifted his head. I walked round to the side of the bed and held the cup out to him, making sure he could reach it.

"What's this?" he shouted loudly, pushing the cup so that the liquid spilt all over Jeffery's bed. He jumped up, grabbing my arm with one hand and slapped my leg with the other. It hurt and burned. Again he slapped me.

What was happening? Why was he hitting me? I didn't understand. What had I done wrong? He pushed me onto the floor, and slapped me again on the back of my legs. My flesh felt as if it were melting under the intense heat. I'll stay still, I thought. If he thinks I'm dead, he'll leave me alone and go away. He didn't and pulled me up by the arm so hard that it cracked, pushing me onto the bed. My mum mustn't know, I thought. I won't tell her. I didn't want her to worry. I was lying on my tummy, my head buried in the mattress, my lips biting on it. Then I felt his hand on my burning skin. He's making it better. He's sorry he hit me, I was thinking. He was very strong. If I pretend I'm asleep, he'll go away. He carried on pushing me, almost suffocating me in the mattress. He was shaking me, pulling me, prodding my legs. He was holding my feet and bending them back, he was pulling them and parting my legs. I knew he would see my bottom. I didn't want him to. My mind was trying to force my legs to close. I didn't want him to see my bottom. He pulled my legs apart so hard, I was sure he had snapped them. He got onto the bed. My eyes were tightly closed. I could feel something on my leg. I knew it wasn't his arm, it was something else. Perhaps he had taken it out of his pocket? Whatever it was, it moved. It seemed to be on hinges. Then he pushed me off the bed, I crashed onto the floor.

"Get out and let me sleep, and don't disturb me." He looked at me. "Your big mouth will get you into trouble one day."

"Yes, Dad," I said, fighting back the tears, not wanting my mother to worry.

My mother shifted about on the couch, but didn't wake up. I took my place on the floor beside her. It was difficult to sit so I lay on my side, making sure that, if she did wake up, she wouldn't see the marks. My father stayed in bed for a while and slept on. I couldn't sleep while he was in the flat. When he got out of bed, I stayed very still, pretending to be asleep. He left the flat. He hadn't called me by my name, I thought to myself. Perhaps he didn't know it.

Jeffery came home from school. I stayed on the floor. He walked into his bedroom, and stayed there till morning.

"Mummy, wake up." The morning had come, I had just opened my eyes. "Come on Mum, take your insulin." I shook her gently. "Come on, Mum, take your insulin. Take your tablets, here's some water." I lifted her head. "Here you are." I placed the tablets on her tongue and gave her the water. "Don't fall asleep until you've had something to eat," I told her as I went to get the last tin of spaghetti. She pulled me back by my skirt:

"What's that mark on your leg?" My skirt was so long, it covered most of the marks.

"It's a handprint, there's blood." She looked at me. "The *momzer*! Hikey, did he do that? He'd better never come here again!"

She ate her spaghetti and slept. It was frightening to see her fall asleep again after taking the insulin, not knowing if her sleep was a coma. I stayed near her, watching her eyes, making sure they weren't rolling in her head, afraid to leave her.

"I'm going to the Benevolent Society tomorrow for the food parcel. I'll see if I can get some money for the gas and electric," I was telling her, even though she was still asleep.

She woke up later in the day, wanting food and cigarettes.

"There's nothing, Mum, and no money. I'll get the food parcel tomorrow."

"Will you go to the doctor's for Duraphet and breathing tablets?"

"I'll have to wait till later, Mum. Try to go to sleep."

"Hikey, go to the shops at the top of the road, and see if they will let you have some food till Monday. I'll pay then." She begged me to go. I walked up the road, first to the greengrocer. When it was my turn to be served, I looked at the man behind the counter.

"Can my Mum have some food till Monday? We live at 32 Bracknell Court."

"No," he answered.

Then I went to the sweet shop, and again, when it came to my turn, I asked if I could have ten Park Drive cigarettes until Monday. "We live at 32 Bracknell Court," I told the lady.

"No, dear."

On my way home, I remembered hearing a lady telling someone that her daughter had long hair, and she'd sold it to a hairdresser. I went back home to the flat, and found my mother's comb. I combed my hair very thoroughly. It was very long. I thought I would get plenty of money for it. I crept out of the flat again feeling very excited. I made my way to the hairdresser's on Middleton Road. It was at the top of Blackley New Road.

I started to feel more excited as I walked down the path to the shop. Inside, the hairdresser was putting rollers in a lady's hair. I closed the door and looked at her. She told me to sit down till she had finished. When she had finished the lady's hair, she beckoned me over to sit on the chair.

"I can't cut your hair. You have head lice!" She held the scissors well away from my head. "Go home and tell your mum. You can get hair soap to kill them." I ran out of the shop, and cried all the way home.

"Did you get anything from the shop?" My mother shouted.

"No. I'll go to the doctor's soon. Try to go to *shloff*." I wanted to wait for Jeffery, to see if he would come with me. My mother wanted me to go straight away. The doctor gave me a prescription for four tablets and some breathing tablets, as well as some more Insulin.

The morning arrived and it was time once again for her insulin. This time there was no food at all. When she had taken the insulin I was very frightened. There was nothing anywhere in the flat. It was very early morning. What could I do? She needed food desperately, or she would go into a coma.

I shook her hard. "Mum, what should I do? Wake up."

"Doris, go and see Doris. It's Birkdale Street."

I vaguely remembered where the house was and left the flat. It was a long way down Cheetham Hill Road. I ran and ran.

"Please can I have some bread?" I was practising, for when I got there, crying and running, looking down, searching the pavements to see if anyone had dropped some money, frightened I wouldn't get back in time to save my mother's life.

I reached Auntie Doris's house, and started banging on the door, begging her through the letter box, to open it. She opened the door. I could see she was very angry.

"My Mother's had an insulin tablet, and there's no food for her," I gasped, banging my foot on the pavement to keep my heart beating. She wasn't interested. She went through to the kitchen, and came back with an onion. She gave it to me, closing the door. I ran back home holding it very tightly, knowing how important it was.

"Mum, come on, get up." She didn't know what was happening, her body was shaking all over. I put some sugar in a cup of water and made her drink it, then I pulled the skin off the onion and made her eat it. I sat beside her until the afternoon. It was time to go to the soup kitchen. Knowing I had to leave her was terrible. I made sure she had a cup of sugar water by her side and left the flat. It was raining hard.

When I arrived at the soup kitchen, I made my way to the room where all the boxes of food were lined up, waiting to be collected. I looked round to see if there was anyone about. There were some women helpers. I wanted to take some food out of the other boxes to take home, but it was impossible.

I had to pass the school on the way. As I passed it on the return journey, I didn't care if anyone saw me. It didn't matter if they did: nobody could make me leave my mother.

Walking home with the food, I was thinking about how I could make it last until Monday, trying to think of where I could hide it without Jeffery finding it. I felt very anxious and frightened. I tried to get home as quickly as possible. I kept looking around to see if Jeffery was walking home. I couldn't see him. The flats drew nearer. My clothes were soaking wet. My school uniform was clinging to me, moulded to my body.

It was my lifeline, my skin, my comfort. We never parted.

I waited for someone to come down the stairs and open the main door. I was too frightened to use the lift in case it got stuck. The door opened and I ran up the stairs as fast as I could. I took the front door key out of my pocket, ready to open the door. As I approached the front door, my heart was in my mouth. "Don't die, Mum, I'm here," I was whispering to myself. "Mum, are you alright?" I shouted. There was no answer. I ran down the hall dropping the food on the floor. She was lying on the couch. I rushed to her, and shook her arm. "Mummy, are you alright?" There was no reply. I sat over her, slapping her face and pulling her tongue out of her mouth so that she wouldn't choke. She pushed me onto the floor.

"Stop it. What are you doing? Let me *shloff*!" She slapped me. I didn't mind her slapping me. It meant she was alive. That was all that mattered. I stroked her hair.

"Go to *shloff*, Mum."

I picked up the food from the floor, taking it into the kitchen. I wanted to eat some of the bread, but every scrap was needed for the mornings. At last the food was hidden. I had to think where I could get some money from. I racked my brain as I realised there would be no money till Sunday when, hopefully, the Benevolent Society would be open; maybe they would give me some.

Jeffery arrived home from school. I was sitting on the floor beside my mother. He walked down the hall and into the kitchen. He was looking for food.

"Where's the food parcel?"

"I don't know, Jeffery?" I hoped he would believe me.

"Where is it?" he screamed, pulling my jumper and pushing me over. "Where is it? I'm starving!"

"Mum needs it," I replied, longing to give him some bread.

He walked into the kitchen, and started banging everything, making a terrible noise: "I've found it." I ran into the kitchen, begging him to save it for my mother. I tried to take the bread off him, feeling frightened that there would be no food for mum.

"What's the noise about? Let me *shloff*. I'll kill you both." She wanted some bread and jam. I made her a jam sandwich with a small piece of bread that was left. Nearly all the bread and jam had been eaten. I managed to hide a small piece of crust, I knew it wasn't enough. My mother had fallen asleep again.

Jeffery came into the living-room. We tried to read some comics. It was getting dark. My mother woke up, screaming that she couldn't breathe. I went into the bedroom. There was just one breathing tablet left.

"Found one, Mum." I gave it to her.

"Is there any chocolate?" She was gasping for breath.

Jeffery and I started to look all over the flat for a few pence, but there was nothing.

"Get some, get some," she was crying.

"OK, Mum. I'll see if there's anything on the landing outside. Perhaps someone's dropped a penny." When I came back into the living-room, she was begging Jeffery to find something.

"Stop it. Get up off the couch. Please Mum!" he begged her. "I'll kill you if you don't get up," he was shouting. "Please, Mum," he kept repeating, and walked towards his bedroom.

"Hikey, will you go to the doctor tomorrow?"

"Yes, Mum."

"I need some tablets, Hikey."

"I know, Mum. Don't worry. I'll go first thing in the morning." She fell asleep again.

When morning came, I gave her the insulin tablet. I'd hidden the crust of bread, and got it for her. After waiting a while, I went and stood outside Jeffery's bedroom. The door was lying on the floor, and he saw me standing there. "Will you come to the doctor with me?"

"No," he replied, and covered his head with the blanket.

I left the flat, and started the journey to the surgery. Gasping for breath, I touched the wall for comfort, that always made me feel a bit better. I waited in the surgery. "The doctor will see you now," the receptionist said. The corridor to his room seemed so long. "Please," I was saying to myself. I knocked on his door.

"Come in." As I pushed the door open, the words spilled out of my mouth. "Please can my Mum, Mrs Levene, have some tablets?" He looked at me. "Duraphet tablets," I told him. It must be a new doctor, I thought. Perhaps he will give me some. He looked at the notes on his desk:

"No, she's already had some."

"Can I have some Hydroderm cream for my lips? My tummy hurts badly, as well." He wrote me a prescription. I walked towards the chemist, not knowing what to do, desperately wanting to ask the chemist for some Duraphet tablets. I didn't want him to say "No."

I counted the steps to the chemist. I wanted to know how many steps there were from the doctor's surgery. It was just down the road. I could see people going in and out. A few more steps and I would have hold of the door handle. As I pushed the door open, the number of steps I'd walked vanished from my mind. There were two people before me.

The chemist was working alone as usual. I held onto the prescription until my turn came.

I looked at him as I passed it over. "Will you change it, please?" He took the prescription into the back of the shop. When I saw him come back with a little white box I knew it was the Duraphet tablets. I closed my eyes and thanked God for them.

My mother took two tablets as soon as I got home. I waited for them to take effect, nothing seemed to be happening. She wasn't coming round or coming back to life. Then she opened her eyes. "Please, get me some chocolate and cigarettes. I need them," she pleaded, holding out her hand towards me. "Get me a pencil and paper." My mother wrote out a small note. It read: *Please can you lend me a shilling till Monday morning, when I get my National Assistance money.*

"Take it to your father. He lives in the big green house on the corner of Cheetham Hill Road and Smedley Lane, in one of those flats." I took the note. "Don't worry, Mum. I'll see what I can get."

Walking down Cheetham Hill Road, I felt very frightened. Praying that he would give me some money, I kept my eyes peeled in case I missed the house.

The synagogue was around the corner. I was trying to hide from view, hoping no-one would see me. It was *Shabbas* morning. My uniform was in tatters. I was wishing and praying that somehow my clothes would be transformed into nice ones, so I could walk on the same side of the road as the families walking to the synagogue. I had promised my mother that I would take my brother, David, to the synagogue when he came home. I had very little recollection of him. I couldn't even remember his voice.

Carrying on my journey and trying to remember David, I came in sight of Smedley Lane. There wasn't very far to go now. I made sure the note was still clutched in my hand. I could see the big house. It must be the right one. It was on the corner. The house was at the bottom of a long driveway. I pushed open the gates. My heart was thumping so loudly that I didn't have to stamp my foot on the floor to get it going again.

There were little white buttons on the front door. I pressed one and waited. My hand started to comfort the blisters on the back of my leg. I could feel them through my skirt, as I tried to protect them from him.

The door opened. "Hello, Dad," I said, wanting him to say, "Hello, Hikey," to me, but he didn't.

"What do you want?" He blew cigarette smoke over me. Sparks were flying everywhere.

"Here's a letter for you. It's from Mum." Suddenly, I could smell his body, his socks, his vest, all his clothes, just as I had smelt them when he was in the bedroom. They frightened me, and I was trying hard not to inhale. I wanted to run away from him, back to my mother, but I needed some money. I followed him into his flat, I was shaking, desperately wanting to be home with my mother. Everything smelt of him. I wanted to be sick, and tried very hard to make the vomit stay in my stomach. I wanted so much to hold out my arms to him, to run to him. I couldn't.

"What does that good-for-nothing fat bitch want?" I just stood rigid as he slowly unbuckled his brown belt and pushed me towards the armchair.

"Bend over." I felt my skirt being lifted, exposing my bare bottom. My body tensed, I felt the strength of the belt as it lashed against my flesh, my body trembled as the burning sensation shuddered over my body. He pulled my arm, but it was difficult to stand up straight.

I watched him take a pair of trousers off the back of a chair and drop them on the floor. I could hear money rattling in the pocket. I smiled at him, hoping he would give me a shilling piece, anything. The amount didn't matter. Taking off his trousers he sat in the easy chair. He beckoned me over and I closed my eyes as I caught sight of the dark triangle between his legs.

"Do you know what they call little girls who tell stories?"

"No Dad".

"Little Miss *News of the World*!" he replied.

I wondered if he would give me some money. The delicatessen was closed today because it was *Shabbas*, but there was the sweet shop. That would be open. I could get some chocolate for us.

As I brought myself back to reality, he was getting dressed. He held a shilling piece. Quickly, I grabbed it.

I left his flat. The most important thing now was to get some food. I stopped at a sweet shop on Cheetham Hill Road, and bought some chocolate and sweets. What had happened with my father didn't seem to have touched me. My desperation couldn't be penetrated. My mother was the most important thing in the world to me. I didn't like my father. I didn't like his flat or the smells that surrounded him. They were fixed in my memory. Why wasn't he looking after my mother? I thought I hated him, but I wasn't sure if I did. He had never called me by my name, he had not talked to me. I couldn't understand why he didn't love my mother the same way I did. I never wanted to go near him again, but I did a few times. I would sit on the step outside his flat, waiting for him to come home, wanting to beg him for money, at the same time hoping he wouldn't want anything in return. But I didn't refuse. My mother's needs were too desperate.

CHAPTER 9

The time came for me to take my eleven plus exam. We were given a note at school telling us where we would sit the exam, the times and the dates. I thought the exams had something to do with leaving school. All I could think about was wanting to get a good job, so I could look after my mother.

We were taken by bus from our own school to a school somewhere in Blackley. I had left my mother in bed. She had had her insulin tablet and a tin of spaghetti. Arriving at the school, we were taken to a room, told to be very quiet and to wait until the teacher arrived. The teacher walked round the room, very slowly placing a paper face down on each of the desks. I looked at the other children. They all looked nervous. We were told to start answering the questions. I wanted to put my head down and start writing like the other children. I wrote my name and my class number, that was all I knew. I wanted desperately to be able to answer the questions. If only I could see what the other children were writing, but it was impossible. I looked at the teacher, even though I knew she couldn't help me. I just sat and waited until it was time to go home. When the exam was over, we were taken back to King David School in a special bus. From there I ran all the way home.

Jeffery was in his room; my mother was still in bed. "Mum, Mum," I whispered, shaking her gently. She didn't wake up. I wanted to tell her I was sorry I couldn't do the exam, but she was fast asleep and I knew she wouldn't wake up. What will I do when I leave school? The thoughts were going through my mind, till my brain felt as if it would shrivel. I sat near the bedroom door, watching her, wondering how I was going to look after her if I couldn't get a job.

She was groaning as she lay on the couch. Her hair was matted and her legs covered in blood. I stood near the door.

"Go to bed, Hikey."

"OK, Mum," I said, not being able to leave her side.

In the middle of the week, Miss Sassoon came to see my mother to tell her that David was coming home in a few weeks' time. She told us that he would go to King David School. My mother was lying on the bed, unable to take notice of what Miss Sassoon was saying. As she was leaving, she told me she had some clothes in her car. I followed her to the car. She gave me some dresses and cardigans. I took them upstairs.

"Mum, look what I've got. I'll take them to the second-hand shop."

My mother was still asleep. I made my way to the shop. I knew I would get a few pennies for them. I was given a shilling for the clothes. It was more than I expected. I went to the chemist to see if I could buy some tablets. He told me I would need at least two shillings so instead I walked to the sweet shop and bought my mother some chocolate.

When I arrived home, I woke her to give her the chocolate. She ate it, and begged me to get her some tablets. I told her I would try first thing in the morning.

Morning came. I gave her the insulin tablet and a crust of bread I had hidden in the cupboard. Then I set out to go to the doctor's surgery. I felt frightened that he would refuse yet again. I turned round and started to walk towards my father's flat instead. I knew he was always in, my mother often told me that he never worked. Maybe he would give me some money and I could buy some tablets.

Eventually, I reached his gate, my heart pounded as I opened it. I could feel the blood pumping through my body as I ran towards the front door, praying he would be in.

I banged on the door and waited, holding my tummy hard to make it stop jumping. I knew he was coming, because the smell of his socks seeped through the cracks in the door. I wanted to run away, but I waited, hoping he would open the door. I could hear footsteps. I held my breath as the door opened.

"Can I have some money?" I blurted out, even before I saw him. "Dad, can I have some money, please?"

He didn't answer, but I knew that I was to follow him to his room. When I left the flat, I had a shilling.

One day, a few weeks later, I heard a knock on the front door. When I opened it, Miss Sassoon was standing there, holding David's hand. His other hand was covering his eyes, and he was pulling away, hiding behind her.

"Come on, David. Say hello to your sister," she told him.

I walked over to him, and took his hand. "Come on, David." He was very quiet and shy. Miss Sassoon handed me a bag, and we all went into the living-room. My mother was lying on the couch. She cried when she saw David. Miss Sassoon told her that David would have to go to school from the next day. Soon after, she left.

David didn't say anything. He sat near the television, and stared at me. "Come on, David," I said, and took him to the bedroom. He was crying.

"Jeffery will be home soon. Don't cry. Get into bed." I lay

on the bed with him, hugging him until he fell asleep. I went back into the living-room and looked in the bag he had brought with him. There were a pair of shorts, a jumper and some sandwiches. I hid one for the morning.

Jeffery came home from school, and went straight into his bedroom. I could hear him and David talking. They both stayed in the bedroom till the following morning.

When daylight came I woke up by the side of the couch. My hand caught the arm of the couch as I tried to stand up. My mother's eyes opened. She glared at me, and pushed me:

"Don't move. Don't breathe. I can't stand it."

"Sorry Mum. I'm just getting your insulin." I knew she didn't mean to hurt me. It was because she wasn't well. If only I could get near her to stroke her hair or hold her. That was all I wanted. It was impossible. I gave her the tablet and found half of one of David's sandwiches which I had hidden for her.

Jeffery and David were getting up. They were both going to school. I went into their bedroom.

"Come on David," I said, taking him into the bathroom to bath him. I took his clothes off and put some water in the bath.

He had a pair of *tsitsi's* on, and didn't want to take them off. All Jewish boys wore them. When I finally managed to make him take them off, he put one foot in the bath. The water was cold and there was no soap. David was crying because he was cold. I took him out, drying him with his shirt. There was no towel. He put on his *tsitsi's* first, and said a prayer in Hebrew.

When he was dressed, he asked me if there was anything to eat. "No," I told him. "Try to wait till you get your dinner in school, and try to get seconds so that you feel full."

I looked for the National Assistance book. "Mum," I whispered to her, "I'm going to get some food. I've left some sugar and water for you." She listened to what I was saying then fell asleep again.

"Come on, David. I'll take you to school." He took my hand and we set off. Jeffery walked ahead of us both. David walked with me, holding my hand and not saying a word.

My heart was thumping. I had to walk as near to the wall as possible, holding it. I looked back at the flat. Please don't die, Mum, I was thinking. When we arrived at the school, I took David into the playground. I showed him where he could stand at break time so he could see Jeffery and talk to him if he felt lonely.

I stayed until the bell rang. "See you later, David. You be a good boy."

When Jeffery and David arrived home from school, they went straight into their bedroom. I took them in some food.

The summer holidays soon came. Jeffery and David spent most of the time in their bedroom, trying to sleep to make the hunger go away. My mother was worse than ever and the only time Jeffery or I went out was to get tablets or the National Assistance money and food parcels.

The holiday passed. The weekend before school started had arrived. I was to go to the High School. I told my mum I was going to school, so that when I left it would be possible for me to get a good job.

On the Monday morning, I woke my mum up, afraid she would hit out at me. "Mum, I'm going to school so I can get a good job."

"I know, Hikey."

"Look, Mum. Each morning when you've taken your insulin and had something to eat, I'm going to leave some sugar and water by your side, in case you don't feel well."

She had been in and out of comas all through the summer. I was very frightened about leaving her. I knew that I would be having free school dinners, and I told her that I would try to wrap the pudding up, and bring it home to her. I hid her insulin tablets so that she couldn't take them while I was at school. Sometimes, she would get up and take one, without knowing what she was doing.

"Jeffery. David. It's time to go. Mum, we're going now. I've left the sugar and water here. Will you be alright?" She nodded her head and touched my hand. "Love you, Mum. See you later," I said, at the same time worried sick, hoping she would be alright. I took the National Assistance book, and put it in my blouse.

We left the flat and started walking to school. When we arrived I took David into the school playground. "I'm going now. Wait for me at break time, and I'll talk to you." He said very little, as usual. I walked through to the High School playground. Jeffery was already there; he ignored me. I stood alone, waiting for the bell to ring, wondering whom I should follow, where I should follow them to.

We all went into the hall. All the new children had to stay behind after assembly. We were taken to a classroom where the teacher called out the class register, then the dinner register. As she read the names, the children took their dinner money to her. My name was at the bottom.

"Jane Levene. You're having free dinners."

"I know," I whispered, holding my head down so that no-one would hear me. I couldn't stop thinking about my mother, hoping she would be alright.

The teacher told us that we would have a small test to see which stream we would go into. She passed the papers round the classroom. I could see the children taking their pens and pencils out of their briefcases. I kept looking around. The teacher sat down and told us to start writing.

"Teacher, I haven't got a pen." She passed one over to me, and told me to bring one with me tomorrow. I didn't know where I could get one from. All I knew was that I wanted to learn everything.

I wrote my name on the paper, this time filling it all in, pretending I knew all the answers. I wanted the teacher to think I was clever, then it would be possible for me to get a good job. I tried to concentrate very hard on my school work, so that I could catch up. I was preoccupied, wondering whether my mother would be alive when I returned home, and panicking at the thought that she needed me with her.

At break time, I looked for Jeffery in the playground. He looked at me, and I knew to stay away. I could see David standing by himself, looking lost.

When school finished I gathered together the books I had been given, and headed towards the Post Office. When I had collected the National Assistance money, I went to the delicatessen, then to the grocery shop, to get some small tins of spaghetti for my mother to eat after her insulin. When all the shopping was done, I waited for the bus. I couldn't wait to get home and show my mother the books from school. I wanted her to think I was clever.

Jeffery and David were already in when I arrived home. I

took all the bags of food into my mother's bedroom, placing them on the floor.

"Mum, look." I was trying to wake her so she could look at my books. I wanted her to be proud of me. "Where's the food?" She was crying with hunger. I piled all the food on the bed so that she could eat it. Jeffery and David followed me into the bedroom, standing, waiting for something to eat. I took the tins of spaghetti and hid them in the kitchen where no-one could find them. My mother gave Jeffery some money for cigarettes and chocolate. There wasn't enough food to last even a few days now that Jeffery and David were both home. I felt very frightened that they might find the spaghetti and eat it.

Jeffery had some change when he came back with the cigarettes and chocolate, and we put a shilling in the electric meter so we could watch the television.

"Mum, are you coming to watch the telly?" I helped her out of bed: it felt good that we were all in the living-room together, watching the telly.

Jeffery had managed to take the slot meter off the television set, so we didn't have to put sixpences in it. My mother had told him to take the meter to Heaton Park, and bury it. She was very frightened that someone would find it, and trace the serial number back to us.

While we were watching the television, I remembered my books and timetable. I rushed over to get them. "Look Mum," I said, bringing them to her, "look at my timetable. It's got Hebrew and *Chumash* and English. I'm going to learn everything," I tried to tell her, but she had fallen asleep. I was frightened to wake her up in case she wanted tablets or food.

Jeffery went into the kitchen. There were a few slices of

bread left, and we decided to make some toast before the electricity ran out.

"I'll get a knife," I told Jeffery, as I switched on the electric fire in the living-room. I put the bread on the end of the knife, and waited for it to go brown. David was sitting in the corner, staring into space. Jeffery wanted to have a go. One slice was ready, we shared it. Suddenly, Jeffery grabbed the knife. "I want to do it." There was a bang; sparks came out of the fire. My mother woke up, and we all stayed very still till she fell asleep again. The fire was broken.

"Don't tell Mum," Jeffery said. "She'll kill us."

"Hikey. Help me into bed, then go to the doctor for some tablets."

It was too late. I told her I would go first thing in the morning. I went back into the living-room. We sat back on the couch, watching the television. There was a comedy on and we were laughing and enjoying it, when the set went dead. The electricity had run out.

Jeffery and David went to bed. I took my books into the bedroom, and placed them under my mattress to keep them safe. I dared not make a noise, or my mother would wake up. I tried very hard to read one of them on the floor. I felt too drained. I covered myself with the coat, and slept till morning.

When morning came, Jeffery was upset because he needed a bottle of ink for school. We looked all over the flat, and managed to find a few pence, just enough to buy a bottle.

Before we left for school, I woke my mother. I told her I would go to the doctor after school for some tablets, and showed her where the cup of sugar and water was.

I carried my books in one hand, and held onto David with the other. I knew how hungry he was, and wished I could have given him some spaghetti, but that was needed for my mother. On the way to school, Jeffery bought the ink. I left David in the playground, and went to the High School. I waited for the bell to ring, wanting the lessons to start so I could learn as much as possible. I tried to take in the schoolwork, but it was too hard to concentrate on anything.

I was too worried, thinking about my mother. All day my heart was pounding and my head was bursting, thinking about her.

At lunchtime I found Jeffery, and asked him to go to the doctor. I wanted to get home as quickly as I could. When the bell rang for lessons to start again, I was telling myself that this time I would try harder to concentrate.

We were lined up in the corridor, waiting for the teacher to come. Mrs Bloughcough, the headmistress, pulled me out of line. "What's your name, girl? Your collar's filthy. Where's your tie? Can't you clean yourself up? Haven't you got another uniform?" The questions seemed endless.

I stood and looked at her. Help me, I was begging inside, please be nice to me, not daring to ask out loud, not knowing how to.

She made a note of my name, and let me go back into the line.

I could hear the laughing, "Jane Levene, the smelly baked bean." The sniggering got louder. Then the teacher came and opened the classroom door. We all sat down. I couldn't lift my head up to look at anybody in the room. I wasn't one of them.

"Jane Levene. Have you brought a note saying why you haven't got a sports uniform?"

"No," I told him, wanting him to go away.

At last, the final bell rang. The anxiety was too much. I found myself running home, sobbing, not knowing what I would find. I was too frightened to put the key in the door in case my mother was dead. David appeared. He had arrived before me, and was waiting on the stairs. Together, we went into the flat. My mother was still asleep in bed. David and I got into his bed and tried to sleep.

Not long after, Jeffery arrived home with some tablets from the doctor. He started shouting at my mother. He wanted some soap to wash his shirt. I got out of David's bed, and crept into my mother's bedroom. Jeffery took the bottle of ink out of his pocket, and smashed it on the wall. The ink splashed everywhere; my mother was covered in it. I was afraid Jeffery would hit her. He was pulling her arm and shaking her, slapping her face.

"He's going to hurt her," I said to David. "Jeffery," I begged, "I'll wash your shirt." Nothing I could say would calm him down. He rushed past me, crying, and got into bed, hitting out at anything he could. I didn't know what to do any more, and just stayed in my bed beside my mother, trying to force myself to go to sleep.

I managed to go to school for a week or two, but I couldn't bear to leave my mother, she was too important to me. I stayed at home to look after her.

CHAPTER 10

It became harder to obtain Duraphet tablets. By now we had changed doctors a few times, and would resort to whatever measures were necessary to get the tablets for my mother. They were having very little effect on her, we clung to the hope that they would enable her to wake up and be normal for a while. She always seemed to know when there was food in the house and stuffed herself with as much as possible. About a month passed, during which time she kept waking up and begging me to go to school in case I was taken away from her. The anxiety of leaving her made me physically ill and more frightened than ever. As soon as the front door closed behind me, I would feel faint, unreal, and breathless, having to gasp for the smallest amount of air.

On one particular Sunday, she begged me to go to school so much that I told her I would. There was nothing to wash my hair with or my uniform. I sat awake all night, wanting to belong in school, but I knew I didn't. I belonged here in this room with my mother.

I awoke early on Monday morning to give my mother her insulin tablet, and managed to scrape together a few bits of food for her. I waited until it was time to leave for school.

"Hikey," my mother started shouting. "Get me some Duraphet. I need some." By now she was crying. I went into our bedroom.

"Yes, Mum. I'll try the doctor, after school." Putting the

National Assistance book in my blouse to it keep safe, I left the flat with Jeffery and David. Jeffery walked ahead of us. He didn't want his friends to see or know about us. "Stay away from me in school!" he said, running off into the distance. I held David's hand, and told him there would be something to eat when he got home from school.

I left David in the school playground, and made my way to the High School. I waited in the playground, wishing I knew as much as the other children, looking to see if they had their P.E. kits or ingredients for the cookery class, hoping that there wouldn't be these classes, so that I wouldn't be embarrassed because I didn't have any of the necessary equipment. I wanted to be at home, away from it all.

When the bell rang, I waited near the school doors. I wanted Philip Nyman to walk past and notice me. Each time I saw him my heart jumped. All the children made fun of him because I wanted to be his girlfriend. He came through the door and ran past me, not stopping in case I followed him. I could hear the children saying to him: "Jane Levene, the smelly baked bean, likes you!" He made sure he kept his distance from me.

The teacher unlocked the classroom door. We sat in our places. He started to read out the register. He came to my name.

"Jane Levene, have you got a letter from your mother to say why you've been absent from school?"

"No," I told him, and hoped he'd forget about me. The teacher told us to stay in the classroom we were having a maths lesson. I didn't have a pen. I looked in the desk and found one. Then Mr Goodwin arrived, looking very stern.

"Sit down. You're going to have a test!" He walked to the

blackboard with his chalk in his hand, and then turned round.

"Levene's sister, stand up and say your tables!" he ordered, staring at me, and letting me know that he hated me as much as he did Jeffery. "Say your tables. We're waiting," he went on.

I stood up and looked around, hoping someone would help me. There was a terrible silence. Then the sniggers came.

"I don't know them, Mr Goodwin."

"Go and stand outside the door. You're a stupid girl!"

My head was aching now and thumping as if something inside wanted to get out. I stood outside the door. The rest of the day had no meaning.

I ran through the playground to get away from that hell. The parents were waiting at the gates for their children. As I ran past, I looked around. One of the girls was hugging her father. How can she do that I thought to myself? How can she bear to smell his body, his socks? I stopped for a minute to see if she would touch him and get some money. She didn't.

I felt too sick to see what was happening. I ran and ran, reciting the *Shama* to myself, hoping that would keep my mother alive until I returned home.

I knew I was supposed to be part of the Jewish Community because my name was Levene and we received a food parcel from the Jewish Benevolent Society. The anti-semitic taunts outside the school left me in no doubt that I was Jewish. I knew I didn't belong in that school, with those children. I didn't know who or what I was.

As soon as I had pushed the front door open, I shouted, "Mum, are you alright?" There was no answer. She was lying on the couch, her eyes closed. "Are you alright, Mum?" I whispered, shaking her. She looked strange. My hand went straight to her mouth, and I pulled her tongue out with one hand and pulled her eyelids open with the other. "*Shama Yisroel!*" I was shouting, hoping God would hear me. She woke up, and pushed me to the floor.

"Hikey, stop it. Let me *shloff.*" I sat on the floor dazed and bruised, but it didn't matter. She was alright.

David came home soon after, he looked lost and hungry. I watched him walk down the hall and into the living-room.

"David," I whispered, "I forgot the National Assistance money. We'll have to wait till tomorrow now."

Jeffery came home later. He had been to the doctor and was unable to get Duraphet from him, but he had managed to get two tablets from the chemist.

The following morning I stayed beside my mother. Jeffery and David left for school. I knew I couldn't leave her to go to school. She woke up, and asked me to go for the National Assistance money. She pulled my skirt.

"Will you go and ask Doris to come and see me? I want to see her."

"Of course, I will. I'll go now." I remembered the address, and left the flat straight away.

I walked down Cheetham Hill Road, looking at the street names very carefully to make sure that I didn't miss the road where Doris lived. Greenhill Road was just past Bookbinder's kosher cake shop, then Birkdale Street was just around the corner. I kept repeating the directions to myself to make sure I didn't get lost. My auntie's house was in sight now. I could feel my heart thumping. I was afraid she wouldn't open the door.

"Auntie Doris. Will you come to see my Mum? She really wants to see you."

"I'm working."

"Please," I begged her, "will you come?"

"If I have any time," she replied, and banged the door in my face.

It was so cold. I desperately wanted to get home. I never expected to see Auntie Doris again.

A few days later, the buzzer on the intercom phone rang. It was mid-afternoon. I knew Jeffery and David would be home soon, but they had a key and wouldn't ring the buzzer. I didn't answer the phone, hoping that whoever it was would go away. My mother was asleep on the couch. I sat beside her, afraid it was someone to take me away from her. I could hear the noise of the lift as it passed our floor, thanking God each time it passed us. Then I heard it stop. My heart was pounding as I willed whoever it was to go to another flat.

There was a knock on the door. I stayed where I was, rigid, trying hard not to breathe in case they heard me. The knocking continued.

"Open the door, will you? It's Doris!"

I started shaking my mother. "Auntie Doris is here." She began to wake up. I went to open the door. Doris walked into the hall, hesitantly. My cousin Eric was with her. They were holding hands. Together they walked down the hall into the living-room. She looked at me.

"The place stinks! Can't you tidy up?" My heart sank. "I'm not staying here!" She started to leave, pulling Eric behind her.

"I'll tidy up," I said. "Please stay for a while."

She walked back, and started talking to my mother. They were talking in Yiddish. I could understand some of what was being said. My mother kept saying "*nisht gut.*" I knew that meant not well. I felt that my heart would break each time I heard her say it. My auntie didn't seem interested, and prepared to leave. I wanted her to love my mother as I did, but she just left.

"Don't worry, Mum. You've got me. I'll stay with you."

Jeffery and I would take it in turns to go to the doctor and chemist or the Benevolent Society. Jeffery would get very angry with my mother for taking tablets. Sometimes she didn't recognise us; most nights she would wake up shouting, wanting things, imagining she could see people trying to take her away. I didn't care anymore about school. I knew that even if I could get a good job I wouldn't leave her. She was all that mattered to me. Looking after her was my life, and I didn't want it to change.

Sometimes when she had been worse than usual in the night, I went to see my father. To do as he told me, was the only way I could get a few shillings to buy some tablets from the chemist.

I left her a cup of sugar and water, as I always did when I had to leave her for any reason, and set out to see my father. When I had the money safely in my hand I ran up Cheetham Hill Road, in the direction of the chemist. I could see the school in the distance, and was hoping that Jeffery and David would be out in the playground so I could tell them that Mum would have some tablets. When I reached the school, it wasn't playtime, so I carried on to the chemist.

When I had bought the tablets, I ran the rest of the way home, feeling very secure with them in my hand, imagining how good it felt when my mother was awake, remembering how warm she felt when I could get near her.

When I arrived home, my mother was on the couch, snoring away, the cup of sugar and water still beside her where I had left it.

I wasn't sure if I should wake her, knowing she would be desperate to eat, and not be able to breathe. I sat beside her for a while, watching her face, reaching out to stroke her plump, warm cheek very carefully, then pulling away for fear of waking her. I sat wondering what to do. Suddenly she opened her eyes and lashed out at me. "Don't breathe near me. It's driving me mad."

"Mum, I've got some Duraphet. I'll get you some water," I told her, taking two of the tablets, placing them in her hand. She gulped them down before I had a chance to bring her a drink.

"Let me *shloff*," she mumbled, turning over on the couch. I tried to straighten the coat over her. She pulled it away. I knew I would have to see if the tablets would make her feel any better. After a while, she started moving about on the couch.

"Hikey, is there anything to eat?"

"No, Mum." I hated to tell her that, wishing I could get something.

"Go to the grocery shop. Ask if we can have some food. Tell them we'll pay on Monday."

"OK, Mum. I'll try."

When I reached the shop, it hadn't reopened after lunch. I waited, practising what I was going to say to the shopkeeper. The lights went on in the shop, the door was opened. A man stood behind the counter.

"My Mum lives at 32 Bracknell Court, and we don't get any money till Monday. Please can we have some food, and I'll bring the money then?" I looked at him, not sure whether or not he had understood what I'd said. "My Mum lives..."

"It's alright," he interrupted. "What did you want?" He was

taking a large book from under the counter. "What's your address again?"

"32 Bracknell Court. Here, here's the National Assistance book."

He looked at the book, and wrote down the address.

"What did you want?"

I looked around. There were some packets of crispy cod balls in the freezer. "I'll take a packet of these, and five pounds of potatoes, and a tin of beans. Can I have a loaf of bread as well?"

"Yes," he told me, and carried on writing the items in his book.

"Thank you. I'll bring the money on Monday morning." I couldn't believe I had the food, and ran all the way home, feeling very pleased with myself.

When I got back to the flat, my mother was still lying on the couch, this time she was awake.

"Look, Mum, look what I've got. These look nice. They're crispy cod balls."

"Hikey, is there any gas to cook with?"

My heart sank. "No, Mum. Here, have some bread."

"Go and try to borrow a shilling."

I left the flat, and started knocking on doors, asking for a shilling till Monday morning, but no-one had any money.

At last, I gave up and went home. My mother asked me to look round the flat to see if there was any money anywhere. I knew there wasn't, but I looked anyway.

"There's nothing, Mum. I'll open the beans for you, we can save the potatoes till Monday."

I put the crispy cod balls in a cupboard in the kitchen. The packet was wet and soggy. The picture on the front looked delicious. I could imagine how they tasted, I left them in the cupboard and opened the beans.

"Here, Mum, eat these. Do you think you'll be awake when Jeffery and David come home from school?"

"I hope so."

When she had finished, she said, "I'm just going to have a *shloff*, Hikey. I'll be alright later." She fell asleep again. I hoped she would wake up later on. There was one more Duraphet tablet left. I hid it with the insulin tablets for the following day.

There was a knock on the door. I stayed very still.

"Jane, Mrs Levene. It's Miss Sassoon. Let me in."

I opened the door, afraid she wanted to send my mum into hospital or take me away.

"You should be at school!" She had a small cardboard box with some clothes in it. She put it in the hall, and walked through to the living-room.

"My Mum's asleep." I wanted her to leave so I could rush to the second-hand shop with the clothes.

"You're going to get your mother into trouble if you don't go to school."

"I can't leave my Mum. She's not well."

"Would you like to go for a day out, you and David?"

"No, I can't leave my Mum."

"You must go to school tomorrow, Hikey," my mother said. She was crying.

"Alright, I'll go, Mum. Don't cry."

Miss Sassoon asked me again if I wanted to go on the day out.

"No."

"I'll organise a lady to stay with your mother for the day," Miss Sassoon said.

"You go, Hikey," my mum told me.

"Look, Jane," explained Miss Sassoon. "The people are called *Lubovitch*. They're religious people, and organise outings for Jewish children. It will be a picnic. You'll go on a train. Here's a list of trips, and the places you'll be picked up. Take Jeffery and David with you. I'll make sure a lady stays with your mother on each of these days."

"Please go, Hikey," my mother begged.

"The holidays start soon, so go to school tomorrow," Miss Sassoon told me.

"Alright," I replied. She left the flat. I watched from the window until I saw her drive off in her car. I checked through the box of clothes to see what was in it, and wondered how much I would get for them.

I laid out the cardigan on the floor and wrapped all the other clothes in it. I set off on the long walk down the road to the bottom of Cheetham Hill Road, it didn't matter how far it was. I knew I would perhaps get a shilling or two. By the time I arrived at the shop, my arms were aching. I dropped all the clothes on the floor.

"Can I have a shilling for them, please?"

The lady looked through the pile. There were boys' trousers and pullovers, skirts and cardigans.

"I can only give you ninepence for them."

"But I need a shilling for the gas meter," I begged her.

"Ninepence," she told me.

"OK, I'll take it."

The next day was Friday. I knew the food parcel would be waiting for me. That made me feel better, I wished I had a shilling for the gas meter so I could cook the crispy cod balls for Jeffery and David. I knew they would be home from school, and rushed home with the ninepence.

Jeffery and David were in their bedroom, eating some bread. I hid the ninepence, hoping the Benevolent Society would let me have a thruppeny piece so I could change my money for a shilling. My mother had managed to get into bed, and stayed fast asleep till the following morning.

I stayed awake all night, not wanting to go to school and to leave my mother. Knowing I wouldn't be able to clean my uniform, I lay very carefully on the bed, trying to make sure it didn't crease even more.

I was still awake when it started to get light. I went through to the kitchen to get the insulin tablet. There was one Duraphet tablet. I woke my mother up so she could take it. There was some bread left. She ate that after her insulin.

"I'm going to school now, Mum. I'll go with Jeffery and David. I'll bring back the food parcel with me, and I'll try to get a shilling for the meter."

She was half asleep. Before I left the flat, I recited the *Shama* to make sure she would be safe till I got home from school. The three of us left together, but Jeffery insisted on walking ahead of David and me.

"You smell. You're dirty!" he shouted back at us, and ran off as fast as he could.

David was holding my hand. When we were nearly at school, I said to him, "Try to eat as much as possible at dinnertime. I'll be getting the food parcel tonight, so we'll have some jam."

I left him at the Junior School gate, and walked through to the High School. I found a corner where I could stand on my own, so no-one would notice me. I hated school, and wanted to be at home. I was hoping there wouldn't be a cookery or maths lesson. The bell rang: we all lined up, ready to go into assembly. I could hear whispers. "It's Jane Levene, the smelly baked bean!"

We were all led into the morning assembly. My stomach was churning. I wanted to be at home with my mother, making sure she was alright. As I looked round the huge hall, everyone was so nice and clean. I knew I didn't belong with them.

The assembly finished, and we made our way to the classroom. It was Class B. There was no Class C now, because there were only two of us in it, so we were put in the middle class. The teacher started to call out the register. When he came to my name, he said, "Jane Levene, do you have a letter from your mother to say why you've been absent from school for such a long time?"

"No," I told him.

"Go and stand outside the headmaster's office."

Once I got outside the classroom I felt like running home. But my mother wanted me at school today. I walked to the headmaster's office and waited. Mrs Bloughcough, the headmistress had just come out of her office.

"Where's your tie, girl? You're a disgrace! You can write me a hundred lines. *I will wear a tie in school.*"

"Yes, Mrs Bloughcough."

"You can bring them in after the holidays, first thing."

Soon, the class teacher came walking towards me. "Wait here, girl, till Mr Linton is ready."

I shortly found myself in Mr Linton's office.

"Why haven't you brought a note from your parents?"

"My Mum's not well."

"Bring one in after the holidays. And you can do a

hundred lines: *I must always bring a note from my parents when I've been absent."*

"Yes, Sir,"

On the way back through the hall, I saw a box in the corner with 'Lost Property' written on it. I could see there was a tie in it, and took it quickly before someone came. When I arrived back in the classroom, all I could think about was my mother. I couldn't hear what the teacher was saying. I desperately wanted to catch up so much, but my mind was full of anxiety about my mother.

The bell rang to change lessons. "It's cookery next," I heard someone shout. We all headed in the direction of the cookery room. Mrs Brookes, the cookery teacher, was very strict. I tried to hide behind one of the other girls.

"Do we all have our ingredients ready?" shouted Mrs Brookes. "Come on, children, get into working groups."

I was still standing by the door, not knowing where to go.

"Jane Levene," she yelled. "Where are your ingredients?"

"I haven't got any."

"Where's your note explaining why you haven't got any, you stupid girl!"

"I haven't got one."

"Well, you can stay there for the rest of the lesson. And don't do it again."

The bell rang at last it was lunchtime. Jeffery was having a P.E. class, and I went to look for him to tell him to go to the doctor. We needed insulin and breathing tablets. I was to go for the food parcel. The changing rooms were just down the corridor. I looked through the keyhole of each door, desperately trying to find him. Suddenly, a hand touched my arm.

"Jane Levene, what are you doing? Go into the dining hall, now." It was Mr Goodwin. "Go on, girl!" he shouted, pointing in the direction of the hall.

I had to find a place, as everyone was already seated. I could see Jeffery. I looked at him. He nodded his head, and I knew not to sit near him. Eventually, I found a seat. When the pudding came, it was a hard jam biscuit. I took mine out of the bowl and put it down my blouse to save for my mother.

"Jane Levene, you dirty, dirty hound!" Mr Goodwin's voice thundered across the hall, everyone fell silent. "Come here on stage, you dirty girl!"

I walked towards the steps leading to the stage.

"Why were you peeping into the boys' dressing room? Why have you put your pudding down your blouse?"

The whole room roared with laughter.

"It's for my Mum," I told him, and started to laugh with everyone else.

"You dirty hound! Go back to your table!"

The room was still full of giggles. My mind felt like ice. All the children knew I was 'Jane Levene, the smelly baked bean.'

I managed to get to Jeffery later on, and asked him to go to the doctor's for insulin, Duraphet and breathing tablets.

When school finished, I made my way to the soup kitchen, and picked up the food parcel. I had the ninepence with me, and asked one of the ladies if she could give me a shilling in return for it, so we would have money for the gas meter. No-one would change it, so I hung on to it, hoping something would turn up.

When I arrived at the flat, David was sitting outside the front door. "Look, David, bread and jam."

He looked up at me and smiled, tugging the back of my skirt. "Is Mum awake?"

"I don't know, David." Leading him through the front door, I heard the front door of the next flat bang. I looked back.

"Mrs Pelham?" I called. The next door neighbour looked at me.

"I've got ninepence. Could you let me have a shilling for it, to put in the gas meter? I'll give it you back first thing on Monday morning. Please. I've got some crispy cod balls for us, and there's no gas."

"I think I have a shilling piece, Jane." She went back into her flat. We swapped our money, and I quickly put the shilling in the gas meter.

The cod balls were still in the cupboard where I had left them. They were all soft, soggy and wet. I put them in the oven to cook, quickly peeled the potatoes, and put them on to boil.

Jeffery arrived back from the doctor. He had a box of insulin and breathing tablets. The doctor wouldn't give him a prescription for the Duraphet tablets.

Tea was soon ready. We had crispy cod balls, mashed potatoes, and bread and jam.

CHAPTER 11

I had put the list Miss Sassoon had given me in the kitchen cupboard. The first day trip was on Monday. We would be taken by train to a picnic site. My stomach churned at the thought of being away from my mother, but she wanted me to go. I showed David the list. He didn't take much notice of it. He went to his bedroom and stayed there with Jeffery.

On Sunday morning, I went to the Benevolent Society, to see if it was possible to get some money. When I arrived there, the big room, where the money was handed out, was locked.

"There's no-one here today," I was told by a lady. She was polishing the stair banister.

"Can you let me have a shilling?"

"I'm sorry, dear, that has nothing to do with me. You go home now."

I returned home, keeping my eyes firmly fixed on the pavement, just in case someone had dropped a penny, even better, a thrupenny piece, but there was nothing. I didn't like going home empty handed. I didn't want them to feel hungry. I knew there was nothing else to do.

Jeffery and David were still in bed, huddled up under their coats. My mother was asleep on the couch, waking up now and again to beg for food and breathing tablets, shouting, and getting very agitated when I told her there weren't any.

"Mum, I don't think it's a good idea for me to go on the trip."

"Let me *shloff*. Leave me in peace."

I sat on the floor near her, making sure she couldn't hear me breathe or sniff. That would make her hit out and shout even more.

She woke up shouting. She was sweating. I could see she was wetting herself.

"Open all the windows. I can't breathe, Hikey."

"It's alright, Mum. I'll open them. Don't worry."

Jeffery came into the living-room as I opened all the windows. "Don't open them! I'm freezing cold."

"I must, Jeffery, Mum can't breathe." I went through to the bedroom. Jeffery stayed in the living-room, I could hear him shouting at mum: "Get up! Do something!"

"I can't, Jeffery. I need tablets."

"Get up!" He was crying and screaming.

All the windows were open now, the wind was howling through the flat.

"I'm freezing! I'm closing the windows."

I couldn't stop him, but was afraid that without air, my mother would stop breathing. He went from room to room, banging and breaking anything he could get his hands on. He stood in the kitchen doorway, holding the bottle of insulin tablets.

"I'll take these if you don't get up," he was crying. "Please, Mum, get off the couch." She didn't move. Jeffery started unscrewing the top.

"Jeffery, Mum needs those tablets. She'll die without them."

He stood silent and still, then he threw the bottle. The tablets scattered all over the room. "There! There's your stupid tablets! You're dead anyway!"

I covered every inch of the floor, picking up the tablets, putting them back in the bottle. Jeffery went back into his bedroom, and stayed there with David. I stayed beside my mother until the morning.

As soon as daylight came, I woke mum to give her the insulin tablet. I had hidden some mashed potato and a crust of bread in the kitchen cupboard, behind some plates. She ate them, and fell asleep again. Jeffery and David were playing in their bedroom. They were fighting and laughing.

"Shut up. Please let me *shloff*." She couldn't stand any noise.

I stood outside their bedroom, and told them to get up. We had to be at the bus stop in Upper Park Road by ten o'clock. It was still very early. I took the National Assistance book to the Post Office. I had to wait a long time until the shop opened. I was first in the queue. As soon as the money was handed over to me, I ran to the delicatessen and bought as much food as possible for my mother. I rushed home to give her the food, taking the bags straight into the living-room.

"Come on, Mum. Look what I've got for you."

She was almost awake, and pulled over the bags. She dragged everything out, and stuffed as much as possible down her throat.

"Will you be alright, Mum? I'm frightened to leave you."

She didn't answer me. She carried on bingeing and pulling food out of the bags. Nothing else seemed to matter to her.

Jeffery knocked on Mrs Pelham's door to ask what time it was.

"If we don't leave now, we won't make it."

"Will you be alright, Mum?"

"Go on, Hikey, I'll be alright."

Jeffery and David were standing outside the flat,

wondering what we would be given to eat.

"Come on!" Jeffery shouted to me.

My mother was asleep again. She looked peaceful. I prayed before I left that her coat wouldn't fall off, as I didn't want her to feel cold, and that God would keep her alive until we arrived back home.

"We won't be long," I whispered.

"Jane, come on!" He and David were running down the stairs. I left the flat quickly, before I had a chance to change my mind, and ran after them, making sure my hand didn't touch the iron banister. If it did, my mother would die. There seemed to be hundreds of things I must do to keep her alive. Jeffery and David were well ahead of me.

"Slow coach!" Jeffery shouted. It didn't matter. All I wanted was to get the day over, and get back home.

We arrived at the bus stop on Upper Park Road. I was hoping we were late and that no-one would arrive to pick us up. We hadn't waited long when a rabbi came to the bus stop. His clothes were all black, his coat long, his hat huge.

"I think you are waiting for me, Jane, Jeffery, David?"

"Yes," we all replied at the same time.

"Follow me," he said, leading us to a large house. It wasn't very far. There were lots of children standing around when we got there. My stomach started jumping about. All I could think of was my mother. I was so frightened that she would fall into a coma, or wake up and notice that I was gone.

"Jane, come on. We've got to get on the coach. We're going to get the train." David was pulling at my arm.

We all sat together on the coach. As the engine started, and we were being driven down the road, my heart sank more and more.

"Stop the bus. I can't breathe. Please let me off." Nobody seemed to take any notice.

"Sit down!" the rabbi shouted. "Join in the singing."

All the children were singing folk songs and clapping their hands. I didn't like them. I desperately wanted to be at home with my mother. Jeffery and David were sitting beside me, looking out of the window.

"You must eat as much as possible," I told them, "and try to get some to take home for Mum."

They sat holding hands, not saying anything.

"Hurry children. We're getting on the train."

The coach had pulled up outside the railway station.

"Quickly!" shouted the rabbi. Before we knew it, we had been ushered onto the train. My heart was pounding. I was being dragged away from my mother, and it felt unbearable.

The train appeared to be full of rabbis, *davoning*, "*Baruch ato adoinoi.*" Prayers were coming from all directions. We seemed to have been travelling forever. If only I could close my eyes, and wake up back at home. That was all I wanted. It didn't feel right: we didn't belong. Eventually, the train stopped.

"We're almost at the picnic site!" the rabbi shouted. "Come, children. Single file."

I tried to keep hold of David's hand. There was a huge surge forward.

Once we were off the train, we had to board another coach. "Only five minutes now," shouted the rabbi.

The rabbis were still *davoning* and praying, swaying backwards and forwards constantly. The coach stopped near to a field, by the side of a huge house.

The rabbi shouted, "Make your way to the tent." He

pointed to a big tent in the middle of the field, not far from the house.

I didn't like it. My mother was on her own. It frightened me so much.

"Are we staying here forever?" I asked the rabbi.

"No, just for a few hours."

Jeffery and David had walked to the tent with the other children. I followed them. There were wooden tables and benches in the tent. Jeffery and David were already sitting and waiting. I sat down as near to them as possible.

"*Baruch ato*," the rabbi was reciting. Everyone joined in the prayer before we could start eating. They all started singing Israeli folk songs. One of the rabbis went outside the tent to start the barbecue. I felt sick. My stomach wouldn't rest. I didn't belong.

The rabbis brought plates of barbecued salami and buns. We all started eating. I told Jeffery and David to eat as much as possible. They knew that they had to try and hide some food to take home for my mother.

When we had finished the meal, the rabbis brought in small baskets of fruit and placed them on the tables. I picked up an apple and bit into it. Suddenly, I felt a hand on my shoulder.

"Don't eat it. Throw it away!" the rabbi insisted. I looked at him. He took the apple out of my hand. "It isn't Kosher. It's got blood on it from your gums." He started praying, and threw the apple into a rubbish bag.

The folk songs carried on, the children were dancing outside with the rabbis. They were in a circle, dancing the *Hora*, and singing *Hava Nagila*. I was counting the seconds, counting the blades of grass, anything, to make the time pass so I could go home.

At last, it was time for us to leave. I had some salami and a bun down my blouse, and made sure I didn't let go of them for a second. We were on our way home. I was praying that my mother would be alive so I could give her the food. It took a long time for us to get back; we were dropped off the coach near to the flats. We ran to the lift, holding all the food we had collected for my mother. Jeffery had the key to the front door, and I almost squashed him, in my rush to get into the flat.

"Mum, Mum." She was asleep on the couch.

"Mummy, wake up." I was shaking her arm. Jeffery and David were standing behind me, holding the food. She started to wake up.

"We've got food for you, Mum. Come on." She held out her hand, and grabbed what we had, and ate it desperately. The food was soon gone, and her eyes closed again.

Jeffery and David went into their bedroom. I sat beside the couch. It was obvious that someone had stayed with my mother, because they had tidied up a little. It felt good to be beside my mother again, I knew I wouldn't go on any more outings.

The rest of the holidays seemed to pass quickly. Jeffery and David stayed in their bedroom most of the time, playing 'Cowboys and Indians'. The lady who had stayed with my mother called at the flat to see if we were going on another day trip.

"No. I'm staying with my Mum."

The Sunday before school started, Miss Sassoon called at the flat to tell me that I had to go to school with Jeffery and David.

"Your mum's going to get into bad trouble if you don't."

It frightened me. I promised her that I would go. All night I stayed beside my mother, wishing my uniform could be nice and clean, wishing I had some dinner money. I didn't want Philip Nyman to know we were poor. My mother kept waking up, shouting for tablets and food, not knowing who I was. I stayed beside her, watching her, knowing there was nothing I could do.

When morning came, I gave her an insulin tablet. I had hidden a bun in the kitchen drawer, and made sure she ate it after the tablet.

"I've got to go to school, Mum. Will you be alright?"

She just stared at me. I didn't know if she understood what I was saying to her, but I didn't want to be taken away from her, so I had to go. Jeffery and David had already left, and after I had put the National Assistance book inside my blouse and left a cup of sugar and water beside the couch, I followed them. All the way to school, I touched the wall wherever possible. It stopped me from falling over.

When I arrived at the school gate, I waited. If only Philip would notice me, I waited and waited. At last, I saw him walking down the road towards the gate. My heart started thumping, my legs were shaking.

Please say hello, was the only thought in my mind. He saw me, and turned his head away. He was almost running as he passed me. I stayed near the gate, unable to move.

"Hello, Jane," said a voice. When I looked up, Zelita Reichman was standing near me.

"Come on," she said, "the bell's gone."

I walked through the playground. Zelita was adjusting her skirt. It was almost as long as mine. Her hair was black, very thick and wavy. I knew her father was a rabbi. Sometimes, the other girls would make jokes about how religious she was. We walked down the corridor together. It felt good to be with someone. She reminded me so much of Minnie Shelefski. I wanted her to be my friend.

"You must come to my house for tea one day, and see how a real Jewish family lives," she said.

"I'll ask my Mum. Can I come tomorrow?"

"I'll ask my Mother, and tell you in the morning," was her reply. We smiled at each other, and went into the classroom.

I couldn't wait to get home, to tell my mother I'd been invited to Zelita's house. At last the final bell rang. I ran to the Post Office, then to the shops for as much food as I could carry.

When I arrived home, Jeffery and David were already in their bedroom.

"Come on. I've got some food."

My mother woke up when she heard me shouting. "Give me the bags quick." She was hanging over the edge of the couch, rummaging through the bags.

"Where's the chopped liver?"

I looked through the bag and found it.

"Here, Mum, here it is."

She pulled it off me, ripping the paper away, and stuffing it into her mouth.

"Where's the bagels?" She was almost choking.

"Here, Mum," I said, handing her a paper bag full of bagels and pretzels.

"Mum, can I go to Zelita Reichman's house for tea tomorrow after school?"

She hadn't heard me talking, and carried on pulling at the bagels.

"Mum, will you be alright if I go for a while? I won't be there long."

"Yes," she mumbled, turning over on the couch to sleep.

"Be quiet. I need to *shloff.*"

I couldn't help feeling excited. I wanted Zelita to be my friend, and felt very angry with some of the other children who called her names for being old fashioned and religious.

The following morning arrived. I woke up on the floor next to the couch, and after I had made sure my mother had taken her insulin tablet and had had something to eat, we all left for school. I told Jeffery I was going to Zelita's house, asking him to make sure my mother was alright when he got home from school.

I waited for Zelita outside the school gate. I could see her coming. Philip was just behind her. She stopped. I could see him walking down the road towards the gate.

"Stay here a minute, Zelita," I begged. We both waited.

"I just want to say hello to Philip." He was getting nearer. As soon as he saw me, he ran through the gate into the playground.

"Come on, Jane. We've got to go. Meet me here after school. See you later." She went to her classroom.

All I could think about in class was my mother. My heart was pounding constantly and I had to repeat numbers, which I counted on my fingers, in order to keep my mother alive.

I started to worry at the thought of going to Zelita's house in case I couldn't find my way home. I saw her at lunchtime: she reminded me to wait for her.

At the end of the day, I made my way to the gate. Deep down inside, I felt that I should to go home to make sure my mother was alright. Zelita arrived, and took me by the arm.

"Come on. We're going to have a nice tea. My home isn't far from here."

We started walking. Soon, we were at her front door. Zelita took her key out. She opened the door and beckoned me into the hall. I knew a man lived in the house. The vague smells hit me, and my heart started racing. Zelita pulled me by the arm into the front room. It was full of books. They all seemed to be written in Hebrew. It was like being in a synagogue.

"Come on, Jane. Come and meet my mother and brothers." Zelita led me into a room at the back of the house. Her mother was sitting on a chair, knitting. She was wearing a *sheitel* on her head. Near her were two little boys wearing *yamulkas* and *tsitsis*. They were talking in Hebrew.

"Finish making the tea," Zelita's mother told her.

I began to feel anxious. This wasn't my home. I wanted to be with my mother.

"Wash your hands. You must perform *Negel Vasser*, like this. Fill this jug, and pour the water over each hand three times, reciting this prayer."

I did what Zelita told me.

"Come on, Jane. Help me put the food on the table." At that moment, the front door banged. "It's my Dad. You'll like him," said Zelita.

He walked into the room. I felt very frightened. I didn't want him to come near me.

"I must go now. I have to make sure my mother's alright." I ran out of the house, promising myself that I would always go straight home to my mother from school. Nothing was more important than her.

I was so glad to get home where I belonged. There was a pile of magazines beside her on the floor and a half eaten fruit cake.

"Where did you get these from, Mum?" I asked her, waking her up.

"Adele Bloch's mother brought them for us," she mumbled.

My heart sank. I knew Adele and all her friends were rich, I had told them that we lived in a big house with a swimming pool, and that I had a television in my bedroom.

"Why did you let her in, Mum? Why?" I was sobbing. "How did you manage to get off the couch? Why did you let her in?"

I felt sick. They would know now that we didn't have a swimming pool, and I didn't have a television set in my bedroom like she did. My mother had fallen asleep again, with a piece of cake in her hand. I took it off her, and hid it for after her insulin, in the morning. The rest I took into Jeffery and David's bedroom. They were both asleep, so I left the cake on the floor beside Jeffery's bed. I went back into the living-room and stayed beside my mother. I knew Philip would find out, and now he would never like me.

The following day when I went to school, I waited outside the gate for Adele. When she approached, I took her to one side.

"Adele, I'm sorry the place was such a mess when your mother came round, but the curtains and suite covers are at the cleaners, and the carpets are away being repaired." I was hoping she wouldn't remember what I had told her and the other girls about the big house and the swimming pool. She looked at me.

"Please believe me." The unspoken words pounded in my head. Suddenly, I could sense that my heart was going to stop. The only way to get it going again was to stamp my foot hard on the ground to make it start.

When I looked up, Adele was almost at the school doors with all the other children. I had to hold onto the gate to make sure I didn't faint. I made my way into school. I knew that everyone knew I had lied about my house, and wished hard for the day to pass so that I could get back to my mother. The time passed very slowly. All I could think of was my mother, just hoping she would be alive when I got home.

When I arrived home, there was a letter behind the front door. It was from the hospital. My mother had to attend the Diabetic Clinic for a check-up. I took the letter into the living-room to show her. She was hanging off the couch, her coat covering her.

"Mum, wake up. There's a letter from the hospital." She moaned and groaned, thinking I had brought her food and cigarettes.

"No, Mum. It's a letter from the hospital. It's an appointment for next week." I was moving her arm, trying to keep her attention.

"Will you tell the doctor you can't stop weeing yourself?"

"Yes. Let me *shloff*."

The appointment was for the following Wednesday. Jeffery was in his bedroom telling David about the clothes he was going to buy with his wages. He had just left school, and was to start work on Monday, and we were all starting to feel very excited.

By the weekend, my mother was getting much worse. She didn't seem to know where she was. The comas were very frequent. She kept pleading desperately for Duraphet and breathing tablets. Jeffery stayed in his bedroom most of the time. That made me feel better because he would get so angry with her for being on the couch. I knew I couldn't go back to school and leave her.

On Sunday evening Jeffery found it hard to settle in one place, he was so excited about starting work. He had a job in a canteen, and was relieved that there would be food about him. Eventually, he went into his bedroom. It was getting dark, and there was no food or heating. I took my place beside my mother on the floor, and sat watching and listening for any signs of a coma. She woke up many times in the night, sometimes not knowing who I was. I tried to tell her that Jeffery was starting work tomorrow. I wasn't sure if she understood what I was saying.

The night dragged before I managed to fall asleep. Jeffery had woken up. It was almost daylight; he couldn't wait till it was time to leave. My mother had taken her insulin and I had managed to hide a small tin of spaghetti. By the time she had eaten it Jeffery had left. It was still very early in the morning but he couldn't wait.

When David had left for school, I went back into the living-room, and stayed with my mother. She would wake up now and again.

"Is Jeffery home yet?"

"No." I stayed by her side, making sure she was alright. She woke up again, later.

"Will you get me some breathing tablets?"

"I'll try tomorrow morning. Don't worry, Mum." I stroked her arm. She needed more insulin and Duraphet tablets as well.

"If the doctor won't give me any Duraphet or breathing tablets, I'll swap a prescription. Don't worry, Mum."

She fell asleep again. I knew she would need some Duraphet to be able to get to the hospital on Wednesday. The ambulance was to arrive at 9.30 a.m. She turned over on the couch, and I tried to straighten her coat. Her legs were covered in blood and she was wetting herself constantly. I looked for something to wash her down with. There was nothing. I ripped a piece of lining from the coat, and wet it. I didn't understand what the blood was, but it didn't frighten me anymore. I knew she wasn't bleeding to death.

I was waiting for the National Assistance book to arrive in the post. The money had to be reduced because Jeffery had left school. They had told me the book would only take a few days to come back and I was praying it would arrive soon.

When David came home from school, I told him to get into bed to keep warm.

"We should have some food tomorrow when the National Assistance book arrives." I tried to find a comic or magazine for him to read.

It wasn't long before the buzzer rang. I knew it was Jeffery, and picked up the intercom phone very excitedly.

"I've got a surprise, Jane. Let me in, quick!"

I ran to the front door to open it, and waited there for the lift to arrive. Jeffery walked out of the lift with two huge unmarked tins under his arms.

"What's in them, Jeffery?"

"One's peaches and one's spaghetti." I rushed in to tell my mother.

"Mum, wake up. Jeff's back home, he's got a surprise for us." She opened her eyes.

"Look Mum, we've got food." We all started laughing. The tins were huge. I ran into the kitchen to find the tin opener. I opened one of the tins on the floor in front of the couch, while Jeffery and David watched me.

The peaches were delicious. I managed to put some to one

side for my mother. She could have them after her insulin in the morning.

I went over to Jeffery and kissed him. He told me he would try to get whatever he could whenever possible. There was still the tin of spaghetti left, so I wasn't too worried about the National Assistance book arriving in the post.

CHAPTER 12

Next morning, the National Assistance book arrived. I ripped the envelope open, and told my mother I was going to get the money.

"I'll go to the doctor this evening, but I'm going to get the food now." She didn't answer me, and I left the flat straight away.

After arriving home with the food, I waited until it was time to go to the doctor. My mother had to have some Duraphet tablets for the next day, to be able to get to the hospital. In the late afternoon, I left the flat and went to the surgery. I was early so I was the first one in to see the doctor.

"Can I have some Hydroderm cream and something for a tummy ache?" I asked the doctor quickly, knowing that if he wouldn't give me Duraphet tablets, the chemist would probably change the prescription for me. I watched him as he started to write out the prescription.

"Doctor, can I have some insulin tablets and breathing tablets, the pink and white ones, for my Mum?" He didn't lift his head; as soon as he had finished writing out my prescription he ripped it off the pad and wrote another prescription for my mother.

"Doctor, please can she have some Duraphet tablets? She's going to the hospital tomorrow for a check-up. She'll need some to be able to get up."

He looked at me. "I'll add four onto this prescription."

I watched his hand very carefully, making sure the pen spelt out Duraphet, watching him cross the 't' and write the amount.

Thank God! I thought. "Thank you, Doctor." I folded the prescription for Hydroderm cream, and put it down my blouse, knowing that I could probably change it next week.

When I arrived home, my mother was asleep on the couch, surrounded by half eaten food. I tried to take some away to hide for her after her insulin. Each time I tried, she woke up, and ate what I was holding. There was less money for food now, then I remembered the large tin of spaghetti that Jeffery had brought home, I wasn't as worried as I might have been. I didn't give her the Duraphet tablets, but put them in the drawer for the morning. It was hard to sleep that night. I was worried that she would be kept in hospital, and I didn't want her to go away.

At last, the morning came, and I took all the tablets I needed out of the drawer. I knew the ambulance would arrive soon.

"Come on, Mum. Take your tablets. The ambulance will be here soon."

"When you've been to get the National Assistance, go to the doctors for some Duraphet tablets. I don't think I could manage the hospital without them."

I explained to her that she had taken the tablets, and that I had collected the National Assistance. She didn't seem to know what was going on.

Soon, she was fully awake. The tablets had worked. She was sitting up and eating the rest of the food from yesterday.

"Mum, you're going to the hospital soon. I'm coming with you." She looked at me and smiled. "The ambulance will be here soon. Come on, get off the couch." I held her arm as she pulled herself up, and tried to straighten her dress.

"When you see the doctor, will you tell him you can't stop weeing yourself? I didn't tell our doctor because I didn't want him to put you in hospital."

"Come on, Hikey," she said, and hugged and kissed me. "I'll be alright. Don't worry."

At last the buzzer rang, and I knew it was the ambulance.

"Ambulance for Mrs Levene," came the voice on the intercom.

"We're coming straight down," I answered. "Come on, Mum, get your coat."

We left the flat and waited for the lift.

"Are you OK, Mum?" I asked as she was stepping into the lift. Suddenly, she held onto the door and crossed her legs. Water started to dribble all down her legs, there was a sudden gush.

"I can't stop it," she sobbed. The lift was flooded.

"Don't worry, Mum. You'll be at the hospital soon." We got out of the lift quickly, so no-one would see us.

The ambulance driver was waiting outside the front door to help my mother into the ambulance. "I'm coming with her," I told him, and sat beside her.

We arrived at the hospital, and found our way to the Diabetic Clinic. We waited for a while then a nurse came and shouted:

"Mrs Levene."

"Don't forget to tell the doctor," I called after her.

I waited and waited. After about an hour, she came out. The doctor was with her.

"Your mother has a prolapsed womb. It's resting on her

bladder. That's why she can't stop passing water," he explained to me, very slowly. "She will have to have a small operation." I looked at her. She had another diet sheet in her hand. "Your mother must keep to her diet, and lose weight. I'll contact your doctor," he went on.

My heart sank. He didn't understand how much she needed to eat. I knew she would never be able to diet. We left the hospital, and were taken home again in the ambulance.

Back in the flats, we waited for the lift to arrive. My mother was desperate to go to the toilet. "We'll be home soon," I told her.

The lift door opened, and two other women followed us in. A notice had been placed on the wall of the lift. It read: *Please do not use the lift as a toilet.* The two women commented on how disgusting it was.

"Yes," agreed my mother, "it's disgusting." She was trying very hard to keep her legs crossed, and we smiled at each other. I desperately wanted to put my arms around her.

"We'll be home soon," I whispered.

As soon as we arrived home, my mother went to bed. The Duraphet was wearing off. I was wishing it wouldn't, but I knew the signs too well by now.

When Jeffery and David arrived home, I told them that mum would have to go back into hospital. I could see that they felt very sad about it; we all got into our beds and stayed there till the morning.

I awoke early. My mother had been very restless during the night, unable to breathe and not knowing where she was. I looked over at her bed. She wasn't there.

"Mum, where are you?" I shouted, running through to the living-room. She was sitting on the couch.

"I'll get your insulin."

"I can't remember if I've taken it."

I panicked. I didn't know how many tablets there had been in the bottle.

"Please try to remember, Mum, please try," I begged her.

"I don't know."

I went into the kitchen. "Where's the tin of spaghetti, Mum? It's gone."

"I don't know," she shouted back.

"Please try to remember something." She couldn't. I gave her an insulin tablet. Jeffery came into the kitchen, looking for something to eat.

"Where's the spaghetti? You've eaten it!" he screamed at her. "Why must you eat everything? I'm leaving home," he shouted, as he walked down the hall. "And I'm taking my drum with me. I'm not staying here anymore. I'm going now!"

"Jeffery," my mother cried, "don't go." But he had already left the flat.

My mother fell asleep, and I stayed beside her, hoping she hadn't taken too much insulin. She had been sleeping for about an hour, when suddenly she hit out at me.

"Where's Jeffery?" she shouted.

"Don't worry, Mum, he'll be back."

"Has Jeffery taken anything with him?" she sobbed.

I walked down the hall to his bedroom. "His drum's still here," I shouted, climbing over the bedroom door, which was lying on the floor. Jeffery had brought the drum home from Delamere Children's Home, and wouldn't be parted from it.

I remembered that there was a prescription for Hydroderm cream in the drawer, and decided to take it to the chemist to see if he would change it for Duraphet tablets. I knew they would make her feel better. When I went back into the living-room, she was asleep again.

I took the prescription to the chemist, and he changed it for two tablets. I ran home quickly, touching the wall for support and trying to ignore the terrible fear that my heart would stop, or that I would die before I got back to my mother.

When I arrived home, the first thing I did was to wake her up.

"Here, Mum, take these." She could see they were Duraphet tablets. "Here, Mum. Sit up, and drink the water." She gulped down the tablets and fell asleep again. I sat beside her, watching her, hoping the tablets would make her better. About half-an-hour later, she began to open her eyes.

"I love you all," she whispered to me.

"We know that, Mum."

"I'm going to make you all a nice tea. Get me a pencil and paper, and I'll write you a list for the grocery shop."

We thought about what we would need. There was no gas or electricity, so there was no point in getting any food that had to be cooked. We decided on bread, jam, frozen chocolate éclairs and a tin of beans.

I took the list, setting off to the shop at the top of the hill. I was hoping I wouldn't get breathless. As soon as I left the flats, I had to start gulping for air and stamping my foot so that my heart wouldn't stop completely. Holding the wall made it a little better, and I couldn't wait to get home.

My mother stayed on the couch all day, opening her eyes now and again, and smiling at me. I sat watching her. If only next year would come quickly. It would be time for me to leave school and find a job; I could look after her properly. She had a lovely face. It filled me with warmth. I wanted to lie beside her, and sink my head into her warm, huge body. It was nice to daydream about it, but I knew how irritable she became if I got too close to her. I knew it was because she was ill. She had always told me that she loved me when she was able to.

It felt so cold in the flat. I went into the bedroom. The need to sleep was overwhelming. I curled up on the bed with my arms wrapped around myself, pretending it was my mother holding me. If only we had some blankets, if only I had another uniform to wear for school, so that all the other children could see me looking nice, especially Philip. My eyes started to fill with tears, and I fought hard to stop myself from crying in case my mother heard me.

My mind drifted to all the nice things I wished for, my mother to be well, to have enough food for her, money for electricity. My head was pounding, "Mummy!" I was screaming inside. Suddenly, I could hear her shouting for me.

"Hikey, quick!"

I jumped off the bed, trying to dry my eyes and straighten my uniform.

"Coming, Mum,"

"Where's Jeffery?" she was shouting.

"He'll be back soon, don't worry," I told her.

"Why are you crying?"

"I'm not, Mum. My tummy's hurting me, that's all, I'll be alright." She fell asleep again. "Don't worry, Mum, I'll be working soon. Everything will be alright." I hoped she would stay asleep, and not get hungry or want cigarettes.

David arrived home from school. When my mother heard him, she woke up.

"Is Jeffery home yet?"

"No," I said. She fell asleep again.

I waited for Jeffery to come home, it was getting late, past his usual time. I didn't wake my mother because I didn't want her to worry. At last, the front door banged.

"I love you, Jeffery!" my mother shouted. "There's a nice tea waiting for you."

Jeffery went to his bedroom, and stayed there with David. The tablets were wearing off, and my mother was sleeping deeply again. I stayed beside her.

Later in the evening, there was a knock on the door. We all stayed very quiet, not knowing who it could be.

My father's voice called "Open the door!"

Jeffery went to open the door for him. I couldn't bear to.

"Where's your Mum?" I heard him ask Jeffery.

"On the couch."

"Mum, wake up. He's here," I told her. I couldn't say Dad. It brought back all the smells and memories. I stood in the far corner, out of his way, when I heard him walking down the hall. He walked into the living-room. A woman followed him in.

"Mum," Jeff whispered, "Dad's here."

She opened her eyes and looked up. "What's he doing here?" She was very distressed at seeing this other woman and I wished she would go. My father told my mother that he would give her money if she would agree to a divorce, so he could marry this woman.

"No," my mother told him. She started to cry, she held her head in her hands, and we all told them to get out and leave Mum alone.

"We've had a child and given it up for adoption," my father told my mother.

"Get out," she told him.

"Get out! Get out!" Jeffery was shouting, over and over again. They soon left, and we all ran to the kitchen window, knowing we would be able to see them walking to the main road. Jeffery pushed the kitchen window open, and picked up an empty milk bottle off the floor.

"Stand back!" Jeffery pushed us away. As soon as they came into sight, he threw the bottle at them.

"*Momzer*," he screamed. "We hate you! I'll kill you!"

My mother was still on the couch, crying. She had recognised the woman. They had attended the old Jewish School together. She cried and cried for ages, and eventually fell asleep again. I sat beside her, stroking her hair, telling her I would look after her, and that I loved her.

The next day was Friday, and Jeffery would be getting his first wage packet. We were all feeling very good about it.

The following morning, Jeffery left early, the day dragged as we waited for him to return with his wages. I had collected the food parcel in the afternoon, and made David some jam sandwiches when he arrived home from school.

At last, the buzzer rang. I answered it.

"Is that you Jeff?"

"Yes."

I pressed the button to open the main door, then ran and opened the front door of the flat. Then I went back to stay with my mother.

"Mum," I shook her. "Mum, Jeffery's home, come on, wake up." She started to open her eyes. "Jeffery's home, he's just coming up in the lift."

"Will you go and get some food?" she asked me.

"Of course, I will."

We heard Jeffery get out of the lift and walk into the hall. He was being very quiet.

"Jeff, what are you doing?" my mother shouted.

Jeffery didn't answer. He seemed to be taking a long time. Eventually, he came into the living-room, looking very sheepish.

"Where's your wages?" My mother asked. Suddenly, there was a squawking noise.

"What's that?" my mother shouted.

"It's a bird. I've just bought it," Jeffery told her, and went to fetch it from the cupboard where he'd hidden it.

"Look, Mum, isn't it nice? I'm going to call him *Yankel the bagel fresser.*" Jeffery handed my mother the rest of his wages.

"We need all the money!" she shouted at him. "You'll have to take it back."

She gave me some money to get food. As I left the flat, I could hear them shouting about the bird. I knew that Jeffery would have to take *Yankel the bagel fresser* back to the shop, and I felt very sorry for him.

CHAPTER 13

The summer holidays came round again. I seemed to spend the time in bed or going to the doctor. Jeffery would bring home food whenever possible. I wished the holidays away so that David could go to school. I always felt better when I knew he was getting his dinners there.

As the holidays drew to a close, I started to feel excited. I knew it would be my last year at school. I desperately wanted to be able to get a good job so I could get money to buy nice things for the flat and for my mother. I knew I could get food 'on tick' from the grocery shop if I was desperate, that made me feel good. I knew my mother would get better if I could afford to look after her properly. I was determined to work hard in school during the last year.

One day, in the late afternoon, I was waiting for Jeffery to come home from work, hoping, as usual, that he would have some food with him. The buzzer rang. I thought that Jeffery might have forgotten his key, so I answered it.

"Mrs Levene?" a voice enquired. I didn't answer. "Is Mrs Levene there? You've won some money." I let go of the phone, and started to tremble.

"Mum, there's a man on the phone. We've won some money!" She looked at me, I handed her the mouthpiece.

"Mrs Levene, you've won the pools. I'm from Littlewoods."

"Let him in." I replaced the phone. "Quick, Hikey, tidy up: Open the front door for him."

I moved some papers off the floor, and opened the front door. Just then, Jeffery walked in.

"Jeffery," mum shouted, "help Hikey tidy up."

"Mum…" Jeffery interrupted.

"Jeffery we've won some money. There's a man from Littlewoods on his way up. Tidy up a little."

Jeffery tried to break in again. "Mum…" She took no notice of him.

At last he managed to get her attention, "Mum, it was me. We don't do the pools."

She stretched her arm out and pulled him towards the couch. She looked at him.

"Sorry, Mum," whispered Jeffery.

One morning, I was woken up by a letter being pushed through the front door. My heart sank. I was worried sick that it was from the School Board. I held the letter for a while before finding the courage to open it. At last, I ripped open the envelope, immediately looking at the signature. It was from Doris. I read the letter. *Dear Annie, I'm very ill, and need help.*

I started waking my mother. She loved Doris, and I knew she would be upset.

"Come on, Mum. There's a letter from Auntie Doris. She's not well." My mother was lying on the couch, and turned away from me.

"Mum, Auntie Doris isn't well."

She half turned towards me. "Go and look after her for a few days."

"I can't, Mum. I can't leave you."

"Please go, Hikey, she needs you." She turned her face back towards the wall, and fell asleep again.

I knew I couldn't go, and walked around the room frightened, not knowing what to do. My mother wanted me to go. If I go now, I can be back soon, I told myself. I checked that there were enough insulin tablets, putting them on the floor beside her, where Jeffery could see them. There were a few bits of food left; I placed them beside the tablets, along with a cup of water.

"*Shama Yisroel*," I was praying, hoping it would keep her safe. "I'll be back tomorrow," I whispered.

I ran all the way to my auntie's house. I wanted to rush everything, so I could get back to my mother. I reached her house, and knocked on the door. There was no reply; I looked through the letterbox.

"Auntie Doris, are you there?"

"Come round the back," I heard her shout.

I pushed the back door open, walking through the kitchen into the living-room. She was lying on the couch, crying.

"What's the matter?"

"I can't move. I'm waiting to go into hospital to have a sinus on my spine drained. I'm in agony," she cried.

I sat on the floor beside her. "Do you want me to do anything?"

"Will you go to Itchkey Abramson's shop? It's on the corner. Get some salami, chopped liver and bagels." She gave me a ten shilling note.

I was just about to enter the shop when I heard someone call out my name.

"Are you Jane Levene? Did you go to the school at the top of Crumpsall Lane? The Open Air School for sickly children?"

I looked at the little girl's face. It was Sheila Bloor. She had played 'twizzers' with me.

"Do you want to come to tea at my house?" She pointed to where the street was, and told me the house number.

"Well, I'm looking after my auntie. She's very ill." I looked at her. All I wanted to do was to go back to my mother. I wanted to be with her in case she died. Sheila was watching my face.

"I'll tell my Mum you might come for your tea," she smiled at me.

"Alright, I'll ask my auntie."

Sheila walked away; I went into Itchkey Abramson's shop.

"Can I have some food for my Auntie Doris? She lives just up the road."

A young man served me. When I had paid for my groceries, he told me to tell my auntie that Jeffery Caplan would pop in to see her later. When I arrived back at my auntie's house, I placed the small box of food beside the couch where she was lying.

"Sit down, and don't move. My nerves are bad. I'm in agony!"

"Auntie Doris, I've just seen a girl. Can I go to her house later? Can I go just for a while?"

"Shut up till I've had a *shloff!*" She started snoring. I sat and waited for her to wake up.

After some time she woke up, and asked me to cut the bagels and spread the chopped liver on them. "Eric's gone to *Chedar* to learn Hebrew. He won't be home for a while."

When I had finished spreading the chopped liver on the bagels she told me I could go to Sheila's house for one hour, and no longer. I walked down the street that Sheila had pointed to; I started to feel very nervous. I knew I should be at home. "Please be alright, Mum," I was whispering under my breath.

Sheila was playing outside her house. She showed me in, taking me to her mother, who was in the kitchen. Sheila pulled my arm.

"Come and see my bedroom." She was showing me her clothes when her mother put her head round the door.

"Do you want any of these skirts, Jane?

"No, I like my skirt," I whispered.

"You two have a wash. There's some cake on the table."

"I don't want a wash."

"Come on, Jane, we'll have some tea." She took me downstairs.

Her mother and father were sitting at a small table, waiting for us. I could smell her father's body and wanted to run away, as far as possible. I couldn't look at him, and hoped he would disappear.

We sat down. Sheila's mother sliced the cherry cake. She placed a piece on each plate. I couldn't take my eyes off my plate. Some moments later, I looked up, to be greeted by three smiling faces. I had eaten the cake, picking out all the cherries, and putting them to one side.

"Why have you done that?" asked Sheila's mother smiling at me.

"They are so nice, I wanted to leave them to the end." They all laughed.

I stayed with my auntie overnight, in the morning returning home as quickly as possible. Jeffery had given my mother the insulin tablet, she was fast asleep. I was pleased about that, I hoped that she hadn't realised that I wasn't there. I didn't want her to miss me.

Some weeks later, we received another letter from my

Auntie Doris. She wrote to tell us that she and my cousin would be going away for a few days, and we could stay at her house. I tried to wake my mother.

"Mum, Auntie Doris is going away." I shook her and she woke up. "Mum, Auntie Doris is going away. We can stay at her house. I'll get you some tablets. It'll be a holiday for you." She nodded her head, and went back to sleep.

It was Friday morning. I left the flat to go to the doctor's surgery. If my mother had tablets, we could all get the bus to my Auntie Doris's house. Life felt so good now.

I arrived at the surgery and I begged him for some Duraphet tablets and breathing tablets. I knew my mother had enough insulin. I also asked for a prescription for a tube of Hydroderm cream in the hope that the chemist would change it for me. The doctor gave me a prescription on which I could see he had written four Duraphet tablets. They were enough to keep my mother awake for one day. He had also put some breathing tablets on the same prescription. Then he started writing out another prescription for the cream. I was going to pick up the food parcel in the afternoon. I remembered my Auntie Doris's cupboards, full of food.

When I arrived home, I hid the tablets. My mother didn't need them till Monday, the day when my auntie was going away.

When David and Jeffery came home, I showed them the letter and told them about the tablets.

"It'll be a holiday. All of us together and there's lots of food in the house."

During the weekend, my mother was constantly waking up and begging for tablets. I couldn't give her the tablets, and prayed she would just sleep till Monday morning. There were four tablets. They would, hopefully, last for a day. I knew I had to get her home before Tuesday afternoon.

I stayed by her side throughout Sunday night. As the hours passed by, I became more and more excited. I was imagining all the food for my mother, Jeffery and David. There was also the National Assistance money to cash, first thing in the morning. That meant more money for food. Morning came. Before Jeffery left the flat he told me he wouldn't be coming to stay at Auntie Doris's. I walked David to school. I had to get the National Assistance money so that we would have the bus fare to my auntie's house. When I arrived home, I gave my mother two Duraphet tablets, and waited for her to wake up.

"I've got the National Assistance money, Mum. Come on, put your coat on. We'll go now."

I checked to make sure I'd put all the tablets in her handbag. I noticed the empty lipstick carton and the empty rouge carton. I could smell them both faintly.

"Mum, when I start work I'll buy you some nice lipstick and rouge."

"What would I do without you, Hikey." She smiled. We set off towards the bus stop.

When we arrived at my auntie's house, I walked round to the back, where she had told me in the letter that the front door key would be left under a brick. I opened the front door, leading my mother into the house.

"Isn't it nice, Mum? It'll be a holiday for you." I left her on the couch, and went straight into the kitchen to get some food. I remembered that most of it was kept in a large sideboard in the living-room and kitchen unit near the back door. I went into the kitchen first. I pulled at the door handle: nothing happened. It was fastened tightly with string round the handles. All the other cupboards were empty.

My heart sank. I went into the living-room and tried to open the cupboards in the sideboard, the doors were tightly tied with string and the drawers were empty. I told my mother. I took some money from her handbag. "I'll go to Itchkey Abramson's, and get you some nice things." I kissed her on the forehead, and went to the shop. I bought all her favourite food and enough for David as well.

When I got back, she was asleep. I stood beside her, watching her, holding the carrier bag full of food. She woke up and pulled the bag off me.

"I'll make some bagels and chopped liver, Mum." Before I could go into the kitchen, she had the bag on the floor, and was pulling at all the packages, and forcing the food down her throat. Later that evening, my mother started crying. She wouldn't stop, so we all went home.

Some days later, when I went to the shop at the top of Riverdale road, I noticed all the Mother's Day cards on display. It was also my mother's birthday soon after. I had never been able to buy her a card. When I had left the shop, I stood looking in the window, wondering how I could afford it. Perhaps I would be able to buy a card for her next birthday.

On the following Monday morning, when I had collected the National Assistance money, I walked home to save tuppence.

Carrying all my bags, I went to the shop at the top of the road. I saw the card I wanted. It was in a box with a blue and gold surround. It had a dog's face on the front, and looked very cute. I left the shop and started walking home, thinking all the time about the card. My heart started racing, I ran back to the shop, and told the man behind the counter that I wanted the card for my mother, for her next birthday. He put it in a brown paper bag, and I carefully placed it in one of the carrier bags. I paid for it, and ran all the way home. I couldn't wait for her next birthday to come round.

When I arrived back at the flat, I listened at the front door before walking down the hall, to make sure my mother was asleep. She was. I took the bags into the living-room, and I looked for somewhere to hide the card. We had an old sideboard; I decided to hide it inside that. I put the carrier bags down on the floor, easing the paper bag out, making sure I didn't damage the box or the card. The sideboard door was hanging off, it was held on by a rusty hinge, it creaked as I opened it and placed the card inside. I put it on top of a pile of old papers, then I went and sat by the couch.

"Mum, I've got some food. Wake up." It took her a while to come round. "Look, Mum," I said, pointing to all the food laid out on the floor.

She turned and faced me. Just then, the sideboard door creaked open and the card fell out. I knew that I shouldn't have bought it, that we needed the food more. She looked at it.

"It's a birthday card for you, for your next birthday." I looked at her.

"Let me see." I passed her the box, and she looked at the card.

"It's lovely, Hikey, but it's very unlucky. I might not be here on my next birthday."

"Don't be silly, Mum," I told her and put the card back

into the cupboard, "I can't wait till your next birthday, Mum."

At school, I was now in Four Commercial. I was learning to type and I was trying very hard. When I went to school I tried desperately hard to answer the written exams, it was impossible. I would write anything just to make the teacher think I was clever. I was determined I would be able to look after my mother. After managing to keep going to school for a short time, it became too difficult for me to concentrate and not become anxious and worried about her.

One day, after lunch, I was unable to go back into the school. I had to be at home with my mother to make sure she was still alive. I ran out of the playground, stamping my foot to keep my heart beating. I had no money. There was a policeman walking nearby, I ran up to him, crying.

"Please can you lend me thruppence for my bus fare? My Mum's not well, I don't know if she's dead and I have to get home." He took thruppence out of his pocket and gave it to me. "Thank you!" I shouted, as I ran to the bus stop. I was panicking terribly.

I shouldn't have left my mother, not for anything, I kept saying to myself. The bus arrived and I jumped on it. Please hurry home I was thinking. Suddenly, I couldn't feel my heart beating, and felt faint. Standing up in the bus I stamped my foot, to try to get my heart going again. Everybody was looking at me. "Stop the bus!" I asked. "I need to get off!"

I jumped off the bus, and ran the rest of the way home, somehow thinking that by running and banging my foot on the ground, my heart wouldn't stop.

At last, the flats were in sight. The door to the stairs was open. I ran up the stairs as fast as my feet would carry me.

Counting the stairs and touching the banister would keep me safe. I was praying my mother would be alright. My body was shaking as I approached the front door. I was trying hard to find my key. Please don't be dead, I was thinking to myself. The key finally turned in the lock, and I ran inside.

"Mum, Mum!" I shouted. She was fast asleep. "I'll never leave you again," I promised.

A few months passed by. Then one day a letter arrived from the hospital to say that my mother would be admitted for an operation. An ambulance would come for her in two weeks' time. When Jeffery and David arrived home, I told them the news. David hardly ever said anything, but I could see he was upset.

"She's going to be better this time," I told him.

My mother hardly ever moved off the couch now, just lying there even when she had tablets. The days passed slowly. I gave her the insulin, then the food, making sure she was still breathing, wanting her to survive. Next year, I would leave school, and I wanted to be able to earn money to make her life as comfortable as possible. I would find somebody to look after her during the day, to keep her company. Perhaps if she had a friend to talk to, she would get a little better. I wanted nice blankets and sheets for her. When Sunday came, I went down to the Benevolent Society to try to get some extra money for a nightdress and slippers for her. They didn't have a room like the Jewish Board of Guardians where you could go and sort out second-hand clothes; I wished they did. I was refused money for the slippers and nightdress.

"Your mother will have to come and see us herself," said the man with the cigar.

CHAPTER 14

Mum had been lying on the couch for as long as I could remember. I went into the kitchen, looking through all the cupboards and drawers, praying I would find a crust of bread, no matter how stale or mouldy. I found the jam jar: it was bramble seedless jam that I had collected the previous Friday from the Benevolent Society. It was completely empty except for some bits around the top on the inside. I ran my finger around the inside and licked what little there was off my finger.

"Hikey, where are you?" My heart started racing so fast I couldn't breathe. I felt my pulse to make sure I was still alive.

"What if she wants food" I whispered to myself, how could I tell her there was nothing?

"Coming, Mum," I went through to the living-room and knelt beside the couch, making sure her coat was covering her. She seemed delirious. "Is it *Yom Kippur* yet?" She became very distressed.

"I don't know, Mum."

"I must say *Yiskah* for my Mother and Father." She lifted her head off the cushion. Her hair was matted over one side of her face. I wanted to pull the hair away and comb it. I reached towards her and she pulled back.

I sat back on the floor. "Help me up, Hikey, I need to say *Yiskah*."

She lifted herself by her arm; her legs were almost glued together at the knees with all the blood that had accumulated there. The coat fell off her legs and she rolled off the couch and onto the floor, her stomach completely covering my legs.

"Come on Mum," I whispered, trying hard to push her off my legs. She said nothing.

"Mummy please." I was shaking her arm. "Get back on the couch." I wanted to cover her with the coat, it was very cold in the flat and I didn't want her to catch a cold.

"Is there anything to eat?"

"No, Mum." I puffed and panted, trying hard to get her onto the couch.

"I'm going to buy you knickers and stockings when I leave school and get a job. I'll make sure you have everything you want." I was still trying very hard to move her body and get her back on the couch.

"Will you go to *shul* to say *Yiskah* for my parents?" she begged me.

"Of course I will. Please try to get back on the couch so I can cover you with your coat," I pleaded.

"I need someone to talk to." My heart sank. "You've got me Mum," I said trying to hold back the tears.

"Where's Doris?"

"I don't know Mum." I was still trying very hard to help her get back on the couch.

"Hikey, I'm so hungry, will you go to the shop? Will you go to the doctor?" She was almost back on the couch now and I managed to get the cushion under her head.

"I'm turning over, so I can have a *shloff*." I covered her with the coat and hoped she would sleep until I could find some food. I listened to make sure she was still breathing before I left the flat.

Once outside I tried to pull my socks as far up my legs as

they would go to keep them warm. I rushed down the stairs, I knew if I wasn't back in ten minutes my mother would go into a coma and she couldn't pull her own tongue out of her mouth. I would have to hurry. I rushed up the street to the greengrocer's shop.

There were plenty of walls all the way for me to hold on to; the only thing that slowed me down was stopping to take deep breaths, to keep my heart and lungs working. I stood for a moment to check my pulse. I heard the ice cream van; I wished I had the money to buy us both one. The shop was only five minutes up the road and I ran the rest of the way.

I could see the shops were open; sometimes the sweetshop owner let us have sweets and cigarettes till we had the money to pay for them, as did the greengrocer. I was imagining what I would ask for. My socks had fallen about my feet and they were dragging along the pavement, the elastic had disappeared a long time ago, but I didn't stop. I wanted some food for us: that was all that mattered.

I joined the queue in the greengrocer's shop and waited. I counted how many people were before me, there were four. I counted out four using the fingers on each hand. My hands were outstretched in front of me; 1,2,3,4, I counted on one hand and 1,2,3,4, I counted on the other. That would make time pass quickly and keep my mother alive.

"Yes dear?" asked the lady behind the counter. I put my hands in my pockets.

"Can I have some food till Monday? We'll pay then, It's for my Mother, Mrs Levene?" She pulled a large book out from under the counter and ran her fingers through the pages, suddenly she stopped. She closed the book. "Your mum still owes us fifteen shillings, I think she should pay that back first."

"OK." I looked at the food stacked on the shelves as I walked out of the shop, and had a quick glance in the chest freezer. I could see the crispy cod balls. My mother loved them very much. I walked out of the shop, my heart pounding. There was nowhere else to go, no-one else to ask for money.

I stayed very close to the wall, looking at my hands: 1,2,3,4, I counted on one hand, then 1,2,3,4, on the other, repeating it until I reached the front door. I put the key in the front door lock to open it.

"Mum," I shouted as I ran down the hall, "are you alright?"

I could hear her shouting and I ran down the hall and stood near the living-room door.

"Why did you wake me? Did you get any food?"

"No, Mum, sorry," I told her, praying she would fall asleep again.

I gently sat down near the door: 1,2,3,4, I counted on one hand under my breath, then 1,2,3,4, I counted on the other. I rushed to the couch, turning her head towards me, so I could see her mouth. I listened very carefully, putting my hand near to her mouth. She shrugged her head and I let go. She was alive. I sat on the floor beside her, tucking my legs under my skirt. I rubbed my hands together to warm them: 1,2,3,4, I counted on my fingers, 1,2,3,4, I counted once more on my toes. I thought about the food parcel from the soup kitchen. I loved the smell of the fresh bread creeping out of the box as I carried it home. I could smell it very clearly as I sat on the floor.

For a moment the smell turned to fire and I sat up panicking, my body rigid. I sniffed with all the force I could muster. I ran down the hall and lifted the letterbox slightly, sniffing all the time; I could hear the sound of crackling wood.

I opened the front door and ran to the door that led to the staircase. I knelt and felt the stairs with my hands, still sniffing about. I knew the stairs would be hot if they were on fire.

I looked through the window of the refuse hopper to see if smoke was billowing from one of the flats below. I looked all around; there was nothing to be seen.

My heart started pounding as I remembered I had left my mother on her own. I closed the door to the hopper and hurried back to the flat. The door was still open. I closed it behind me. I opened it again. I must repeat it four times or mum might die.

I noticed the light switch near the door. There were no bulbs in the fittings but I had to turn it on and off four times before I could move. It had to be repeated four times, no more, no less, or mum might die.

I crept along the hall, counting my footsteps, four at a time, to ensure she was kept alive.

"Hikey."

"I'm here, Mum."

"I'm having a *shloff*."

I didn't breathe too loudly or it would wake her up and make her irritable. "OK Mum, see you soon, love you." They were the last words I had said to her, and I knew I had to repeat them four times.

For each object I looked at in the room I blinked four times, repeating what it was also four times. All this would help keep her alive.

My heart skipped a beat. What would she have to eat after her insulin tomorrow morning, I thought to myself? I couldn't breathe; I crept into the bedroom so I could gasp for air and get my heart going again without waking her. The bedroom floor was full of crumpled and ripped up comics that we had found in the refuse hopper. I picked up a handful of the paper and moulded it into a ball, Jeffery had told me I was the only girl of nearly fourteen he knew that was flat chested. I put the moulded paper down my blouse and looked at the shape. It looked real so I moulded another ball and put that down my blouse as well.

"Hikey!" I heard my mother shout.

"I'm here, Mum," I went into the living-room.

"Will you go and get me some Duraphet?"

"Yes, Mum, I'll go when the children come out of school, don't worry." She was still facing the wall and hadn't noticed my newly formed breasts. I sat beside her until I heard children's voices, then I knew it was time for me to go to the surgery.

"Mum, I'm going to the surgery," I whispered, "I'll leave a cup of water with sugar next to the couch in case you need it. See you soon."

As I left the flats, I opened my jacket and stuck my chest out. I walked along the road towards the doctor's surgery, staying near to the wall and counting how many steps it would take to get there. I still had my jacket wide open so I could show off my not so flat chest. I glanced up for a moment and saw two young boys laughing and pointing at me. I looked down at my chest and noticed one ball was still in place, the other had fallen down to my waist.

I found an entry, stopped and adjusted them. Walking along the road I wondered if the doctor would give me some tablets for my mother. I didn't feel very hopeful. It was difficult to get a prescription for them and I knew my mother would soon beg us to change doctors.

I could see Victoria Avenue in the distance and my body started to fill with all the usual anticipation and excitement. If only he will give me some, I thought to myself, she would be able to sit up and I could give her a cuddle.

I stopped dead in my tracks; I had lost count of how many footsteps I had taken. Perhaps I should go back to the flats and start again? The urge to do so was very strong. I could see I was almost at the surgery. I decided it would be better to count them on the way back instead. I pushed the gate open as I reached the surgery. I hated the building, it looked so nice and clean, as did all the people sitting on the chairs waiting to see the doctor. I wished I could have all their tablets to take home for my mother. I wished I could have this house for her to live in. I knew they weren't really nice and clean, they were pretending. The receptionist told me to sit in the waiting room.

There were six other people waiting to see the doctor, sitting on the chairs that lined the wall. I found a seat that was well away from them all. I didn't like any of them. I looked to see how many posters were stuck on the walls and how many were over the fireplace. There were six altogether. My hands were placed firmly under the seat and with each finger I counted six, six times. Then I looked to see how many words there were in large print. After I had counted them all I started tapping out the amount on my fingers, each one touched the wood underneath the chair. I knew I had to finish before the receptionist called me or my mother would die.

"You're next," the receptionist said, pointing at me.

"I won't be a minute; I've got to finish counting." I hurried to finish my counting, then ran to the doctor's room.

I entered the doctor's room and my heart was pounding.

"Please can I have some Duraphet tablets for my Mum,

Mrs Levene?" He was looking at my chest, and when I looked down I could see one of the balls had fallen to my waist again. I put my hand down my blouse and adjusted them once more.

"Can I, Doctor, please?"

"No," was the reply.

"Can I have some cream; my lips are very sore, please Doctor." I watched his every move as he started writing out the prescription and handed it to me.

"Thank you, Doctor." I held it tightly in my hand and started walking towards the chemist.

It started to rain. I could feel my socks getting heavier with the water as they dragged behind me. I stopped now and again to try to pull them up but it made no difference.

I waited in the chemist until he had served the people who were already in.

"Can I have some Duraphet tablets for this prescription?" I begged him. He took it off me.

"No, I can't do it all the time; do you want the cream?"

"Yes, please."

He passed me a small white bag with the cream inside. Once outside the shop I opened the small tube and rubbed it on my badly cracked lips. The pain disappeared. It took longer than usual to get home as I was so breathless.

During the week before my mother was due to go into hospital, I stayed near to her as much as possible. I hardly left her side. Jeffery and David remained in their bedroom. My brothers and I all looked forward to the time when she would come home and would be well at last.

CHAPTER 15

Sunday arrived all too quickly. The atmosphere was cold and damp as I lay in bed next to my mother. I looked at her, wanting to tell her she would never have to do without heat once I left school and found myself a job.

I reached out, shaking her gently. "Mum, wake up. Here's your insulin," I whispered, lifting her head and placing the tablet on her tongue. Her legs were shaking. "Drink the water, Mum." She drank it, and rested her head back on the cushion. "I've put a tin of baked beans away for you. I'll go and get them." She ate the beans, and fell asleep again.

About half-an-hour later, I heard a knock on the door.

"It's Mrs Pelham. I've got some cake for you."

I opened the front door. "Mum's going into hospital tomorrow. We're going to the Sarah Laski Home," I told Mrs Pelham. She passed me the cake and asked me how mum was. "Not very well. I'm frightened." She looked at me, but didn't say anything.

"Thank you very much for the cake. We'll eat it now," I told her, closing the door.

I took the cake to Jeffery's room to show him and David, we all started to pull pieces off it and eat them.

"Jeffery, will you come to the Benevolent Society with me?"

"Yes," he answered.

"David, will you look after Mum? I'll bring you some food

back if we get any money." He looked at me and nodded.

I put the rest of the cake away for my mother, Jeffery and I set off towards Cheetham Hill Road, my mind encased in ice, afraid of the coming week.

We arrived at the Benevolent Society and waited, hoping we would get a shilling or two. At last, we were sitting in the big room, pleading silently with the man smoking his cigar. He handed me a shilling. We left quickly and headed home.

Jeffery was walking ahead of me. I wanted to hold his hand but dared not ask. The memories of last night came flooding back. My mother couldn't breathe. She was imagining there were people in the room wanting to take her away from us. She was begging me to put the light on so she could see them, but there wasn't any electricity.

We stopped at the delicatessen nearest home. It was at the top of Blackley New Road. We bought what we could. Jeffery started running ahead of me. I wanted him to tell me that our mother was going to be alright, but I couldn't catch up with him.

The rest of the day passed very slowly. We all slept to keep the cold away. At last night fell. I sat beside my mother all night, watching her face, hoping that this time when she came out of hospital she would be well.

Again, during the night, she was hallucinating and shouting, wanting someone to help her breathe. We didn't know what to do for her, or how to make her better.

"Hikey, don't let them take me away!" she was shouting.

"Don't be silly, Mum. Nobody's going to do that."

The next minute, she was asking who I was. "Are you going to take my children away?" she asked. She managed to fall asleep again. I stayed awake throughout the night, and as soon as morning arrived, made sure she took her insulin.

"I'll get you some cake. Mrs Pelham brought it yesterday."

"What's going to happen to my kids?" She was crying. "What's going to happen to you?"

I didn't like her talking that way. It frightened me too much.

"I'll go and wake Jeffery and David."

Jeffery and David were already awake. I told them to get up because the ambulance was due to arrive early. My mother had managed to sit up and I helped her to put on her coat. She asked me to pass her handbag. It was Monday so she made sure the National Assistance book was in it. She wrote a note for me, and told me to take it to the sweet shop at the top of the road.

The note read: *3 packets of Maltesers and 3 packets of Treats, and I'll pay you at the end of the week. Thank you. Mrs Levene.*

I left the flat, and ran to the shop, touching the wall and stamping my foot to ensure my heart carried on beating. I soon had all the packets of sweets in a paper bag, and ran home. When I arrived home, Mum took the bag off me, and shared the sweets out. We all sat on the bed together.

"What's going to happen to my kinder? All I want is to see you all married."

Suddenly, the intercom buzzed. I answered it.

"Ambulance for Mrs Levene,"

"We'll be down in a minute."

"Come on, Mum." David started crying. I put my arms around him. We all helped mum off the bed, and made our way down the hall to the front door. I checked to make sure she had her tablets and National Assistance book, closing the front door behind me.

When we arrived at the ground floor, the ambulance driver was waiting, and led my mother by the arm into the ambulance. She kissed us all.

"I'll come and visit you tonight! Love you Mum!"

The doors closed, and she was driven away. Jeffery left us to go to work. David and I made our way to school. I left David in the playground and I went down the small path to the High School.

The children were all in their classrooms. I managed to find the classroom where I should be, just as the bell rang. All the children rushed out into the playground, and I followed. As I stepped outside, a group of girls were skipping and singing:

"*Oy avey, as mere,*
tatties on the beer,
mamma's maching loction soup,
Oy avey as mere."

I stood and watched a while, my stomach knotted in anticipation of visiting my mother.

When break time was over, I followed the children to the classroom. Mr Price, the English teacher, was waiting. "We're going to watch a film today." He closed the door and curtains. The film was about concentration camps, people dying. I couldn't watch.

"You must never forget any of this," he said.

I was thinking about my mother, and remembered the larder door near the kitchen in the Sarah Laski Home, hoping it would be open so I could get some food for her.

At last, the bell rang. It was home time. I rushed to collect David, we both ran all the way to the Home. We stood at the front door, and I rang the door bell. The Matron opened the door. "Hello Jane, hello David. Come in. We'll get you cleaned up."

We were taken upstairs to the bathroom.

"I'm going to see my Mum tonight," I told the nurse as she was washing me."

"That's fine. Hurry and get dressed. We're having tea soon."

"I'm taking your uniform to wash," the nurse told me. I felt lost. My mother wouldn't recognise me without it. The nurse wouldn't allow me to put it back on and led me to a large room with shelves full of clothes. I found a small cardigan. It was white with two small flowers on each side. I grabbed it, and ran downstairs.

"What are you doing, Jane? Go and get dressed!" The Matron yelled.

"Will my Mum recognise me if I wear this?"

"Of course, go and get dressed."

The cardigan looked very pretty, and I wanted my mother to think it was pretty too. Suddenly, I couldn't breathe. I started gasping for breath. The Matron went to her office and phoned for the doctor. I couldn't understand why. I knew it would pass soon.

The nurse took me back upstairs and I got dressed. Soon, the doctor arrived, and examined me. He told the Matron that there was nothing physically wrong with me.

"Please can I go to the hospital to see my Mum?" I begged the Matron.

"Yes," She replied.

"I'm just going to get a drink of water." The larder door was open. I rushed in and picked up some oranges and a packet of biscuits for my mother.

It wasn't far to the hospital. As soon as I arrived, I started looking for the ward. I followed the signs. They led me to a flight of stairs. At the top of the stairs I could see people waiting to go into the ward. I was trying to reach the little round windows in the door, so I could see my mother. The double doors were opened and we were all ushered in. I walked into the ward, looking for my mother, excited because I had presents for her.

"Hikey!" she shouted. I ran and hugged her.

"Look Mum, my cardigan. I've brought you some oranges and biscuits."

"You look lovely, Hikey." She showed me off to the women in bed on either side of her. I sat down on the bed, she opened the bag with the oranges and biscuits in it. She kissed and hugged me. "What would I do without you?"

Her operation was to be tomorrow, I told her I could visit tomorrow night.

"Pass me my handbag, Hikey." She pulled out her National Assistance book.

"Tomorrow after school, I want you to take this and buy yourself some nice dresses."

I didn't want to take it, but she insisted. We were talking for quite a while. Then the bell rang. Visiting time was over. My mother begged me repeatedly to ask Doris to come and see her. I got off the bed, and arranged her bedside table. As I leant over to kiss her and say goodbye, she pushed me away. I felt very frightened.

"I'm not kissing you goodbye. I'm not saying goodbye to you." I felt even more frightened, desperately wanting to hug and kiss her.

The nurse came. "You must all leave now. Visiting time is over."

My mother and I looked at each other. "I love you, Mum," I said, and started to walk out of the ward, turning to wave to her.

My heart sank as I left the ward. I wanted to run back. As I walked to the top of the stairs, my mother was shouting, "Hikey!" She had run after me. She put her arms around me, and started hugging me and kissing me all over my face and on my lips.

"I love you."

She clung on to me until the nurses came to take her back to the ward.

When I arrived back at the Home, Jeffery and David asked me how mum was. I told them she was having her operation in the morning. I felt drained, and only wanted to sleep. I went to my bedroom, getting into bed, and made sure the scarf was over my blankets. That was to make sure my mother would be alright.

I slept all night, waking up occasionally just to make sure the scarf was still over me. When it was almost light, I felt myself waking up. On checking the scarf, I found that it had fallen off me. I felt sick and frightened, thinking it meant that my mother was dead.

I took the National Assistance book out of the drawer of the little bedside cabinet, and got dressed in my school uniform. I put the book inside my blouse so that I wouldn't lose it.

The day at school didn't register. I couldn't stop thinking about seeing my mother. I wished every minute, every second away, sitting in the classes doing nothing, saying nothing. Then the bell rang for home time.

I ran out of school, heading for the Post Office at the top of Cheetham Hill Road. I cashed the National Assistance book, and started to get very excited, knowing what I would do with the money. I would go to my auntie's house to plead with her to go and see my mother. She desperately wanted to see Doris.

My first stop was Boots the Chemist. My heart was pounding with excitement as I stood at the counter, holding my money. "Can I have two bars of Diabetic chocolate?" I asked the assistant. My eyes were all over the place, looking around. I wanted to buy the whole shop for my mother. The assistant put the chocolate in a bag.

"That will be two shillings, dear,"

"I haven't finished. I want some talcum powder and bath cubes." Then I noticed the perfume. "My Mum would like some of that, as well."

The shopping list was endless. Eventually, when I had bought all the things I wanted, I clasped the carrier bag very tightly, handing over the money. "Thank you," I told the assistant, and left the shop.

My next stop was at a shop further down Cheetham Hill Road. It was a ladies' wear shop. As I approached the shop, I could see an orange nightdress in the window. The shop was empty. I looked at the lady behind the counter. "Please can I have the orange nightdress in the window?" I begged her. "It's for my Mum."

"What size would you like?"

"I don't know, but she's big."

She bent down to open a drawer behind the counter, and lifted a plastic bag out.

"This should be fine. It's a large women's."

I was feeling so excited. I couldn't wait to surprise my mother. Then I noticed the slippers. "Can I have some orange slippers, and a dressing gown to match?" I asked the lady.

Feeling on top of the world, I watched her wrap them all up, then I placed them neatly in the carrier bag. I left the shop, and ran and ran, swinging the bags from side to side, feeling so happy.

Then I passed the fruit shop. I turned back and went in. I bought oranges and apples and another carrier bag. Once out of the shop, I ran and ran towards my auntie's house which was just round the corner now. I could see the street, then the house. My heart was pounding. I was so happy with all the surprises I had for my mother.

Suddenly, I was at the bottom of the steps. I reached for the letterbox, banging on it. There was no answer, I banged on the door. There was still no answer.

I bent down to look through the letterbox. My auntie was standing in the living-room, holding a letter. When she saw me looking, she walked down the hall to open the door. She opened it, and stood silent, with the letter in her hand.

I looked at her. "My Mum's dead, isn't she?" I asked her.

"Yes," she said.

PART TWO

SILENT IN THE SHADOWS

CHAPTER 16

1966

My auntie was standing in the doorway holding a letter. My heart sank:

"Mum's dead, isn't she?"

I looked at her face hoping she would say no; instead she handed me the letter. I didn't want it and fell back down the steps still holding the carrier bags. I looked up at my auntie again, panicking inside, hoping she would say my mother was alright. She didn't. I picked myself up off the pavement, still making sure I had all the presents to give my mother. I turned around and started running down the street towards the hospital, Jeffery Caplan was walking towards me. I stopped him. "Where's my Mum?" I was screaming. He looked at me and I could see he wasn't going to answer. I started running again, this time across the road in front of a car that screeched to a halt.

"Get hold of her. Get her in the house!" I was sitting on the couch, someone tried to take my carrier bags. I wasn't going to part with them. They were for my mum. I remember being helped into a car, hearing voices saying I was being taken to the Sarah Laski Home, to tell Jeffery and David that mum had died. I sat quietly, not sure what was happening. I felt happier, it must be a dream. I still had the carrier bags for my mother. I hadn't noticed the car had stopped until I looked out of the window: we were at the Sarah Laski Home. "Jane, go to the Matron's office," someone said as I got out of the car.

I walked through the front door and down the corridor. The Matron's office door was open and I could hear voices. I wanted to be sick and wake up. "Come in, Jane." I stood in the office still holding both my carrier bags. Jeffery and David were standing close to the Matron's desk.

"Mum's dead," I sobbed, holding my tummy in disbelief.

David said nothing and suddenly Jeffery shouted out, "The chemist used to sell us tablets. I never wanted my mum to take them." He looked at the Matron, his face was screwed up with pain. "Can we all stay together, in the flat? We can look after David." I looked at the Matron for a response.

"No, you're too young." My arm was being tugged, "Come on Jane." I was being taken towards the front door. "The father doesn't want them," I heard the Matron say.

I was in the car again, being driven down Cheetham Hill Road, past Levy's delicatessen. My carrier bags had gone. I didn't know what had happened to them. Perhaps they had been taken to my mum. I was back at my auntie's house. My clothes were being pulled at. Before I knew what was happening, I was wearing a navy jumper: the rabbi was standing in front of me reciting *Yiskah*, the prayer for the dead. He held a pair of scissors and cut the jumper at the neck. "You must wear this for the seven day mourning period," he told me. All the mirrors in the house were being covered over. My auntie's neighbours and relatives were bringing food and wishing her a 'long life'. I had never seen any of these people before. I wanted to be at home with my mum, Jeffery and David. I didn't belong here. I didn't know what was going on.

"Can I see my brothers?" I asked the rabbi.

"You can't leave the house for a week, while you're sitting *shiva*," was his only reply.

People were coming and going, talking to my auntie. I sat waiting for the nightmare to end. I lived at 32 Bracknell Court. I wanted to go home. I sat on the end of the couch. Hours had passed. I hadn't noticed. "It's your bedtime!" Auntie Doris told me. The mirror in the bedroom had been covered over. I was glad. I didn't want to see any monsters' faces in them. A *Minion* had congregated in the front room downstairs: they were wailing and praying in Hebrew, and the chanting seemed to carry me away. I awoke some hours later. It must have been the middle of the night. It was very dark. I wanted to see my mum. I turned to the mirror hanging on the wall to see if I could see her face in it. I started to panic. "*Shama Yisroel*," I was repeating to myself, frozen and petrified in the dark. I opened the bedroom door, and started walking towards my auntie's room. "*Shama Yisroel*," I kept on repeating to myself. My hand touched the door handle, I pushed the door open. She was fast asleep, snoring. I stood beside her.

"Auntie Doris," I whispered, keeping my eyes on the door, in case a monster tried to grab me.

"What do you want?" she groaned.

"Can I get into bed with you, Auntie Doris, please?"

"No. Don't think you're going to stay here. I can't cope with you!"

I went back to my room, and pulled a blanket off the bed, wrapping it around myself, sitting on the floor near the door. I covered my head and face, and prayed for daylight to come. I wanted to wee. I went back to her room, gently pushing the door open.

"Auntie Doris, I need to wee."

"Get downstairs. Open the back door. You know where the toilet is!"

"It's dark, the monsters will get me."

"Get out and stay out"

"OK, Auntie Doris." I closed the door behind me. I was shaking and trying to hold my wee in. I stood at the top of the stairs, looking down. It was dark. I was very frightened. My legs froze at the thought of going outside in the dark. I ran into my bedroom, my heart pounding. I sat on the floor, not being able to keep it in any longer. At last I could see shadows on the wall: morning had arrived. There was banging on the front door. My heart lifted. Perhaps it's a nurse from the hospital. It was all a mistake?

"Come on Jane. Get up!" Eric, my cousin, said in a raised voice.

"Eric, open the door for Uncle Asher," she shouted. My heart sank. It wasn't the nurse from the hospital.

"Leave the front door open," she told Eric.

The door had to be left open for the rest of the week during the day until *shiva* was over. I stayed in the bedroom, still wearing the jumper the rabbi had cut. He told me not to wash: that applied to all of us. I didn't want to go downstairs. I was afraid I would be able to smell Uncle Asher's body and socks. I knew it would make me feel ill. My auntie shouted for me to go downstairs. I put my shoes on and left the room. I could hear her voice from the top of the stairs:

"I can't cope with this, it's the last thing I need."

"Don't worry," Asher told her, "she won't be here forever!"

I crept into the living-room, sitting down on the corner of the couch.

"She can't go to the funeral," my auntie was saying, placing plates of bagels and hardboiled eggs on the table.

"My Mum's dead," I whispered. I felt so ill at this thought that I ran to the toilet and was violently sick. I walked back to the living-room. Mrs Pelham was standing near the door. She was holding a white paper bag.

"Mum's dead."

"I know," she said, "I've brought you these grapes. I wasn't sure what to do when a Jewish person dies."

I wanted her to take me back to the flats, where I belonged.

"Your mother loved you very much. Where are Jeffery and David?"

"I don't know." She clasped my hand.

"Jeffery wanted us to stay together in the flats, and look after David."

"I know," she said and started walking towards the front door.

I sat on the couch: things were happening, voices were coming from all directions, prayers were being said.

"You can't go to the funeral," my auntie told me.

Two children I vaguely recognised from school were standing in the hall. They came over to me and wished me a long life. I lowered my head as they shook my hand, ashamed of what I was. They soon left.

"Is my Dad going?" I asked Auntie Doris.

"He's been asked. He said no. It's your bedtime!"

"Yes, Auntie Doris."

I awoke a few times and could hear the Hebrew chanting. Then I noticed the silence. The chanting had stopped. It was the middle of the night. I was desperate to go to wee. I held it in for as long as possible. I made my way to my auntie's room.

I pushed the door open and crept to the side of her bed.

"Auntie Doris, I want to wee."

"Get to the toilet outside," she said through gritted teeth.

"It's dark out there, Auntie Doris. I'm frightened."

"Get out of the bedroom, and let me *shloff!*" She put her head under the pillow.

I made my way back to the bedroom, leaving the door slightly open in case a fire broke out. I couldn't hold it in any longer. I sat on the floor. It felt comfortable sitting beside the bed. The noise of the water broke the silence.

The week passed. Tomorrow was the last day of *shiva*. After lunch we would have to go to a non-Jewish house or shop and leave all our *tsoriss* there. I had overheard my auntie discussing it. "That was the custom," she told one of the visitors. I sat on my bed and didn't want to go downstairs.

"Jane, we'll go to the flat tomorrow, to collect your belongings!" Uncle Asher shouted from downstairs. I wasn't sure if it was still a dream.

"Jane, get down here, now!" Auntie Doris shouted.

I could hear all the praying and chanting again, and didn't want to face it. I sat on the couch wishing the time would pass so I could see my mum, Jeffery and David.

"Auntie Doris, is my Dad coming?"

"No."

I stayed on the couch till it was time for bed. I was worried about leaving my *tsoriss* with another person: I didn't want to make anyone unhappy. The morning arrived soon enough.

"Come on, Jane!" my auntie yelled. We all walked up the street on to Cheetham Hill Road. Auntie Doris walked on ahead, and beckoned for us to follow her into the sweet shop. I didn't want to go, but we all had to stand inside the shop while my auntie bought a box of matches, or it wouldn't work. Soon we were back at the house. Someone had left some second-hand clothes.

"They're for you." Auntie Doris pushed the box towards me. I noticed a duffle coat placed on top. I put it on, hoping it would stop me from shivering. Uncle Asher told me we would have to go to Bracknell Court. We walked to Upper Park Road, and waited for the 145 bus, which stopped very close to the flats.

My heart was banging. Stepping off the bus I looked up at the kitchen window: there was no smiling face waiting, looking for me. He walked into the flat first. "It stinks, talk about *ipish!*" I followed him into my mother's bedroom. "Why is there blood and piss everywhere? It's filthy." He was holding up a piece of torn blanket covered in blood. He dropped it. I could see him screwing his face up. "It's disgusting!" I walked into the living-room, to get the candle sticks. I held on to them tightly, there was nothing else to take.

When we arrived back at my auntie's house, I took the candlesticks to my room. *Shiva* was over now. The house wasn't filled with the sound of chanting and praying for the dead. All the mirrors had been uncovered, the curtains opened. "Perhaps it's all a mistake," I whispered to myself. Uncle Asher was just about to leave, and make the journey back to London. He took a ten shilling note out of his pocket.

"Here, Eric, buy yourself a record." He hugged Eric and Auntie Doris. I sat on the couch and pretended not to notice. They walked down the hall to the front door.

"Get in touch soon 'kid' and don't forget to contact the Benevolent Society, about the furniture for her room, don't forget." I could hear them whispering. Then the front door closed. Auntie Doris and Eric walked past me and went straight into the kitchen.

"Why me?" I heard her say.

"Don't worry, Mum. I'll make you a cup of tea." They stayed in the kitchen, then came back into the living-room, both holding a beaker of tea. They sat at the table. I waited to be asked to sit at the table with them, or to be spoken to. Nothing was said. I made my way upstairs to my room. Eric opened the living-room door and shouted up to me.

I darted out of my room and looked over the banister.

"Yes, Oric?"

"My name isn't 'Oric'. It's Eric. When are you going to learn English? My mum wants you downstairs early in the morning, to help with the housework!"

I went back to my room, and looked in the mirror. I watched my mouth carefully as I tried to say Eric. All I could hear was Oric. It was difficult for me to pronounce certain words, and I stammered quite badly. I went out onto the landing: "Auntie Doris."

She came out of the living-room and looked up at me sternly.

"Don't worry. I'll be up very early in the morning, to help you."

She disappeared, without saying anything. I went back into my room, making sure the door was left slightly open, so I would smell fire as soon as it started. My bed was in the same room as the bath. Auntie Doris told me she had been going to make the room into a bathroom and toilet. She told me that her plans had been ruined. She let me know how angry she was about it, especially as the plumbing couldn't be done for a few weeks. I got into bed. I could hear the television, and muffled giggling. I wrapped the blankets around myself and soon fell asleep.

I woke up in the middle of the night, wanting to wee. Please God make it go away, I was praying to myself. I was very frightened and wouldn't put my feet out of bed, in case a monster was waiting, to pull me to pieces. I wrapped the blanket tighter around myself for protection and started to recite the *shama*. I managed to get one foot out of bed and rushed to put the light on. I couldn't leave the room, or go outside to the toilet, in case something killed me. I walked towards the bath and sat in it. It felt cold and hard in the bath, so I sat on the floor, holding myself, trying to keep it in: the warm water felt so comforting, I didn't want to move. I reached over to the bath and picked up the flannel. I mopped the wee up with it, and got back into bed.

"Go to *shloff*, Hikey. Yes, Mum," I whispered to myself. I pulled my arms through my coat and jumper. My flesh felt warm, and I cupped my breasts in my hands, squeezing them, trying to extract as much warmth as possible. "I love you, Hikey," I whispered once more, before falling asleep.

Two weeks passed. The Jewish Benevolent Society had delivered an old chest of drawers and a wardrobe for my room at my auntie's request. The sight of them in the room made me breathless. I was expecting to go home to my mother soon. It was Friday now, and Auntie Doris had told me to wash my uniform, so it was ready for school on Monday.

"There's a letter for you," Eric shouted.

I felt so excited. It must be from the hospital. He passed it to me. My hands were shaking, at last the envelope was ripped open. It was a notelet with a picture of a flower on the front.

Dear Jane, I began to read it, my eyes caught the signature.

It was from Miss Sassoon. The address, at the top of the note was Christie's Hospital, it read: *Dear Jane, I was so sorry to hear of the death of your poor mother.* I panicked at the words, and hid the note under my mattress.

"Auntie Doris, do you want me to do anything for you?" She came out of the living-room and stood in the hall. I smiled at her.

"Tidy your bedroom. It's time for bed!"

I stayed on the landing for a while, and could hear them talking.

"I'm not paying for her to come on holiday. The Benevolent Society will have to. I'm not missing my holiday!" I could hear her saying.

"Don't worry, Mum, they'll probably pay for it," Eric told her.

CHAPTER 17

Monday morning, I awoke early, my heart banging. It was insulin time. I stayed motionless closing my eyes. I'm going back to school so I must make sure Mum has her insulin tablet: something to eat, before she goes into a coma. It's important that she's as warm as possible. David has to get ready. Jeffery has to go to work. I opened my eyes, I wasn't at home with them. I held my stomach, digging my fingers into the flesh, trying hard to comfort it and wanting the terrible pain to go away.

"Get dressed!" Auntie Doris shouted as she walked past my bedroom door. My uniform was folded neatly on the chair, next to my bed. I looked at it. I could smell washing powder on it. I reached out and touched it, the last time I wore the jumper I had been at home with my mother, Jeffery and David. "Come on, you'll make me late!"

"Coming, Auntie Doris." I fastened my skirt and pulled my socks up. I didn't like taking the uniform off to wash, "it won't happen again," I whispered, stroking the skirt. I reached to a small shelf at the top of the wardrobe. The candlesticks were tucked in the corner. I pulled them out, holding and kissing them, before placing them back gently in the corner. My auntie gave me a key and list of instructions, for when I arrived back at the house. "This is what I want you to do," She told me. I looked at the note; *peel potatoes, put meatballs in the oven and tidy up.*

"Bye Auntie Doris, see you later."

I wanted my old jacket to wear. It had been thrown out in the rubbish. I put on my duffle coat, pulling the hood over my head. It felt comforting. I closed the front door behind me. I felt very faint as I left the house and almost fell off the steps. My legs felt like they might give way under me. I was trembling, wanting to run back in the house. I walked along the street, staying as near to the wall as possible, touching it. It felt safe, comforting and warm. I had to cross Greenhill Road, to get onto the main road. Suddenly, I couldn't breathe, my heart had stopped beating. I tried to inhale as much air as possible and stamped my foot on the ground. I felt my pulse, the panic was over, my heart was going again. The road looked too wide to cross. I felt I was becoming smaller. I waited till my heart was definitely working, then I ran across the road, and started walking towards the school, my head lowered, keeping close to the wall and touching it.

I was in the playground. The bell rang. I headed for the main doors, following the children into assembly, keeping my duffle coat on. I was getting used to it and I knew no-one would ever take it away from me. I found my form line and sat down. Mrs Bloughcough was on the stage, "We will say a prayer for Jane Levene's mother who died recently." I didn't take any notice. It was someone else's mother who had died. As soon as the assembly was over I followed the children to the classroom, my head lowered, we all sat down. The teacher sat at his desk, and started calling the register.

"Jane Levene!"

"Yes Sir." He looked at me.

"Go and hang your coat in the cloakroom!"

"No, Sir, I'll keep it on," He left the classroom and Mr Suffrin walked in. He was a rabbi.

"Get your books on your desk. Jane Levene take you coat off and hang it in the cloakroom!" I sat and opened the book that had been placed on my desk. I could hear voices, and see people moving around. I wanted to run out of the classroom, my stomach was churning. I knew there was nowhere to go. Mr Suffrin, started to collect all the books together. He picked up mine. It was still at the first page. He left the room and Mr Goodwin walked in. He turned to the blackboard and wrote a page number on it, without turning his head he shouted very loudly.

"Jane Levene, take off your coat. Now!" I stood up. My body was vibrating with the sound of his voice. I left the classroom and walked down the corridor, holding the wall. I hung my coat on a spare hook, and went back into the classroom.

"Levene's sister, stand up and recite your tables!" I stood silent, for what seemed to be a very long time. "Sit down, you stupid girl. As stupid as your brother!" he looked at me. "Well are you?"

"Yes Mr Goodwin." The bell rang, it was dinner time. I lined up to get my plate filled, then sat at a table. I ate everything on the plate. It wasn't enough. I felt so terribly cold and hungry. There were so many plates with leftovers on, I wanted them all. I rubbed my tummy to try to make the hunger go away, it didn't work.

The lunch break was soon over, the next lesson was cookery. The cookery room was upstairs. We were all waiting for Mrs Brooks to arrive. She unlocked the classroom door. We went into the room. I knew I didn't belong here. My mother could never afford to buy the ingredients for the cookery lesson. Mrs Brooks always shouted and got very angry.

"I want my Mum," I whimpered. She looked at me. "Mummy," I sobbed, "where's my Mum?" Through the haze of tears I could see the other children staring at me. I could smell the washing powder on my uniform. It smelt so false and unreal I wanted to rip it off and throw it in the bin. "Mummy!" I cried till my head ached so much I had to hold it. I sat down, oblivious to what was going on around me. I didn't care anymore if the teacher shouted, I wasn't frightened of her. The final bell rang. I ran to the cloakroom. I could see it was very sunny outside, it made me feel uncomfortable. The other children were carrying their blazers and playing in the playground. I put my coat on. It was warm and thick, it felt protective. I fastened it up and put the hood on. As I walked out through the main door, leading to the playground, my heart was pounding. I looked to see how many footsteps it would take to get near to the wall. As I reached the wall, the sun was beating down. It felt hot to touch. It felt comforting and I wanted to sink into it. I could see all the fathers in the distance, waiting at the gates for their daughters. I turned away. I didn't want to see what they were doing with each other. I didn't want to smell them or get too close.

Arriving back at my auntie's house, I read my list of instructions. First of all lighting the fire, that wasn't on the list. I wanted the house to be nice and warm for her. The next thing to do was to peel the potatoes and put the meatballs in the oven. I was looking around the kitchen feeling so cold and hungry. I opened the cupboard door and started eating the loaf of bread. It wasn't enough, I turned on the gas stove and found the frying pan. I had eaten most of the bread and what I had left over I dipped into two beaten eggs and I started to fry them. I couldn't wait, I was so hungry. It felt so warm in my tummy.

Eric walked in the back door. "What are you doing?"

"Having something to eat, I'm starving."

He looked in the cupboard, "Mum will kill you. You've eaten all the bread and butter and where are the eggs? You've eaten them as well; you've had it! They're not yours, it's not *your* house." I carried on eating, frightened of what would happen when Auntie Doris arrived home. I checked the potatoes and meatballs, they were cooking nicely. I wanted her to be pleased with me. I stayed in the kitchen, watching the potatoes boil. I couldn't wait for the food to be cooked. Feeling cold, I decided to sit near the fire. The front door slammed, it was Auntie Doris.

"It's a million degrees outside, who's made the fire? What's burning?" Eric went to meet her. I could hear them whispering. Auntie Doris rushed into the kitchen, and went straight to the cupboard. "You've burnt the potatoes!"

"I made the fire for you Auntie Doris. I wanted you to be nice and warm."

"You're a *shmock*. Where's the bread? Where's the butter?" she shrieked. My heart started racing, she looked at me. Her face was purple and completely distorted.

"Sorry Auntie Doris."

"Only a *meshuggina* would make a fire in this weather. You've wasted all that coal, and food. Sorry you say, *shmorry!*" she yelled at me very loudly. "Get to bed, you're *not* having any tea!" I walked through the living-room. Eric was standing near the fire, grinning as I walked past. I left my bedroom door slightly open, in case a fire broke out downstairs. I had to be sure I could smell it, and put it out quickly. I got into bed still wearing all my clothes and coat. I pulled the hood over my head and covered the whole of my body with the blankets, trying not to inhale the smell of the meatballs.

Some hours later, the front door slammed, I tried to listen to hear what was happening. I could hear creaking on the stairs. "Jane, come downstairs, my Mum's gone to bingo." He walked into the bedroom. "Why are you still wearing your coat?"

"I like it. I don't want to come downstairs." I knew if Auntie Doris came back she would be very angry. He left the room and I fell asleep. It must have been the middle of the night. I could hear crackling wood. I could definitely smell smoke.

"Auntie Doris," I cried jumping out of bed. I ran towards her room. "Auntie Doris, there's a fire."

"Get back to bed, there's no fire!" she shouted angrily, pointing in the direction of my room.

"I want to wee, Auntie Doris."

"Well get outside to the toilet. Wake me up again, just try it!"

"Sorry Auntie Doris." I stood outside her room, wondering if I should go and sit beside her bed. I went back to my room and sat on the floor, feeling the warmth of the wee on my legs. I wanted to get a knife and prize the flesh away from my body, put it in an envelope to send to my father. It didn't belong to me, it belonged to him. He had paid for it. I pulled my skirt down so it covered my legs, never wanting to see that part of my body again. I grabbed the flannel from the side of the bath and mopped the wee up. It was part of me, I hid it behind the bath so no-one could take it away from me.

The following morning I waited for Auntie Doris to call me. Hoping she wouldn't get angry.

"Get up. *Now!*" she shouted. I straightened the clothes I had slept in and went downstairs. She was sitting at the table with Eric. They were talking.

"Auntie Doris." There was no response. They carried on talking, ignoring me, I sat on the couch. She looked at me.

"If I come home and find you've been eating our food again, if *you* touch anything that doesn't belong to you, you'll end up dead!"

"Yes, Auntie Doris." She gave me a list of instructions. I left the house and made my way to school. I waited in the corridor to see which classroom we were in.

"Michael," the P.E. teacher shouted. I turned around and looked, recognising the face. He had come with his mother during the week of *shiva*. The teacher walked away from him. He was waiting outside the classroom on his own. I walked up to him.

"You're my cousin?" He looked at me.

"Go away, go away," he whispered insistently, looking around to make sure no-one was watching. I knew I wasn't the person to be seen with and walked away quickly, my head bowed. I noticed Philip was waiting outside the classroom further down the corridor. He was looking at his timetable. I half looked in his direction. I knew he would be embarrassed if I said hello, so I carried on walking past him. The last lesson of the day was Hebrew. I sat listening, wanting to learn everything so my mother would be proud of me. My stomach started churning, the urge to run out of the classroom and home to her was so great I had to hold my tummy to try to make the pain stop. The bell rang and I hadn't heard a single word that was said.

School finished. I started walking down Cheetham Hill Road. Mr Levene; one of the teachers, was crossing over towards the bus stop. I wondered if I should follow him, and ask if he was related to me, but I didn't want to smell his socks and body smells. I waited till he was out of sight and started on my way back to Auntie Doris's house, keeping near to the wall, holding onto it. The list she had written out for me was in my pocket. I looked at it; get saveloys from Itchkey Abramson was at the top of the list. Peel potatoes. I could see Bookbinders cake shop as I approached Greenhill Road. The window was full of cakes and bread. I wished I had the money to buy them all. My tummy was aching very badly with hunger, it was hard to pull myself away from the window.

I wanted to light the fire for her but I knew she wouldn't be pleased. I walked into the kitchen and tried to stop thinking about food. I couldn't. I found some buns in a white paper bag. I pulled at the bag and ran upstairs to my room. I sat on the floor beside the bed eating the buns, quickly stuffing them in my mouth. I went downstairs into the living-room and looked at the sideboard. I knew there was always plenty of food in it. Opening the cupboard door, reaching to the back, I pulled out a packet of biscuits. Then I sat on the floor next to the couch eating one after the other, till the whole packet had disappeared but it wasn't enough. I still felt very cold and hungry. I looked at all the tins of food, wishing I could eat them. I pulled another packet of biscuits from the cupboard and opened them frenziedly. I ate them all. I noticed a bottle of kosher red wine at the back of the cupboard. Almost full, it looked like pop I reached out for it. I had never tasted wine before. I started gulping it down. It made my tummy feel warm but I didn't like the taste. The front door slammed, there was a blur standing in front of me.

"Get off the floor!" Auntie Doris screamed. She ran through to the kitchen, there was nothing cooking. She came back and started pulling my arm. "I don't need this. You're a whore, nothing but trouble!" I tried to lift my head, the room started moving.

"Can't get up Auntie Doris."

"Wait till Eric gets in, he'll get you up." She managed to pull me onto the easy chair, I slid off. She disappeared into the kitchen. I could smell the savaloys cooking. I could hear Eric's voice coming from the kitchen. He walked up to me and knelt down behind me. Before I knew what was happening he was pushing me up the stairs.

"My Mum's going to murder you!" I wanted my head and legs to stop aching. I awoke on my bed a few hours later, the smell of the savaloys was still lingering. I knew they had all been eaten. I was still wearing my duffle coat. I pulled the blankets over me and curled up on the bed, making sure every little bit of me was as warm as possible. "Go to *shloff*," I whispered to myself. The house seemed to be in complete silence. Then I heard the living-room door open. I wrapped my arms around myself, as I heard Auntie Doris banging up the stairs, muttering. My heart was pounding. The bedroom door flew open.

"Go downstairs. I'm having a bath." The bath had been plumbed in the previous day.

"Alright Auntie Doris," I didn't want to get out of bed. I desperately wanted to sleep. She pulled at my coat as I walked past her.

"Get that coat off, and leave it downstairs!"

"Alright, Auntie Doris,"

Eric was in the kitchen. I sat on the couch and waited for Auntie Doris to finish her bath. The ceiling started shaking, the bedroom door slammed. Auntie Doris was storming down the stairs shouting, "you little *momzer!*" She pushed the living-room door open. My heart started thumping, I looked at her. She stopped dead in front of me. She was holding the flannel.

"Why does this stink of piss?" She grabbed my hair.

"Don't know, Auntie Doris."

"Smell this," she rubbed the flannel all over my face till I couldn't breathe. "Get that coat off, hang it up, then put the flannel in the bin, outside!"

"Sorry, Auntie Doris."

"Get to bed!" she yelled at the top of her voice. "Get out of my sight!"

"Are you alright Mum?" I heard Eric ask, as I walked upstairs to bed.

"Sorry, Auntie Doris," I whispered to myself.

CHAPTER 18

I had been given a second-hand briefcase and some pens. I knew there were only a few months before the term ended and I would have to leave school.

My auntie told me Tesco was advertising for Saturday staff and she wanted me to go and enquire after school. School finished and I rushed to the supermarket as quickly as possible, touching the wall all the way. I knew Auntie Doris wanted me to work. I wanted to please her very badly. The counter assistant directed me to the manager's office. It was a small kiosk at the top of a flight of stairs. "The job's stacking shelves. Start Saturday morning."

I could hear Eric walking down the hall. "Oric, I've got a job." He didn't answer. He walked over to the table and emptied his briefcase. I went over to him, trying to look at his books, wishing I could read them without my tummy churning over.

"Go away, don't be nosey," he shouted, almost deafening me. I walked over to the couch and he followed me. He stood in front of me and stared. "Sit down." He put his hand on my breast and pushed me backwards.

"Don't." My heart was pounding. I stood up again, he touched me and pushed me back. I sat on the couch looking at him. He didn't move.

"Don't do that."

"What's going on?" Auntie Doris had just walked through the front door.

"She's arguing with me Mum. She can't even say Eric. She says Oric. She's stupid!"

"Get upstairs."

"I got the job, Auntie Doris," I mumbled as I walked past her.

Saturday morning arrived. I left the house at half past eight. That left plenty of time for me to get there. I waited outside the manager's office. As soon as he arrived he handed me a uniform. "You'll have to work on the provisions counter, we're short staffed."

"What will I be doing?"

"Serving cold meats, bacon and cheese," I followed him to the counter. I saw the scales: if only I knew my tables and fractions I would be able to use them. He walked away. The store was open. I felt light headed and my heart was pounding. I gasped for air. Shortly a queue formed as people were waiting to be served. A lady asked me for half a pound of bacon. I picked up the tongues, placing a few pieces of bacon on the paper. Then I put them on the scales. After about ten minutes of serving, the manager approached the counter and looked at me.

"Miss Levene, I have a queue of people outside my office complaining about you. You've given one woman two pounds of bacon when she asked for a few slices. One woman two ounces of cheese when she asked for a pound. I'm afraid you'll have to come off the counter. You're sacked." I gave him back the uniform and started walking back to my auntie's house.

She was outside the house talking to one of the neighbours. I wanted desperately for her to be pleased with me. I approached her, letting a slight smile creep very slowly to one corner of my mouth. "Auntie Doris, I couldn't do the job." She glared at me.

"Tidy the kitchen." I felt very angry with myself, determined to clean the kitchen without making any mistakes.

Eric walked through to the kitchen. I looked at him, once again letting a little smile creep to my lips. He looked at me.

"Cup of tea Mum?" he shouted in the direction of the living-room.

"Yes, Son."

I stood waiting. Perhaps I would be asked. I stopped smiling and carried on with my work. I could hear them talking in the living-room, and eventually walked through. They were sitting at the dining table, drinking their tea.

"Auntie Doris, I've finished." They carried on talking for a while and didn't seem to notice I was there.

"What are you doing stood there? Are you waiting for *Chanukah*?"

"No, Auntie Doris,"

"Your rooms' upstairs." She stared at me.

"Sorry, Auntie Doris." She turned her head away. I went to my bedroom and huddled up on the floor next to the bedroom door. I wrapped my arms around myself. Still I wanted to please her.

The summer holidays had arrived. Auntie Doris was packing the suitcases. The Jewish Benevolent Society had agreed to pay for my share of the holiday in Blackpool. We would be getting the train first thing in the morning. She gave me some money to go to the public baths on Cheetham Hill Road. I wasn't allowed to use the bath in the house. I walked over the road and paid for a cubicle with a bath in it. I filled the bath with boiling water, sitting on the small wooden chair beside it. The air felt very warm. I sat on the chair for about half-an-hour. I kept looking at the water. I didn't like it. I knew I would be very cold if I took my coat off.

When I arrived back from the baths, I waited in my

bedroom for Auntie Doris to tell me what jobs were to be done.

"Jane, come downstairs. The kitchen, and front room need tidying. Did you have a proper bath?"

"Yes, Auntie Doris, look at my hands." She looked at them then pulled my coat away from my neck.

"Have you had a bath?" she asked again.

"Yes, Auntie Doris, I'm nice and clean." I could see she was getting very angry. I froze.

"What have you done with the money I gave you for the baths?"

"Nothing, I had a bath, honestly."

"You're filthy," I felt her hand on my shoulder, and fell back against the couch. "You're a liar. What are you?"

"A liar, Auntie Doris." I felt her hand smash across my face.

"Get the rooms sorted out, now."

"Alright, Auntie Doris"

When I had finished the work, I went back into the living-room. Auntie Doris was lying on the couch. My heart started banging and I had to stamp my foot on the floor. I sat on the end of the couch.

"Are you alright, Auntie Doris?" Tears were streaming down my face. "Are you ill?"

"Don't move. I'm *shloffing*."

"I won't, Auntie Doris, I promise." I wanted to pat her legs and make her comfortable. A warm glow came over my body. She needed me. She slept for a long time.

There was a knock on the front door. I stayed very still, not wanting to wake her. Eric opened the door. "Is Jane in?" I heard a voice say. "We live around the corner and I go to the same school." Eric let them in. They were sisters. I recognised one of them from school. "Would you like to come for a walk?" one of them asked. Auntie Doris opened her eyes.

"Stay still. Don't move." Both girls looked at my auntie and decided to leave.

"We live around the corner, come and see us," one of them whispered on the way out, making sure they didn't disturb Auntie Doris.

I stayed on the couch until it was time to make tea. When the meal was ready, I sat at the table with them, wondering how much food would be on my plate. They were talking to each other joking and laughing.

"Take your meal to your bedroom," she told me.

"Yes, Auntie Doris." I held my plate with both my hands, making sure not to drop any of the food on the floor. I didn't want to do anything else to make her angry. I got into bed and placed my plate on my lap. I ate my meal and licked the plate clean, too hungry to waste a crumb. I wrapped my arms around myself, all the blankets were covering me. My coat was fastened, my hood over my face. I was as warm as possible, that was all that mattered. Later on I was woken by the front door being slammed. Moments later I closed my eyes. I could hear footsteps on the landing outside my room. I heard my bedroom door creak open, I clung onto myself with even more desperation, my heart was banging. I managed to peep over my hood. Eric was beside my bed, he turned to the chair in the corner of the room, he was holding up some underwear. I stayed silent, hoping he would go away. He didn't. I could feel his hand under the bedclothes. He was pulling at my coat. I stayed very still, trying to secure myself inside my coat. He left the room and I felt relieved when I heard the door close.

"*Gehen shloffen meine kinder,*" I whispered, before falling asleep again.

I awoke in the middle of the night. I had forgotten what my mother's face looked like. All I could see in my mind's eye was her hairstyle. I felt very frightened and desperately wanted to see her face. I had no photograph of her.

Morning arrived and I rushed to Auntie Doris's room. She was still fast asleep. I waited beside her bed till she woke up.

"What do you want?!" She was feeling around her bedside table looking for her glasses.

"Auntie Doris, have you got a photo of Mum?"

"No, now get out of my room and leave me in peace."

I went back to my bedroom.

"Get that coat off," she yelled after me.

I could vaguely remember my mother telling me Auntie Doris had taken a photograph of her, when she came out of hospital and was able to work. I was sure there was a photograph, I hurried back to her room, "Auntie Doris I think there is a photograph of Mum."

"Well I haven't got one, now get out!"

We arrived in Blackpool and headed straight for the guesthouse. Eric told me it was a kosher guesthouse. "Don't show us up." Our rooms were in the attic, Auntie Doris and I shared a room, Eric was in a smaller room next door. I had two dresses and two cardigans, Auntie Doris told me to hang them in the wardrobe. It was lunchtime, we went downstairs, and sat in the lounge. The room was very warm. Auntie Doris told me to take my coat off.

"Please can I leave it on?" I begged, "I'm nice and warm." At that very moment a family came in and sat down. Auntie Doris looked at me. I could see she wasn't pleased, she whispered something under her breath. I couldn't hear what it was. I was praying we would have lots of food for lunch, I was so hungry. I couldn't wait. We were shown to our table. A salad was placed in front of me. The plate had two pieces of chopped and fried fish on it. I noticed a large crusty loaf in the middle of the table. I wanted all of it, so my tummy would feel full.

"Don't you know how to eat?" Eric asked me. "You've got the wrong knife and fork."

The landlady walked over to the table and asked if we had enjoyed our lunch. I looked at her and wished she would bring more food. I was desperately cold and hungry. She was plump and dark haired. I liked her, when I smiled at her she smiled back. She turned and left the room, I wanted to follow her, to reach out and touch.

"We're going for a walk now," Auntie Doris said. "First we'll have our photograph taken, so get your coat off. You look ridiculous." I held my coat while the photograph was being taken. Auntie Doris and Eric went into a shop. Eric needed some shirts. I was told to wait outside. I held onto the wall for support. Then they went to the Post Office. "We need some money. You stay outside. We don't want you to know how much money we've got." When we got back to the guesthouse it was tea time. After we had eaten, we followed her upstairs to the attic room. "We're going out, to see a show. You'll have to stay here."

"Yes, Auntie Doris." After she got dressed I watched her putting her eye makeup on, still wearing her glasses. I wanted to help her. I didn't dare ask. When they left I fastened my coat up and got back into bed. I was frightened in case they didn't come back, or got killed in an accident. I pulled the blankets over me. "Go to *shloff*, Hikey." I whispered to myself and fell asleep. I wished the week away. I wanted so much to get back to Auntie Doris's house. I knew the photographs of my mother must be there, I wanted to find them.

We arrived back in Manchester. A few days later when I had finished school, I rushed home to have a look before they returned. I was in her bedroom, listening out for the door in case they came back. There was nothing except clothes in the large chest of drawers in the corner. My heart was banging. I pulled the chair from the side of the bed, towards the wardrobe. I opened the doors and put the chair firmly in front of it. I stood on it, reaching for the top shelf. I could see about four shoe boxes. Taking the top off one of the boxes I could see lots of photographs. I stepped off the chair and looked out of the window, to make sure Auntie Doris and Eric weren't on their way back. There was no sign of them so I stepped back on the chair and grabbed the largest one. I emptied it on the bed and started rummaging through it. There were so many photographs, but none of my mother. I put it back and quickly grabbed the smaller box. Placing it on the chair, I took the lid off. My heart was pounding with fear. I would never find one. Looking through them one by one, my heart wouldn't calm down in case they arrived home. I couldn't believe my eyes; there were two in an old envelope, one of my mother and her father, I had never seen him before, and one of my mother and Auntie Doris. Her face was in front of me, I put them in my blouse so nobody would see them. I placed the box back on the top shelf and made sure everything was as I had found it. I walked back to my room, pleased that I had found them. I lay in bed holding the photographs next to my cheek, kissing them. I wrapped myself in my coat, listening out for the front door to open, praying that Auntie Doris wouldn't be angry, with me, afraid she would never like me.

A few weeks later I heard Auntie Doris talking to one of

the neighbours outside the house. "Jane, come downstairs."

"Yes, Auntie Doris."

"I've been to see the man who owns the café at the top of Greenhill Road. He's looking for Saturday staff. I've told him about you. He wants you to go and see him. Go over now and tell him you're interested."

"Yes, Auntie Doris." I walked into the café. It was very small and the owner was standing behind the counter.

"My Auntie Doris sent me. She said you need someone."

"Yes, general duties. Can you start Saturday?"

"Yes."

Saturday arrived. I walked over the road and looked through the window of the café. The owner was wiping some tables.

"What do you want me to do? I can't use scales."

"First, take off your coat and put this apron on."

"I can't take off my coat."

"Take it off or go home." He pushed me into the corner and pulled at the coat. I took it off.

"Put this apron on and stir the baked beans in the pan on the stove."

"Alright."

I was stirring the beans in the pan when I felt something on my back. He put his arms around my waist and pulled me into his body. I started trembling. Somehow I managed to get away from him and ran all the way back to Auntie Doris's. I ran upstairs crying.

"What's wrong with you?"

"Nothing, Auntie Doris,"

"Well, get back to work."

"I can't, Auntie Doris."

"You'll never be able to keep a job. You're useless."

"Yes, Auntie Doris."

"Where's your coat?"

"I left it in the café."

"Get back there and get it now."

The weekend arrived and Uncle Asher called at the house early. I was tidying the kitchen and could hear him talking to Auntie Doris and Eric. He had been to see a relative who owned two second-hand shops in Wigan. He had persuaded him and his wife to give me a Saturday job.

"Jane," my auntie shouted.

As I walked through to the living-room Uncle Asher was sitting on the easy chair next to the fire. He was belching and farting. "You'll be starting work on Saturday, in Wigan." He started belching again. "I know the couple. His name is Henry Newman; be at their house for half past six, Saturday morning."

"What will I be doing?"

"You'll have to ask on Saturday morning. No doubt you'll make a *hegdish* of it. He'll pay you one pound for the day."

"You'll give me ten shillings," said Auntie Doris.

Uncle Asher wrote down the address for me and explained how to find the street.

"I'm off now Doris!" He walked over to her, hugging her. "Don't worry kid, I'll be in touch." He pulled a ten shilling note out of his trouser pocket and handed it to Eric. "Buy yourself something. Take care of your mum." He patted him on the shoulder. I turned away. They walked down the hall.

"Isn't it your bedtime?" Auntie Doris said.

"Yes," I replied, and went to my bedroom.

CHAPTER 19

Auntie Doris's alarm clock had just gone off. I felt very excited about my new Saturday job. I knew it would please her. I placed the two photographs of my mother inside my jumper, afraid my auntie would find them if they were left in the bedroom. Auntie Doris and Eric were still sleeping. I took great care not to wake them. As soon as I had eaten my breakfast; three slices of toast, two crusts and any leftovers. It wasn't enough but I didn't dare take anymore. I left the house making sure I had the address in my duffle coat pocket.

I walked down Waterloo Road, holding the wall and trying very hard to keep my heart beating evenly: stamping now and again to make sure it didn't stop altogether. I found the house and walked up the path. The front door was wide open. I stood waiting, wondering what to do. I could hear dogs barking in the house, they raced down the hall towards me. I ran into the garden to get out of the way, they were big dogs.

"Get in the house, naughty dogs. Are you Jane?"

"Yes." I wanted to cry because she smiled at me. She was tall and slim, with ginger hair.

"Come through to the kitchen." I followed her down the hall, past piles of old clothes. "This is Mr Newman." He was small and fat with grey hair. I didn't get too close because I didn't want to smell his body. "Have you eaten?" Mrs Newman asked.

"No, I'm starving."

"Would you like some toast and jam?"

"Yes please, my tummy's hurting me."

"How many would you like?"

"Lots please," I watched as she started toasting the bread.

"Aren't you hot with your hood on? That coat looks too heavy for this weather." Mr Newman said.

"No."

"Sit down if you can find a space." The room was full of second-hand clothes, reminding me of the second-hand clothes shop at the bottom of Cheetham Hill Road.

"Will I be using any scales?"

"No, you'll be helping to stock the shop. You'll do a bit of cleaning. I'll put the dogs out and we'll make a move." Mrs Newman opened the back door for the dogs, and I finished my toast.

"Go and get me a newspaper from the shop across the road," Mr Newman said. He was by the front gate. I walked down the street staying close to the wall, touching it, hoping my heart wouldn't stop while he was waiting near the gate. I arrived back at the house with the newspaper and we set off for Wigan.

"Well, we're here. These are our shops," Mrs Newman said. They looked very old, a bit like Johnson Street. The windows were packed solid with second-hand clothes, and new electrical goods. Mr and Mrs Newman went through the front door. I followed, we had to move all the boxes out of the way before the light could be switched on. It was very dark and creepy.

"Turn on the lights, already," Mr Newman yelled. "Jane, sort out these boots." He pointed to the corner, piled high with black ex army boots. "They're army seconds. After that tidy all the price tags and dust around the place." I was so relieved there were no scales.

"You must be hot with your coat on?" Mrs Newman said.

"No, I'm OK."

"You can take your hood off if you want."

"No, thank you." I carried on with my work.

People started walking into the shop. They were buying all sorts of items second-hand and new. The black boots seemed to be very popular. I would be sent to rummage through the pile to find the right size. Lunchtime arrived. I was sent across the road to buy sandwiches. I was so hungry I wanted to eat everything in the shop.

Later in the day a lady came in for a cotton bra, she had seen one in the window. Her husband was busy buying himself a second-hand suit. It was navy blue. He picked it off the rail.

"Jane, there's a box upstairs. It's full of cotton bras. They're packed in plastic bags. Go and get me a size 32a. Get one with roses on it," Mrs Newman said.

"Which room are they in?"

"The attic." My heart started thumping and I couldn't get enough air into my lungs. All I could think of was fire creeping up the stairs and monsters waiting to get me.

"Go on, girl." Mr Newman shouted. I pushed the large boxes out of the way and headed for the stairs. "*Shama Yisroel*," I started reciting as I made my way upstairs, holding on desperately to the banister, praying a fire wouldn't break out while I was up there. I thought I heard a monster's voice. I couldn't move. I was petrified.

"Hurry up, girl." Mr Newman insisted.

I climbed the next flight of stairs and could see the attic door. I started sobbing. "Please stay away from me," I was whispering. The huge box was in sight. I stood staring at it, afraid to open it in case something jumped out. I heard a creaking noise. I crept to the corner of the room and huddled up as much as I could under my coat. I pulled the hood over my face and stayed completely still, so that whatever was there would leave me in peace.

"Jane, what on earth are you doing?" Mrs Newman was standing by the door.

"I couldn't open the box." She opened it and pulled out a bra.

"This will do. Get off the floor. Come on." She pulled my coat and my hood fell off.

"What on earth is that on your neck? I've never seen a rash like that before. Your neck's very dirty."

"Don't know. Can we take the box downstairs? I don't like it up here."

"No, don't be silly, come on," She rushed down the stairs, handing the woman the bra.

"That took you long enough," Mr Newman said. I looked at him saying nothing, hoping he would never ask me to go to the attic again.

"Jane, there are *shmates* in the back room for dusting. Take them as you need them."

Before long I was dusting. When I had finished the shop window, I was sent into the other shop to tidy and dust. I hoped I wouldn't get sacked for taking so long in the attic. I was told to put some of the army surplus boots in order of size. I sat looking, trying to make sense of what I had been told.

"She's a bit slow. Do you think she's all there? A bit strange I think," Mr Newman said.

"I see what you mean. I think she is trying hard."

We carried on working till about nine o'clock, when they decided to close. Mr Newman locked up. We started our journey back to Manchester.

"Here's a pound." Mrs Newman passed me the note from the front passenger seat. "Would you like to work next week?"

"Yes please," I answered, placing the pound note down my jumper. The car turned onto Birkdale Street. Auntie Doris's house was in sight. I climbed out of the car and ran to the front door. Before I could get my key in the lock, Auntie Doris had opened it.

"Hello, Auntie Doris." She looked very angry. My heart started thumping. I could hardly breathe.

"Get in here. Have you been taking money out of my purse?" She dragged me by my hood, almost choking me. Have you been taking my money?"

"No. Auntie Doris."

"Get up those stairs," She pushed me out of the living-room.

"I'm starving, Auntie Doris." She looked at me. I stopped halfway up the stairs and turned. She was standing at the bottom.

"I'm going to see your headmaster on Monday, and the police," she yelled from the bottom of the stairs. "I need this like a *loch in kop*."

"Yes, Auntie Doris,"

I put my arms around myself, pulling all the blankets over me so I was covered all over. I kept hold of the pound note all night. It was for Auntie Doris. I couldn't wait to give it to her.

Monday came around slowly. It took such a long time before daylight shone through the window. I heard Auntie

Doris's door creak open. She walked past my room, banging on the door.

"Come on, get up!"

"Alright, Auntie Doris," I put on my shoes and made sure all my photographs were still intact. I crept downstairs so I wouldn't annoy her. She walked into the living-room.

"Well, where are your wages? That should replace some of the money you stole from me." I handed her the pound note.

"Get in the kitchen and make your toast."

"Alright, Auntie Doris. Can I have some crusts as well? I'm very hungry."

"No."

I ate my toast. Before I set off for school I made sure my photographs were tucked into my blouse. I got my briefcase and started walking up Cheetham Hill Road. My heart was banging. It was getting more difficult to make the air stay in my lungs. I took very deep breaths which made me feel faint. The school was in sight and I was very pleased to get into the building. My first stop was the toilets. I pulled out my photographs. My mother's face looked so kind. I wished I had known my grandfather. They were standing beside a large fireplace, linking arms, looking very happy. I couldn't stop thinking about Auntie Doris. I wanted her to believe that I hadn't stolen the money from her.

It was almost lunchtime. I was so desperate to eat. The cold and hunger were unbearable. The classroom door opened and Mrs Bloughcough beckoned the teacher to her. She whispered something to him and left the room.

"Jane Levene, the headmaster would like to see you in his office. You can go now." I left the room walking down the corridor, holding onto the wall for support. I knocked on his office door.

"Come in,"

"Are you Jane Levene?"

"Yes Sir," I sobbed.

"Your auntie's been to see me. She tells me you've been stealing money from her purse." I stood rigid, trying hard not to sniff up the smell of his body and socks.

"Well?"

"I didn't Sir, honestly." I edged towards the door, away from him. I could see he didn't believe me.

"Your auntie will go to the police, if you do it again." He looked at me. "Your auntie took you in out of the goodness of her heart. I don't think she should have to put up with that behaviour. Go back to your class, and remember what I have told you." I left his office, still sobbing. I walked back to the classroom, wishing the rest of the day away so I could sleep.

On the way back to Auntie Doris's, I pulled out my list of instructions and walked home. We were having saveloys for tea, with chips and lots of bread. The list read; *potatoes need peeling, and chipping.* In block letters she had written:

Don't burn anything. Stay away from the cupboards and don't look for any money to steal.

I started preparing tea. I was so hungry I had to hold my tummy whenever possible, to stop the pain. I looked in the fridge and saw a large piece of cheese. I cut a chunk off and ate it. Eric arrived home. Auntie Doris came in through the back door.

"I've put the saveloys in the pan Auntie Doris,"

"Have you burnt them?"

"No, Auntie Doris." She shook her head.

"Get upstairs. You're not having any tea, not till you've learnt your lesson."

"Alright, Auntie Doris,"

I was in the bedroom, in bed, holding my nose, trying desperately hard not to smell the savaloys and chips, then it got too much for me. The smell was driving me mad. I put the blankets over my head so I couldn't smell anything.

My door was slightly open, even under the blankets I could hear the muffled sound of the television. There was a knock on the front door. I hurried out of bed and listened by the bedroom door to see who it could be, wondering if she had called the police.

"Come in Anita. Where's Morris?"

"He's locking the car."

"I've had terrible trouble with her, she's been stealing."

I heard David's voice. Anita told Auntie Doris the adoption had gone well. I wanted to run downstairs and put my arms around him. I knew I should be looking after him. I desperately wanted to talk to him.

"We're his family now. We don't want any contact with her. She wouldn't be a good influence on him. We've bought him a dog. That will take his mind off her."

"Yes, you're right Anita. I don't need this. I wish my Henry was here."

"That *momzer* Wilfred was overheard in Lee's delicatessen moaning that his wife had died leaving him with three kids to look after."

"In *dread*," Aunty Doris said pretending to spit, "the *momzer*."

I was holding my tummy, trying hard not to be sick, the voices carried on floating up the stairs for a long time. I crept back into bed and pulled the blankets over my head, so I couldn't hear what was being said. I managed to fall asleep, holding the photographs and wishing Saturday would arrive so I could go to work to get money for Auntie Doris.

The week was almost over. On Friday morning I awoke with terrible pains in my tummy. I rubbed my breasts and tummy hard to soothe the pain away, nothing helped. It was getting light and I noticed one of my photographs was marked. I picked it up and looked closely at it, it was covered with blood, I pushed the blankets back. My legs and skirt, my hands and hair were covered with blood.

"Auntie Doris. Auntie Doris, quickly." I was about to get out of bed when she walked into the room.

"You're covered in blood." She grabbed my hair. "Get out of bed and get washed. Get that uniform and that bloody coat off and cleaned, now."

"My tummy hurts badly, Auntie Doris."

"My *kops draying*, because of you, and you tell me you're in pain." She pulled me off the bed. "*Nebach*," She hissed in my ear.

She left the room muttering to herself. I looked in the mirror and my hair had blood in it. My hands were covered. I lifted my skirt and saw my legs too were covered with blood. I recognised it, feeling comforted by it. Auntie Doris came into the bedroom, and put some money on the mantelpiece. "Before you go to school, get yourself a packet of sanitary towels from the chemist." I remembered the pieces of towel I had seen my mum use. I wondered how many pieces I would get in a packet.

"Get washed."

I stayed near the mirror. She pulled at my coat. "Get this off."

"I don't want to, Auntie Doris. I don't want to wash the blood off."

She pushed me back, and I landed on the floor. I pulled my skirt up as far as possible.

"Look Auntie Doris, I've got public hair."

"Pubic, *shmock*, now get off the floor, get washed, get to school and out of my sight." I didn't want to part with the blood, it was mine. I wanted to keep it. Auntie Doris came back into the room with a towel under her arm.

"Is that a sanitary towel, Auntie Doris?" She wet it in the bath and threw it at me.

"You're not going to make me late for work." She glared at me.

She placed a pair of Eric's grey school socks on the bed, "You'll have to wear these." She wet more of the towel and rubbed my face, then my legs.

"Can I have that towel, please Auntie Doris?"

She said nothing. I picked the money off the mantelpiece and went downstairs. Auntie Doris was about to leave the house. She left my list of instructions on the sideboard. I looked at the clock, it was nearly nine o'clock. My heart started racing. I didn't want to be late for school. I waited outside the chemist shop for it to open. I stood looking, expecting to see bath towels to wrap around myself, or bits of towels.

"Can I help you?" The assistant asked.

"I need some sanitary towels," I told her. Looking around again, I couldn't see them.

"Here you are. Do you need a belt as well?"

"I don't know."

"Have you started your periods?" I looked at her.

"Have you started bleeding?"

"Yes." I felt very confused.

"Well in that case you'll need a belt and sanitary towels."

She placed them in a paper bag and handed them to me. I put them in my briefcase and ran to school. My tummy was still hurting. I could feel my legs were getting wet again. I reached the school and headed for the toilets. I didn't like the sanitary towels, they seemed false and unreal. My photographs were still in my jumper, I waited till break time to try to clean most of the blood off them. As I was putting them back into my shirt I noticed my house key was missing. I always kept it around my neck, tied to a piece of string, and wore it like a necklace. My heart was pounding. My head ached. I felt faint and had to sit on the floor. I looked everywhere, in my case, down my jumper, I realised it must still be on the mantelpiece in the bedroom. I had taken it off to wipe the blood from my neck. I looked at my list of instructions: *put meatballs in oven, peel potatoes and put into pan to boil; Don't let them burn.* She expected tea to be almost ready when she arrived home. I didn't know how I could get in. School finished and I ran back to the house, hoping Eric would arrive home early. I sat on the doorstep, praying he would come home. Eric didn't arrive. I stayed on the step, for what seemed to be ages.

I looked up. Auntie Doris was walking down the street.

"I've forgotten my key, Auntie Doris," I shouted, giving her plenty of warning. Her face was red with anger. I was shaking. I felt my pulse and found that my heart had stopped. I stamped my foot on the ground. I knew I wasn't going to have meatballs for my tea, or anything, I was sure of that. She took out her key, and stormed through the front door. "Sorry, Auntie Doris,"

"Get upstairs." She turned to me, holding my head with

her hands and directing her mouth at my ear, "out of my sight."

I went to my bedroom. "Go to *shloff* Hikey," I whispered to myself, holding my photographs. "Alright Mum," I replied. Later that evening she left the house. The slamming door woke me. She had gone to play bingo.

Eric shouted me. "Come down and watch the telly." She was usually gone for a few hours. I prayed she wouldn't come home early and find me in the living-room. I crept downstairs, in case it was a trick, in case she hadn't really gone out, and wanted to catch me out.

"Come on, watch the telly." I pushed the living-room door open and sat on the end of the couch. I was very cold and hungry. Eric was sitting near the fire, on Auntie Doris's favourite chair. "Take your coat off."

"No, I don't want to." He walked towards me.

"Take it off." He pulled my coat and I reached for the door, to go back to bed. I didn't want to take my coat off. He turned towards me, and pulled me back away from the door. I was standing in front of the couch.

"Sit down," he said, pushing me back by my breast.

"Get off." I pushed him back. "Leave me alone." I went back to bed and soon fell asleep. I was woken up later that evening. I could hear very loud voices. Eric was crying. I pushed the blankets away from my face, and crept onto the landing.

"Why did you steal that money?" I could hear Auntie Doris shouting. Eric was still crying. She smacked him. I felt relieved that she had found out it was Eric who was taking the money. I hoped she would tell Anita, Morris and David. I wanted her to tell the headmaster. I got back into bed, pulling the blankets over my face, and fell asleep. The following morning, when I went to make my toast she told me I could have six slices of toast and the crusts.

Saturday arrived and I made my way to the Newman house. I got there early so I would have plenty of time, before we left to make the journey to Wigan, hoping I would be offered more toast.

"Have you had your breakfast?"

"No, I'm really starving," I said, almost crying with relief that I would be getting more food. She made me four slices of toast and a crust with jam. I was still very hungry. Before lunchtime Mr Newman arrived back in the shop, he had been working next door sorting out all the stock. He whispered something to Mrs Newman then he left the shop. I was relieved when he left. I had smelt his body as I sat in the car. It made me feel ill. I noticed Mrs Newman was holding a small radio.

"Do you have a radio?"

"No."

"Would you like this one?"

"Yes please."

"I'll leave it here, on the side. You can take it home with you."

I arrived back in Manchester very late. I wanted to show Auntie Doris my new radio and give her the pound note I had earned. All the lights in the house were off. Auntie Doris and Eric were in bed. I went straight to my room. I switched the light on and noticed there was a cardboard box beside my bed. I quickly opened it and looked inside. I stared at the blue leather mini skirt on top of the pile of jumpers and blouses. I walked down the corridor to Auntie Doris's room, my heart banging. I pushed the bedroom door open very gently and looked to see if she was asleep. Her eyes were open.

"What are the clothes for, Auntie Doris?" I couldn't understand what they were doing in my bedroom. I could see they were new.

"They're for you. My boss bought them for his daughter. They don't fit her. You can have them."

"Thank you, Auntie Doris." I bent down beside the bed and hugged her. "I love you."

"Get to bed."

I wasn't sure if they were my size. I pushed the box under my bed and turned off the light. I could feel the warmth and comfort of my school uniform and duffle coat. I knew I couldn't give them up, even for all these nice clothes. They belonged to me, they were my friends. They loved me. I checked the door was slightly open, in case of fire and hurried into bed so the monsters wouldn't get me. I pulled my hood over my head and hid under the blankets. I couldn't sleep with all the excitement. I felt very sad they were nice girls clothes. They were false and clean. I imagined the boss's daughter. I knew she was pretending to wear clothes like these, I knew deep down, she wore her school uniform and duffle coat.

Early the following morning, I heard noises and quickly got out of bed. Auntie Doris would be angry if I overslept. I went downstairs. She was sitting on the arm chair near the fire. In the corner was a huge pile of rain coats. She was a hand finisher, and sometimes worked from home. She had a thimble on her finger and was pulling the thread through a small block of bees wax to strengthen it. She was working very quickly.

"Can I do that for you, Auntie Doris?"

She showed me how to pull the thread through the wax. I

sat on the floor beside her. "I love you, Auntie Doris. Do you want me to peel the potatoes tonight, Auntie Doris?"

"Yes."

We sat for a while. She carried on sewing and I carried on pulling the threads through the wax. "Go and get the box of clothes from your bedroom." I walked upstairs. I hoped she didn't want me to try them on for her. Taking my clothes off made me feel too cold and hungry. She picked out the leather skirt first. Turning it inside out she picked up the tape measure and started measuring the length.

"They're not for you." She looked at me. "They're for my boss's daughter, they belong to her. I'm altering them for her. She's very pretty. Her head was bent over the skirt and she was pulling at the threads. I opened the living-room door.

"Jane," she was grinning. "I saw your mum on the bus yesterday. "Get to your bedroom."

"Yes, Auntie Doris."

CHAPTER 20

"Get up!" I was woken by the shrill of Auntie Doris's voice. "Come on. I want you to take the laundry." It was Sunday morning and I had overslept. "Come on. It's *Yom Kippur* in a few days. I want to get the house ready." My heart sank at the thought of having to go a full day without food. I didn't know how I would manage.

"I'm coming Auntie Doris." I ran down the stairs, the laundry bag was already waiting for me. She had stuffed it all in her shopping trolley.

"Bye, Auntie Doris." I walked around the corner to the launderette, holding on tightly to the trolley with one hand, feeling the warmth and comfort of the wall with the other. My heart started pounding. I could feel it in my throat. I felt faint. My mum's dead. Where are Jeffery and David? It was four months since it happened. How was I going to get through the next minute or the next day I wondered, looking in the direction of my father's flat. His smell was embedded in my mind. I had to look away. I knew it would be impossible to go near him. I walked into the launderette and started putting the washing in the machine. I sat down and huddled up inside my coat, soon the pain disappeared. I wanted to make sure the washing was clean so Auntie Doris would be pleased with me.

It was the evening before *Yom Kippur*: a day of fasting and praying for the dead. Auntie Doris was preparing tea. It was to be a feast. She was making chopped liver, *lockshen* soup, *matzo* balls and potato *kuggle*. I couldn't wait to go to the synagogue and say *Yiskah* for my mum. I was hoping that somehow she would be able to hear me. I wanted to say *Yiskah* for her parents. I could remember lighting a memorial candle for them and my mum reciting *Yiskah* as she was lying on the couch, crying because she wasn't well enough to go to the synagogue. All the food was ready, my auntie lit the *Yartzeit*. She started dishing out the food. We all sat at the table. I wanted to eat as much as possible so I could feel warm and comfortable inside. I watched Auntie Doris and Eric. They were having a conversation. I was wondering if they would talk to me, there were such long periods when they didn't. I waited but nothing was said. I ate my meal then sat on the corner of the couch. Auntie Doris finished her meal, then decided to lie down on the couch. I could see she was falling asleep.

"Don't move."

"Sorry, Auntie Doris." I stayed as quiet as possible. Eric was getting his clothes ready for the synagogue, along with his *tallis* bag and *Yamulkeh*.

"There's someone at the door, Mum,"

"Is Jane in?" I recognised the voices. It was the sisters who had visited previously. They walked into the living-room. I smiled at them, wanting to cry because they had mentioned my name. "I'm Melanie and this is my sister Andrea.

"Which *shul* are you going to tomorrow?" Melanie asked. I was still sitting very stiff, trying to mime my answer.

"Shut up," Auntie Doris said, kicking me. I looked at them and put my finger to my lips. They realised I couldn't talk and left the house. I slowly moved off the couch and crept up the stairs.

"Get that coat off, you'll dirty the sheets," Auntie Doris shouted as I reached the top of the stairs. It was impossible for me to survive without my coat. I went into my bedroom. A second-hand dress hung over the chair for tomorrow. It had been given to me by the Benevolent Society. I looked in the chest of drawers to see if I had any stockings to wear; there were none. I looked under the bed; again there were none, I held the mattress up with one hand and checked that my bag of used sanitary towels were still there: they were part of my mother and myself. I couldn't bear to be parted from them.

First thing in the morning, I crept along the corridor to Auntie Doris's room. As usual when I approached the door, my heart started banging, having to gasp for air. The door was already open and very quietly I put my head around the door. "Auntie Doris," I whispered in case she was still asleep.

"What do *you* want?"

"I haven't got any tights or stockings, have you got any?"

"No, go back to your room. I want you on your best behaviour today. Show me up and you'll see what happens."

"Yes, Auntie Doris."

I put the dress on over my school uniform, I was bulging out everywhere, and the zip wouldn't fasten. I put my duffle coat on. I went back to Auntie Doris's room.

"Auntie Doris, where are my school socks?"

"In the dirty washing," There was no dirty washing. I looked through the clean washing but they weren't there. When I went into the living-room Auntie Doris and Eric were sitting at the table talking. All dressed up in their best clothes.

"Auntie Doris, can I have some money to buy a pair of tights?"

"No. Why should I? Help me put my coat on Eric."

"OK, Mum,"

"Come on."

They left the house. I followed behind them. They were walking towards the synagogue linking arms. They didn't look back. I just carried on following them, staying as close to the wall as possible. They stopped outside talking and shaking hands with people. My head lowered, I followed Auntie Doris inside, through the main doors and up the stairs where the women sat. I was almost at the top of the stairs and could see the doors that led to the balcony. Two women walked towards me, stopping in front of me.

"You can't come into the synagogue bare legged," one of the women said. Her friend agreed with her.

"You can't do that in an Orthodox synagogue, not at all. Go home, get dressed. You must cover yourself."

I walked down the stairs, my head banging. I ran out of the front doors, all the way back to Auntie Doris's. I wanted to tell mum how much I loved her. I pulled out my key and put it in the lock, my hands trembling. I ran upstairs into Auntie Doris's bedroom, sitting on the floor beside her bed. My stomach aching with hunger, I knew there was nothing to eat till tonight. I noticed something under the bed. It was two plates of food. "She mustn't know I've seen them," I whispered. I went back to my room and got into bed. I was desperate to sleep. Hours later they arrived home. I heard the stairs creaking. They both walked down the landing to her room. I heard the door close.

In the evening I awoke to the smell of food. I needed to eat. I crept downstairs, and into the kitchen. The smell of chopped and fried fish greeted me. I could see chicken soup boiling away in the pan.

"Can I help you Auntie Doris?"

"No, if I need any pans burning, I'll let you know. You can wash up later."

I sat on the couch. Eric had already laid the table. He brought plates of pickled cucumber and olives. He went back, returning with plates of chopped and fried fish and gefilte fish. We all sat down. I ate as much as possible, looking forward to washing up and eating all the leftovers. When we finished eating, Auntie Doris went into the living-room sobbing. She had taken her glasses off and was wiping her eyes.

"What's the matter?"

"I wish my Henry was alive," she sobbed.

"Don't worry Auntie Doris. I love you. I'll wash up for you."

The clothes from the Jewish Benevolent Society didn't fit me anymore because I had put a lot of weight on. Auntie Doris told me I could open a Post Office account and keep ten shillings back from my Saturday job. I made my breakfast. As much toast as I was allowed and any other leftovers lying around. I walked down Waterloo Road, staying close to the wall, holding it, getting as much comfort as I could. It stopped me from falling over and fainting. I remembered where all the alleys were in case I couldn't breathe and needed to stamp my foot on the ground to get my heart beating again. I reached Mrs Newman's house. I hoped she would offer me some toast. The front door was open, I knocked on the door.

"Come in. Have you had any breakfast?"

"No, I'm starving and very cold." She made me four pieces of toast and one crust. I had lost the button off my school skirt and the zip had broken some time ago. It was kept up by a piece of string held around my waist. She handed me the toast.

"What's the matter with your skirt?"

"It doesn't fit." I lifted my jumper and showed her the string.

"Eat your toast and we'll see if there's anything you can wear."

As soon as I had finished the toast she led me upstairs to her dressing room. There were rails of clothes. Pairs of shoes lined the wall. We looked through everything for a skirt but they were all too small. I felt relieved that I didn't have to change my skirt. She pulled out a box from the drawer. "I've got some elastic. I'll sew it on for you." When she had finished the skirt was held more securely. "Would you like a trouser suit?" I didn't answer. "We're leaving Manchester shortly. I'll pick you up one day next week at your auntie's house. We'll go to C&A. They always have a good selection. Would you like that?"

"Yes, please. Thank you," I whispered trying hard to hold back the tears.

I rushed into the house and couldn't wait to tell Auntie Doris. She was in bed. I waited till morning.

When school finished on Tuesday, I was picked up by Mrs Newman. I sat watching out of the window. I could see buses. Auntie Doris had told me she had seen mum on a bus. I wondered which one it was. We went to the trouser suit section.

"Go on. Have a look around. You choose one."

I looked through the rails. I knew they were for girls who were nice and clean. I would put mine over my chair, for safekeeping.

"Jane, would you like a skirt?"

"No, thank you." My school skirt kept me warm and secure. I didn't want to change it.

"Here's a nice trouser suit. Do you like this one?" She was holding a tunic and trousers. The tunic had a mandarin collar and belle sleeves. It had a psychedelic pattern, with matching bell bottoms. "Try it on."

"No, it'll be alright." I started feeling very cold and didn't want to take my clothes off.

Mrs Newman walked over to the cash desk. I waited near the rail, she handed me the carrier bag. "Here take it."

"Thank you." We drove back to my auntie's house.

"See you next Saturday." She waved. I couldn't wait to show it to Auntie Doris and Eric. I let myself in and rushed through to the living-room.

"Auntie Doris." She was in the kitchen making tea. "Look, Auntie Doris." I pulled the trouser suit out of the bag. The hanger was still attached. I held it up so she could see it fully.

"It's very nice, wish you well to wear it, *gaygazintahate*, and all that *drek*," she said without lifting her head.

"Is tea ready yet, Auntie Doris? I'll help you. I'm starving. I'll wash up, later." I took my suit upstairs and put it over the back of the chair. After tea I made sure I had any leftovers.

"Isn't it time you were in bed?"

"Yes, Auntie Doris."

Some weeks passed I had been to work on Saturday and given Auntie Doris the pound I had earned. She hadn't mentioned the Post Office savings account or given me ten shillings out of my wages. I was sure she would, soon. On Sunday morning I got up early. I wanted to do all the house work. I wanted it to be nice for when she got up. If only she would be pleased with what I had done. It wasn't long before I heard her footsteps vibrating along the length of the landing, I could tell her mood by how heavy and violent her footsteps sounded. They seemed quite gentle. I settled down on the end of the couch and waited. The door opened, she walked past me and went into the kitchen. She walked back.

"Did you never learn to say good morning?" My heart sank. "Eric, I've made you a cup of tea," she shouted.

"Good morning, Auntie Doris." I wondered if I should smile at her.

"It's too late now. What the hell's that?" She pointed to the scatter cushions on the couch. "You don't tidy up by putting things under the cushions. There's no chance for you. You've got a sieve for a brain. Take the laundry. Get upstairs. Put on one of the dresses from the Benevolent Society. I want your uniform washed."

"I don't want to take it off Auntie Doris."

"Oh, yes you will." She pulled me by the arm leading me upstairs, "G-e-t it off now." She pushed me. I put the uniform in the laundry bag. I picked my duffle coat off the floor and put it on. On my way out Jeffery Caplan arrived.

"Doris."

"I'm pleased to see you Jeffery. Asher's been in touch. Jeffery's run away.

I wondered if she was talking about my brother Jeffery and rushed up the steps.

"Auntie Doris,"

"What the hell now."

"Were you talking about my brother Jeffery?"

"Yes. Your hearing's fine isn't it."

"Yes."

The laundry was done and I was about to leave when a man approached me.

"Are you Jane Levene?"

"Yes." I moved away from him so I wouldn't smell his body.

"I'm Melanie's father. Melanie and Andrea pointed you out to me. Why don't you come and visit us?"

"I'll ask Auntie Doris." When I arrived back, I could hear people talking in the living- room.

"Jane."

"Yes, Auntie Doris."

"Come and say hello to Mrs Roth." I looked at her. She introduced herself as my voluntary social worker from the Jewish Social Services.

"Hello Jane." We spoke for a while. She asked if I had seen Jeffery and David. I told her that I had not seen them since the day my mother died.

"Your cousin Eric is going to a disco at the Jewish Lads Brigade next week. I would like you to go with him." My head bowed I started shaking.

"I don't want to."

"I would like you to. It's all arranged and Eric has agreed to it. Do you have anything to wear?"

"Yes. I have a trouser suit. I get very cold, without my uniform."

"Don't be silly," Mrs Roth said.

Monday arrived. When school finished, I rushed home to do my chores. After tea Auntie Doris told me to go to bed. Later in the evening she went out to play bingo. I was in bed looking at my photographs, trying to get some music on my radio. I heard my door creak. My heart was banging. I felt faint. I closed my eyes tightly, pretending to snore. It was dark. I opened one eye slightly and could see Eric was edging towards my bed. He stopped at the chair beside my bed and started rummaging through my clothes. I stayed as still as possible. He was still moving around. I felt his hand under the blankets. His hand was on my leg.

"Stop it Oric." His hand didn't move. "Please stop it," I begged. I sat up and moved the blankets away. He carried on touching me. I sprang out of bed, pushing him over. We were fighting. I pulled his shirt and a button came off.

"Mum will kill you. You wait." He left the room. I got back into bed and fell asleep.

I was woken in the morning by a voice in my ear. Auntie Doris was standing beside my bed.

"Hello Auntie Doris," I smiled at her.

"Don't you ever touch my Eric again," She grabbed my hair and I felt my jaw crack as she pulled my hair back. I closed my eyes. She pulled me out of bed. "Don't ever do that again, whore." She screamed in my ear.

"What's a whore, Auntie Doris?"

"It's what you are." I was lying on the floor watching as she left the room, relieved when I heard the door bang. Eric stood at the door. "I'm not taking that from her. Come on Eric."

I held my breath for fear she might come back in the room. My new trouser suit was on the floor. I noticed it as I got up. It had been shredded with a pair of scissors. I put it in the rubbish bin. I put my shoes on and went downstairs. "Can I have something to eat, Auntie Doris? I'm very hungry."

A few weeks passed. It was the evening of the Jewish Lads Brigade disco. Eric went straight from school. I was to meet him there. I wore my school uniform and duffle coat. I started walking up Cheetham Hill Road, staying close to the wall, counting on my fingers and repeating what I had counted. I looked down at my shoes and socks. I had managed to find two elastic bands which held my socks in place. The shoes had parted from the soles. Auntie Doris had asked the Benevolent Society for some shoes. I was waiting for them to arrive. I was in the grounds of the JLB. I could hear music. I hoped there was plenty of food to eat. If Eric wasn't hungry I could eat his too. I went through the main doors.

Two girls came past me laughing. I recognised one of them from school. They were both dressed up, wearing makeup. They stopped and looked at me, then at each other, they walked off. I went into the disco. There was a small table near the door with a cash box on it. I looked at all the young people dancing. They were all dressed up. No-one else had their uniform on. A young girl came to the table and told me it was sixpence to get in to the disco. I didn't have any money on me.

I made my way back to Auntie Doris's house.

CHAPTER 21

It was getting more difficult to leave the house. My legs would tremble, the panic was unbearable. I knew it was a matter of months before I left school. Each day I attended I would try desperately hard to learn as much as possible. Opening a book made my heart pound. I would break out in a sweat. The more I tried to concentrate, the harder it was to absorb what was going on. Nothing had changed. The Hebrew classes came around. I tried to listen to each word for my mother's sake. It was useless. My mind was a terrible confusion of atmospheres and intensely painful feelings which took control of my whole body. I was cold and hungry all the time.

One day in school I found some face makeup in the toilet. It was almost white. I put it in my briefcase. When I arrived back at the house I read the list of instructions. I rushed upstairs. I stood in front of the mirror putting all the makeup on my face and neck. I heard Auntie Doris's voice downstairs, my heart started racing.

"Where are you? Why haven't you put the tea on?" I rushed downstairs. "I'll do it now, Auntie Doris."

"Now 'shmow,' you won't be getting any, that's for sure." She looked at me.

"Have you got powder on your face?"

"No, Auntie Doris," my heart was pounding. She disappeared into the kitchen and came back with a towel.

"Come here, now!" I walked towards her, my heart

banging, convinced I was going to faint. I closed my eyes and felt her rub the towel all over my face.

"What's this?"

"Don't know, Auntie Doris."

"I'll tell you what it is *meshuggina*. It's bleeding powder. Whore. Put that *drek* on your face again and you're out."

"Sorry, Auntie Doris." She laid the table and called Eric. I sat on the couch.

"Take yours upstairs."

I fell asleep. I was woken hours later by knocking on the front door. It was Anita and Morris. They went into the living-room: I crept out on the landing.

"Doris, Doris, I don't know what to do. David keeps running out of the house. I don't know what to do with him. All we wanted was a nice *yiddishy* boy, go to college become a doctor or solicitor."

"You think you've got problems," Auntie Doris said.

"We've got tutors for him. I don't know what to do," Anita said.

"*You* don't know what to do. Try living here for a while. Then you'd know what suffering is. We've got a *meshuggina* upstairs"

I got back into bed and fell asleep.

I was back in Johnson Street. It was night time. I had crept downstairs to make the fire for mum. I made sure I had enough lino from the landing and kept reciting the shama to keep us safe. The fire was burning bright. When I thought the room was warm enough I closed the living-room door behind me and went upstairs to the bedroom to get her up. I was floating up the stairs, along the landing, into the bedroom till I was standing at the foot of mum's bed. She had nice blankets and sheets covering her. She looked so calm and loving, she was smiling slightly.

"Mummy, come on." She opened her eyes and looked at me, her face started to change. It was decomposing, I turned and panicked. I wanted to run, but my feet were stuck to the floor.

"Mummy," I cried. Her face was like that of a monster, her hair had fallen out. "Mummy, Mummy," I cried once more. She sat up in bed staring at me, still I couldn't run.

"Wake up, Wake up!" My body was shaking. I opened my eyes. Auntie Doris was by the bed looking very angry. I looked at her, realising I was having a nightmare.

"Sorry, Auntie Doris."

"I've got to get up early in the morning for work." She left the room. I didn't get out of bed in case something grabbed me. Quickly I pulled the blankets over my head. I was sniffing in case a fire broke out. Auntie Doris would be pleased if I could get them out of the house to safety. It was impossible for me to sleep. I looked out of the window. It was getting lighter. I heard voices on the landing.

"Is she awake?" I heard her ask Eric.

"Are you awake?" he shouted.

"Yes, Oric."

"Would you like a fried 'ogg' on toast for your breakfast?" I heard giggles.

I went downstairs. "Good morning, Auntie Doris." I smiled at her. There was no answer. She pointed to some slices of toast on a plate. There was no egg. I ate it very quickly not knowing if saying good morning was wrong. I couldn't understand what I had done.

"I'm not giving you a list. I want you to peel the potatoes and tidy up. Do you think you can remember that?"

"Yes, Auntie Doris."

During the course of the day, we were given the date for leaving school. Eight weeks, that was all I had left to learn everything so I could get a job and look after her. I arrived back at the house. I peeled the potatoes and put them in the pan, then turned the stove on so they would cook. I dusted and straightened the furniture. I picked the letters off the carpet and put them on the sideboard ready for Auntie Doris. She opened them. "This one's for you. It's from the caretaker of Bracknell Court. They want £75.00 for the damage done to the flat." I looked at her, not knowing what I would do or how I would pay. "What are you looking at me for? In *dread*, I'll pay. You can pay for it when you start work."

"Yes, Auntie Doris."

She got her writing pad from the sideboard. "I'm writing to Asher. He can have you for a few days. I don't see why I should have all the *tsoriss*." I smiled at her. She lifted her head. "I am well aware I am Auntie Doris. Do you have to answer everything I say?" Her lips scrunched up at the corners.

"Sorry, Auntie Doris," I mimed, before running upstairs.

"I've had enough of you," she shouted.

Within a few weeks she received a letter back from Uncle Asher. He told her he was visiting Manchester and would take me back to London for his son's *Bar mitzvah*. There was a knock on the front door. Eric was upstairs doing his homework in his bedroom and Auntie Doris was in the kitchen.

"I'll get it, Mum." I listened from the landing. "It's for you Mum." Eric passed her a letter. It was like the one I saw when my mum died.

"What's the matter Auntie Doris?" I was trembling. I ran downstairs.

"Number Seven's dead. Your Auntie Edith is dead." I didn't understand. I had never seen her, she was my mum's other sister. She had lived at number seven Maude Street. Because she had married a Christian man on *Yom Kippur*, no-one spoke to her or mentioned her by name. She was only called Number Seven. "We'll have to sit *shiva* here. I need this like a *loch in kop*." I ran upstairs. I wanted to sleep until it was all over.

"Come down here, now." The front door was open. She was standing with Eric at the bottom of the steps. She had hold of a baby's pram. "I want you both to take this to seven Maude Street, it's off Waterloo Road. Collect all the tinned food from the cupboards. Do you both understand?"

"Yes, Auntie Doris." We started walking, Eric holding one side of the pram handle. I was holding onto the other side. I made sure the pram stayed close to the wall so I could touch it. I didn't want to sit *shiva* again. I desperately wanted to sleep.

"It's at the end of this street. This is number seven. Wait here, Mum told me to get the key from the neighbour."

"I've come for the key," I heard Eric say.

A plump lady was standing near the front door. "They found her dead on the floor. She was a very clever woman, self taught. Did she have a heart attack?"

"I don't know," Eric said. The house was a small terraced. I tried to see through the window. "Help me get the pram in." Eric was steering it from side to side, I gave it a big push and almost fell over. My heart was pounding. It was hard to breathe. The hall was littered and piled high with newspapers. It was difficult to walk.

"Come on, we'll go into the kitchen."

"Wait for me, I'm frightened." I looked in the front room. It was knee-high with newspapers, everything was upside down. She must have had the same illness as my mum. I had to walk through the sitting room, over more piles of paper to get to the kitchen. The cupboards were full of tinned food.

"Come on, help me." The house had a smell of its own. Perhaps she's still here. My stomach churned. I could smell death. I wondered where Auntie Edith had kept her bits of towels and rags to wipe the blood away with.

"Do you think she's upstairs? Please hurry," I begged. He had piled all of the food into the pram. I went into the front room to see if I could find a photograph of her. There were none.

"I'm going," Eric said as he started pushing the pram down the hall. We started walking up Waterloo Road. I wanted to take all the food back in case Auntie Edith wasn't really dead and they sent her home from hospital. We waited for the lights to change at the top of the road. They were on green. We only had to walk around the corner now. Auntie Doris rushed to the front door.

"Get it all out and leave everything in the hall."

"Yes, Auntie Doris." Eric took the pram back to the neighbour.

"Put the tins on the living-room table. Get me a pen and paper out of the drawer." She sat at the table holding each tin and writing. "That lot would have cost me five pounds in the shops. Put them in the sideboard. It's your bedtime."

"Yes, Auntie Doris." I smiled at her. My head felt very heavy, like a block of ice was searing through it. All I wanted was to sleep. All the mirrors in the house had been covered and a *minion* gathered in the front living-room. I didn't like it. I could hear the *davoning*. I placed all the blankets over my head. My bedroom door was ajar in case of fire. I heard it creak. I pushed the blanket away from my face and could see Eric. He crept over to the bed and I felt the blankets move, his hand was near my coat, on my legs. I couldn't breathe. I didn't gasp for air in case he realised I was awake. He wouldn't go away.

"Get away from me. I'll kill you if you do that again."

"If you do my Mum will kill you back." He grinned, turned to the chair and lifted some underwear. I jumped out of bed grabbing my clothes from him.

"Go away, don't touch them."

The *davoning* carried on, it seemed louder than ever. My body was pulsating. I felt drowsy, my eyes closed.

I was in the school playground. One of the teachers told me to go to the headmaster's office. I stood outside wondering what I had done wrong. He opened his door and beckoned me in.

"Why haven't you been home to see your mother? She's ill and needs you." My heart jumped so hard I thought it would come up through my throat. "Why didn't Auntie Doris tell me?" I cried. Why did she give me that letter saying Mum had died? "Please can I have some money for the bus fare so I can hurry home to her?" He looked at me and searched through his pockets. "Please hurry. I want to see her. She might die before I get home."

He handed me a thruppeny piece. I ran towards the bus stop, crying, banging my foot on the ground. The front door to the flats was open and the lift was waiting for me. I pressed the button for the sixth floor. Soon it stopped, the doors opened. It was the fifth floor. I ran out onto the stairs. I opened the door it was the eighth floor. I ran down the stairs. The flat door was open. "Don't worry Mum, I won't be long. Where are you?"

"Hikey, I'm here." I ran through to the living-room, she was laid on the couch.

"Why didn't you tell me you're alive? I thought you were dead." I sat beside her. "I'll never leave you again."

"Let me shloff, be a good girl." I looked out of the window, it was getting light, almost time for her insulin. I found the bottle in the kitchen cupboard and took one out.

"Come on Mum, take this." It was too late, her eyes were rolling around. Her tongue was stuck back in her throat. I pulled at it so she wouldn't swallow it. She couldn't breathe. I could smell smoke. The sound of crackling wood was getting louder. I went to the front door to see what was happening. As I ran back to the living-room she was engulfed in flames. My feet were stuck to the floor. I couldn't move. "We're going to die Mum." I sobbed.

I felt my body shaking, I opened my eyes. Auntie Doris was standing over me.

"My hearts banging, Auntie Doris, I'm dying."

"Get out of bed, now." She looked angry. "I'm tired of all this. If I can't sleep, you won't sleep."

Shiva had finished. It was early morning, I could hear voices downstairs.

"She'll be leaving school in a few weeks. I think the best place for her is on a *Kibbutz* in Israel. I've had a word with Mrs Roth she thinks it's a good idea too. I'll contact the Jewish Agency."

I didn't want to go to Israel. I couldn't speak Hebrew. My mum and brothers were here not in Israel. I sat on the floor. It was damp where I had peed. I got some of her talcum powder and sprinkled it on so she wouldn't smell anything. I left my room. Standing on the landing I was stamping my foot on the floor to keep my heart beating.

"Auntie Doris."

"What."

"I love you, Auntie Doris."

"I've left some *shmates* in the *shicel*. When you get home from school wash them and hang them over the maiden."

"OK, Auntie Doris."

"When you finish school I want you to go to the Jewish Agency. It's on Middleton Road next to the JLB. It's called Mamlock House. You're going to live in Israel and work on a *Kibbutz*."

After school I found the Jewish Agency. They were expecting me. I was taken into an office. There were large posters on the walls of Israel and people living on a *Kibbutz*.

"You're Jane Levene?" The receptionist asked.

"Yes."

"What's your date of birth?"

"I'm not sure." She looked at me.

"Fill this form in."

I sat looking at the form. I wrote a few things on it and passed it back.

"You're not English. You are British! We will pay your fare to Israel. The current wage for working on a *Kibbutz* is half a crown a week.

"What if I want to come home?" She said nothing.

"Take these leaflets. They explain about life on the *Kibbutz*."

A few weeks passed. I got home from school and noticed Auntie Doris's writing pad on the sideboard. It had Anita and

Morris's phone number on it. I wrote the number down and found some change in the sideboard. I ran to the phone box around the corner and rang the number. Anita answered. I recognised her voice.

"Can I speak to David please? It's Jane."

"No, he's upstairs. He's busy." She hesitated. "He's not here."

"Can I ring back when he's in?" There was silence.

"That's not a good idea. You're not a good influence on him. We're his family now." The phone slammed down.

On the way back to Auntie Doris's I bumped into Andrea and Melanie.

"Why don't you come round to our house?" Melanie asked

"I'll have to ask Auntie Doris. Will you come with me?"

"No. Why won't she let you move, or say anything when you're sitting on the couch?" Melanie said.

"I don't know, I don't think she's very well." On the way back to Auntie Doris's they showed me where they lived.

"Go and ask her if you can stay here for a while." Melanie said.

"I'm very cold and hungry. I need to go to *shloff*. But, I'll ask her later."

"Auntie Doris, Melanie asked me if I can go to her house."

"Get your dinner." She pointed to the kitchen.

"Is this one mine?"

"No, it's for *Yankel the bagel fresser*. It's your bedtime."

"Yes, Auntie Doris." I felt warm and comforted in bed. I wished I could sleep forever. A few hours later I was woken by a knock on the door. I pushed the blankets off my face and listened.

"Can Jane come to our house?" It was Melanie. Auntie

Doris shouted me and told me I could go for an hour. I closed the front door gently behind me so I wouldn't disturb her. I walked with Melanie, staying close to the wall. She opened the front door. I was taken into the living-room. "This is our brother, and my Mum and Dad." I sat on the very end of the couch away from them and stayed as still as possible in case I got into trouble. I could hear them talking but found it difficult to concentrate on what was being said. Mrs Levy gave me some cake and a cup of tea.

"I've got to go now. Auntie Doris needs me."

"You must come again," Mrs Levy said.

CHAPTER 22

Saturday morning arrived. I crept down the stairs wondering how many slices of toast I could have without Auntie Doris noticing. I was starving. Before long I realised I had eaten half the loaf. I went back to bed. I was desperate to sleep. I heard the letterbox.

"Mum, there's an invitation for the *Bar Mitzvah*." Eric banged on my door. "Get up." I walked into the living-room. She was sitting on a chair in the corner, with a pile of raincoats behind her. She didn't lift her head and carried on sewing the hem of the coat she had on her lap.

"Asher's coming at the end of next week. You'll go back to London with him for the *Bar Mitzvah*. I suppose I'll have to make you something to wear. I've been given a pattern for a kaftan. That should hide your bulges."

"Can I help you Auntie Doris?"

"No."

"Don't worry, Auntie Doris, I'll be working soon. You won't have to work."

"Why, what are you to do? Be a brain surgeon?" They giggled.

Auntie Doris gave me a letter for the teacher saying I would be going to a *Bar Mitzvah* in London so I would miss two days at school. In the evening I was sitting on the couch and Auntie Doris and Eric were sitting at the table having a cup of tea. She told me to go to bed. I heard their voices downstairs

"She won't be here much longer, Mum. She'll be in Israel." She shouted up to me, "Tomorrow after school I want you to come to the factory. I have a lot of shopping to carry, you can help me."

I got the bus. I knew the factory was some way down Waterloo Road. After each stop I asked the bus conductor if my stop was next. I didn't want to miss it and make her angry.

I found the factory and entered through the main doors.

"I've come to see my Auntie Doris."

"Follow me; you must be Jane. Your auntie tells us what a good girl you are and how you help her. She's a good woman. Not many would 'of' taken you in."

All the sewing machines were revving. The smells were so familiar. I wanted to cry. Auntie Doris was sitting at her bench. "Auntie Doris." I tapped her on the shoulder. She jumped.

"Well, I see you made it." She pulled me to her. "Do you see that grey haired lady sitting at that machine?"

"Yes, Auntie Doris."

"That's your grandmother." I thought about what she had said. I knew my mother's parents had died before I was born. I knew my father's father had died. I didn't know if it was my grandmother or not. It could have been. Auntie Doris had often told me she had seen my mother on the bus or out shopping. I didn't know. My mind went blank.

"Go and say hello." I sat at the bench and said nothing.

It was nearly time for the *Bar Mitzvah*. "Asher's due any minute. Eric, make me a cup of tea," Auntie Doris said, rushing around the house. I heard a car pull up outside. He had a key and let himself into the house. I held my breath as he walked past, I didn't want to inhale the smell of his body.

"It's your bedtime."

The following morning she gave me a bag with some clothes. The kaftan was on top. I heard a car pull up outside.

"Come on, the taxi's waiting," Uncle Asher shouted. I closed the front door behind me. Uncle Asher was already in the taxi on the back seat. I sat on the end of the seat well away from him. After a long journey by train we arrived in London.

"I'm very tired, Uncle Asher. Can I go to *shloff* when we get to your house? Will I see Jeffery?"

The house was different from the ones in Manchester. The road was full of very large houses. I felt faint. They reminded me of the children's homes. I followed him up some steps into the house then to the living-room.

"This is your Auntie Francis." I looked at her. She was big like mum.

"Hello," I said to her.

I wanted to go to bed away from them all. Two young boys ran into the house. Uncle Asher shouted loudly, "I'll get the belt out."

"Leave them alone," Auntie Francis said. She looked frightened.

"This is your cousin, Jane," Uncle Asher said.

"Hello." I didn't move and wished I was back in Manchester.

"Are you hungry?"

"Yes, Auntie Francis. I'm very hungry. I'm starving." She brought me a plate of sandwiches and cakes. I ate them quickly. "I'm very tired. Please can I have a *shloff*."

"I'll show you where you'll sleep." She took me upstairs. I had hold of my bag. There were other people living in the house, they were very old. She told me they were her relatives.

"Auntie Doris said I've got to wear this kaftan for the *Bar Mitzvah*." She walked over to a chest of drawers, opening a brown paper bag.

"You can wear this." She laid out a dress on the bed. It was white with a starched underskirt. It had little pink flowers sewn on all around the bottom. She held it against my body. "It should fit."

"I don't like it. I pulled away. Please can I wear the clothes I have on?"

"No, you'll have to wear this dress for the *Bar Mitzvah*. Here are some white socks"

"Can I have a *shloff* now, I'm very tired?" The urge to curl up and sleep was so great that nothing could have stopped me. I awoke with a jolt, sure I could smell fire. My heart had stopped. Jumping out of bed I felt my pulse: I stamped my foot on the floor and ran to the top of the stairs to see where the fire was.

"What are you doing, Jane?" Auntie Francis asked.

"Starting my heart."

Uncle Asher was standing in the hall.

"Can I come down?" I asked.

"Yes, breakfast is nearly ready. Go and play with the boys outside." I sat on the step watching them. There was plenty to eat at breakfast. I was shivering and lightheaded, longing to be back in Manchester.

"I need to have a *shloff*." I told Auntie Francis.

"Go upstairs. You know where the bedroom is." Out in the hall I looked up the stairs. I could see an old man on the next landing. I was at the top of the stairs. He passed me. I looked at him. He looked like someone's kind grandfather. I moved near to the wall so I couldn't smell him. He stopped and put his hand up my jumper.

"Let me touch them." He touched my breasts. I froze for a moment. I ran downstairs until I found a safe corner in the living-room. I stayed huddled up in a ball.

"Get up," I heard Uncle Asher say.

"What's the matter with you?" Auntie Francis came into the room.

"Doris has to put up with this all the time."

Eventually, I picked myself up off the floor. I went to my bedroom and stayed there.

The evening before the *Bar Mitzvah* I was taken to see Jeffery. He was lodging with a woman called Mrs Shapiro. He told me he had joined the army. We talked a little. He told me he thought I was mum's favourite, that I was always with her, sitting beside her, that she loved me more than him. I said nothing in reply.

The day of the *Bar Mitzvah*, Auntie Francis and Uncle Asher took me to the synagogue along with the rest of the family. Once inside I started sobbing and ran out. They agreed that I could wait outside. It was too difficult for me to stay in the building; the feelings of rejection and hurt were too strong. When the ceremony had finished, I went home with them. Little was said. Back at the house I ate as much as possible. Taking some food to bed with me, I slept till it was time to get ready for the evening celebration. Auntie Francis knocked on my door. "It's time to get ready. We're going in an hour. Have a wash, put your dress on." We arrived at a large building. There were so many people I felt faint. Everyone was seated. I found a table in the corner of the room. It didn't have a table cloth on but I wanted to stay there.

"She's being awkward. Leave her to it." I could hear different people making speeches. I felt so drowsy. The buffet was open. I joined the queue and filled my plate high with food. I went back to my table and stayed there, refilling my plate two or three times.

It was late evening the following day when I arrived back in Manchester. I hoped Auntie Doris would be up. I had missed her terribly. I remembered little of the *Bar Mitzvah*. The taxi stopped outside the house. I looked up at her window to see if any lights were on. There was a faint glimmer of light through her bedroom window. That meant the landing light upstairs was still on. She must be awake. I paid the taxi driver. My hand was shaking as I pushed the key in the lock, my legs were like jelly. I knew that feeling would go as soon as I entered the house. I closed the door behind me. Standing in the hall I tried to catch my breath.

"Get up these stairs." Auntie Doris shouted very loudly. She was at the top of the stairs. I could only see her legs. "Get up these stairs." I looked at her.

"Alright, Auntie Doris, I'm coming." My heart was pounding. My head banging, I didn't know what I had done wrong. She was in my bedroom holding the door open. I walked over to my bed and watched as she closed the door. She walked over to me. I felt my pulse to make sure I was still alive.

"Are you alright, Auntie Doris?" Before I could finish she pulled my hair from the back and I felt my teeth clash together. She held my hair with one hand and scrambled under the mattress with the other. "What's this?" she screamed in my ear. She was holding a bag full of used sanitary towels. There was another bag under the mattress. She left them. "What's this?" she whispered in my ear. Her mouth was touching it. She pushed the bag and rubbed it on my face.

"Brought up in *drek* always *drek*."

"Yes, Auntie Doris. Sorry."

"Sorry isn't enough, not this time."

She threw the bag to the other end of the room, and pushed me onto the bed. I didn't want her to throw them away. I couldn't bear the thought of being parted from them.

"You're a *meshuggina*, only a *meshuggina* would do something like that. I've had enough. Get all this mess into the bag and get them burned on the fire."

I took them downstairs and placed them on the fire. I could see Auntie Doris sitting on the couch watching me.

"I want to go to bed, but no, I have to sit here till you've finished, because if I don't you'll probably burn the house down." The last sanitary towel had been placed on the fire. When the fire dimmed she got a kettle of water to put it out. "The sooner I get rid of you the better. Get to bed."

"Yes, Auntie Doris."

I didn't want to get into bed. I pulled the blankets off. Wrapping them around myself I huddled up behind the door. I put my hands inside my coat and held my breasts tightly, I felt comforted. I picked up my shoe. I hit myself hard, on the legs, thighs and between my legs. Soon I fell asleep.

CHAPTER 23

The last week of school arrived. The headmaster told us he would be handing out leaving certificates on Friday. It would be a non-uniform day. We were told there were businesses that wouldn't employ you if you had a Jewish name. I begged Auntie Doris to get me a dress from the Benevolent Society. I knew all the other girls would be dressed up and wearing makeup. I desperately wanted Philip to see me wearing something different even though I intended to wear it over my uniform.

"No, I'm not asking the Benevolent Society for anything. You're not staying here. You're going to live in Israel. Here's my cardigan, wear this. Don't get it dirty."

"Thank you Auntie Doris."

Mrs Roth called to see me. She had managed to find a job for me, working as a filing clerk at Marshall Wards, a catalogue warehouse. She gave me a cricket jumper to wear for work and a dress to wear on school leaving day, which had to be returned. I lay in bed for hours wondering how life would be if I never saw Philip again. He never spoke to me. I wished I could look after him like I did with Jeffery and David. He always had lots of girls around him making a fuss of him. I knew one of them would end up looking after him. Nothing mattered anymore. I needed to sleep. Pulling the blankets over my head I whispered, "Don't worry, Hikey, I love you. I know Mummy."

The following morning as soon as I awoke I took off my coat and put on the dress and Auntie Doris's cardigan. I could smell her on it. I put my coat back on and was pleased at how much warmer I felt. The headmaster came into the classroom before the lunch break and handed out the leaving certificates. I looked at mine, my stomach churning over. I wanted to show it to Mum.

After lunch I walked into the playground with all the other children, I found a step to sit on. I realised I wouldn't be going back home to the flat anymore, I wouldn't be waiting for David and Jeffery to come home. Everything seemed so final. I stayed on the step, crying for my mum, I wanted her so badly. I couldn't stop the tears streaming down my face, as I huddled up in the corner near to the door. I knew I would never catch up with all my schoolwork now, it was too late. I badly wanted Mum to be proud of me.

The final bell rang and the school leavers hurried to get their coats and belongings. Most of them were being picked up by their mothers or fathers. I started walking through the playground staying near to the wall. I didn't lift my head as I approached the main gates. I didn't want to smell them or see what they were doing. I pulled my hood over my head as far as it would go, all I could see was the pavement beneath my feet. I stayed close to the wall. Reaching the main road, passing the sweetshop that had always been out of bounds, because the shopkeeper was not Jewish, I carried on towards Auntie Doris's house. I didn't look back at the school, or the children. I couldn't bear to see the bus stop on Upper Park Road, where I had waited when I had the money to go home to mum.

I carried on walking near to the wall, touching it, being able to lean on it and extract comfort from it. The library was in sight. My stomach ached as I saw children walking in through the main doors, with their briefcases. I wanted to be able to follow them, to sit and read the books with them. I couldn't pick up a book or start reading one. Anxiety crippled me. I carried on walking, holding the wall. I noticed the bus stop, I could see a familiar figure standing next to it. She was a small, slight woman with thick black wavy hair. It looked like Minnie Shelefski. I walked up to her.

"Are you Minnie Shelefski?"

"Yes." She looked at me.

"I'm Jane Levene. My Mum's dead."

"I know," she said. I carried on walking.

I looked at my list of instructions to see what Auntie Doris wanted me to do. Food from Itchkey Abramsons; we were having pickled meat, salami and bagels for tea. I had to peel the potatoes for chips. I took off her cardigan and put it on her bed. I waited for her to come home. I was grown up now, about to start work the following Monday. I couldn't wait to see her to tell her that I would look after her. I tidied up the best I could. My eyes were closing so I went to bed. I heard the front door bang. "Where are you? Go to Itchkey's and get me some candles," she shouted from the hall. I got out of bed and hurried to her.

"I've left school now, Auntie Doris."

"Ten out of ten for brains." She handed me the money. "God help Marshall Wards," she shouted after me.

"Can I have a bath tomorrow? Before I start work?"

"If you want a bath go to the public baths."

"I haven't got any money."

"Well you'll have to do without."

I was pleased at her reply. The water made me feel miserable, uncomfortable and cold but I knew people had a bath before going to work. I waited till Sunday morning, asking again. Perhaps this time she would say yes. Again the reply was "No." I found a piece of paper with Mrs Roth's address written on it.

"Can I go for a walk, Auntie Doris?"

"Yes," she said without lifting her head. She gritted her teeth. I knew I always made her angry. I decided to go to see Mrs Roth. I wanted to know if she thought I should have a bath. I started walking. The house was on Bury Old Road, it was a continuation of Cheetham Hill Road. My heart was banging in case I got lost. It was difficult to see the numbers on the houses. They were huge, set right back off the road with very long driveways leading to them. My heart sank, all the feeling of being in the children's homes racked my body. As I approached Mrs Roth's house I felt light headed and faint. I gasped for air. I waited outside the house for a while, plucking up the courage to ring the door bell, afraid she would shut the door in my face or tell me off. Eventually, I rang the bell and waited. I could see her outline through the huge doors: she was a small, slim woman with fair hair. I felt my pulse just to make sure I wasn't dead.

"What do you want, Jane?" I knew I shouldn't have come here. "What is it?"

"I'm sorry for coming to your house. Auntie Doris won't let me have a bath. I'm starting work tomorrow." My arms were shaking. I couldn't stop trembling.

"Come in." She led me through the inner doors, into a large square hall. I could smell the children's homes. I wanted my mother. Voices were coming from one of the rooms. There was a strong smell of cigars, my mind wandered to memories of the Jewish Benevolent Society. I could see men through the glass doors.

"Come on, Jane," I followed her upstairs. We walked past her bedroom. I could smell her husband's socks. I looked away so I couldn't see the bed, rushing after her into the bathroom.

"Why won't your Auntie Doris let you have a bath?"

"I don't know, Mrs Roth." I looked around. The bathroom was very large. She put the plug in the bath and turned the taps on. She placed two bath towels on the side of the bath. I could smell the children's home, it made me heave. She left the room. I pulled the chair over that had been placed in the corner, sitting on it next to the bath. My duffle coat was still buttoned up, the heat of the water made me feel nice and warm. I leaned over, putting my finger into the water. "You're false and unreal. I don't like you." I loved my uniform, my duffle coat, they protected me. I wouldn't let the water take all that away from me. There was a knock on the door.

"Have you finished?"

"Yes, Mrs Roth. I'm going back to Auntie Doris's. I'm very tired." I pulled the plug out of the bath and unlocked the door. I showed her my hands. "Is that alright?" She looked at me.

"I must get back to my visitors." I followed her to the front door.

"I'll tell your auntie she must let you have a bath."

"I go to the baths off Cheetham Hill Road."

"Make sure you wear the cricket jumper for work. I brought you some clothes in a box"

"They don't fit me."

"I'll see if anything's been donated to the Benevolent Society. I must go"

"Yes, Mrs Roth."

When I got back to the house Auntie Doris was cooking a meal. I didn't tell her I'd been to Mrs Roth's house.

"You can wear my cardigan for work. Mrs Roth mentioned your wages. How much will you be getting?"

"Five pounds."

"Your bus fare to work and back is a shilling. You can have some pocket money on top. You can take sandwiches for your lunch"

"How many Auntie Doris?"

"You'll get what I've got. You need to lose some weight. *Grobbo tochas.*"

I was wondering about the job I would be doing. I couldn't wait to tell her about it. I got frightened hoping I wouldn't need to sleep in the toilets. "I won't be able to peel the potatoes for you anymore. I won't be home in time." She looked at me sternly.

"I know that, don't I, *Shnorror.*" I longed to talk to her.

"I'll get up early and tidy up for you." There was no response. I went to my bedroom and put the radio on. I pulled the blankets over my head, holding the radio. The music I was listening to couldn't keep me awake. I felt drowsy, happy I was going to sleep.

Auntie Doris put the alarm clock on the landing so I would hear it. It seemed to ring forever. I wanted to sleep. I crept out of my room and turned it off. I took great care to make sure I didn't wake her. It was six o'clock: I had plenty of time to tidy up before getting ready for work. I dusted the furniture and straightened the cushions on the couch and chairs. I crept into the kitchen, making sure I didn't make a noise. I looked in the fridge and cupboards to see if there was anything I could eat without her noticing. I took some biscuits and stuffed them in my mouth. I made some toast, and then made cheese sandwiches. The cupboards were full of tinned food. She knew exactly what she had so I left them.

I heard footsteps, stamping along the landing. I felt faint, taking deep breaths because the air wouldn't go deep enough into my lungs. I felt my pulse, there was nothing. I stayed very still for a moment. I couldn't hear her, I couldn't breathe. I knew I'd done something wrong. She couldn't wait to tell me what it was. I sat on the couch waiting for my punishment. She pushed the living-room door open. I opened one eye slightly, she walked past me.

"Hello, Auntie Doris."

"Do you mean good morning?"

"Yes, Auntie Doris."

"Well say it then, *shmock*."

The bus to work was due at eight o'clock from the top of the road. I kept watching the clock. I didn't want to be late. The two sixpenny pieces for my fare were on the sideboard.

"Why didn't you put your sandwiches in a bag? here, take them." I looked in the bag. There were four slices of black bread and butter. She had taken the cheese out. It was time for me to leave for work. I sat close to the back of the bus. I asked the conductor if he would tell me which stop I would have to get off at.

"This is your stop." He pointed in the direction of Marshall Ward.

"Thank you. Please God don't let me them give me scales to use," I repeated till my head ached. People were walking into the side entrance. The building was huge. I could see how easily a fire might start. My heart started banging. I would have to make sure I could sit near an exit. Inside the building everyone was queuing to clock on.

"I'm starting work today." I whispered.

"Knock, on the office door and you'll get your card," someone said. I was told to go to the first floor, to the billing section. I didn't understand what that might be. The room was huge and very long, with lots of filing cabinets lining the walls. Women were sitting next to them. I was relieved when I was told I was working on my own.

"You have to match these statements with your files. Then you file them in alphabetical order."

I couldn't concentrate. I was getting frightened, wanting to run out of the building. If I got the sack Auntie Doris would kill me. I was sure of that. I could smell the black bread, I couldn't wait. Sliding down on my chair, feeling the bag, I pulled at the bread. It felt so good to eat. I wished I had twenty slices.

"What are you doing?" The supervisor's voice shocked me, I looked around.

"Having a piece of bread,"

"You must carry on with your work."

"Sorry." I pushed the bag back under the chair. I looked around and could see her sitting at her desk in the middle of the room. For a moment my heart stopped. "What if she tells Auntie Doris?" The supervisor came back.

"Where are your bad debts?" I felt faint. I didn't understand what she was saying.

"Let me sit down. These have to go to the correspondence clerk." I couldn't understand.

"I'm sorry. I'll do better tomorrow, I promise." She explained the job once more. I tried very hard to make what she had told me stick in my mind.

"Lunchtime," one of the women shouted. I looked up and I could see them all heading for the stairs. I waited so I could walk down on my own. I was still wearing my duffle coat. I don't think anyone noticed. Going down the stairs, the smell of chips was very strong. The sound of the clattering plates from the canteen was making me very hungry. I wanted to eat everything in sight. I looked at all the plates. How could I get to the leftovers? If only I could do the washing up.

I sat in the corner away from everyone. I put my bag on the table there was only a small piece of bread left. I ate it. I tried to remember what the supervisor had told me. I couldn't remember any of it. My eyes were fixed on the serving area; plates of chips, pies, stacks of bread. I could eat them all now and ask for seconds. If only I had some money. Then they brought out bowls of steamed pudding with custard. The assistants were lining them up on the shelf. I wanted them all, if only my tummy could feel full and warm, I would be so happy. I noticed plates with leftovers on. How could people leave their food? Why didn't they need it? I didn't understand. Perhaps they were leaving it because they knew I wanted the food. Maybe they knew how much I needed it. I walked over to the serving area.

"Can I wash up please?"

"Miss Levene. Your lunch break is over." The supervisor was beckoning me.

The canteen assistant looked at me. I realised this wasn't the children's home. I followed the supervisor. If only I was a canteen assistant. I sat back at my desk, confused. Another pile of invoices had been placed very neatly on it. My mind started wandering. I imagined what Auntie Doris would make for tea. I looked at the desk. My body felt very still, my heart had stopped. I felt my pulse, there was no movement. I was going to faint. I stamped my foot on the floor beneath my desk. I felt my pulse again. I had managed to get it going.

"You're alright, Hikey," I whispered.

"Time girls," the supervisor shouted. I looked at my desk. Nothing had been done. Everyone collected their belongings and rushed downstairs to clock off. I waited till they had gone. As I approached the clocking on machine I could see my name written on the top. My heart sank. The only thing I belonged to now was the brown card on the clocking on machine, hanging on the wall. I headed for the bus stop.

Auntie Doris and Eric were sitting at the table eating tea when I arrived home.

"Yours is in the kitchen." She didn't lift her head. I wanted to tell her about my new job.

"Did you take your coat off?" They giggled

"I didn't hear what you said." I replied.

"I was talking to Eric."

"Can I have some money to buy something from the canteen tomorrow, please?"

"Do you think I'm made of money?" She carried on eating. "It's your bedtime."

"Can I tell you about my job, Auntie Doris?"

"You can tell me about your wages." They both laughed.

"Eric's going to the grammar school. He's clever."

"Can I have a piece of paper to write to Jeffery?" She looked at Eric. He went over to the sideboard. Opening the cupboard door, he ripped a piece of paper off the writing pad and passed it to me along with a pen. I wasn't allowed near the sideboard. It was full of their property. I went upstairs to the bedroom. I wrote about my job, asking when he was going into the army. I pulled all the blankets over me. I felt secure. The new hiding place for my sanitary towels was behind the wardrobe. My photographs were still in place down my blouse. I put on my radio and fell asleep.

Later in the week when I arrived home from work Auntie Doris had received a letter from Mrs Roth to say that she would be calling in the evening. After tea I was allowed to sit on the couch and wait for her. She knocked on the front door and Eric let her in. I could see her walking down the hall, holding a carrier bag.

"How are you enjoying your job?"

"It's very nice, thank you."

"Have you made any friends yet?" I frowned.

"No." I didn't like the question.

"Have a look in the carrier bag."

"How are you, Doris?"

"*Nishtgut.*"

I knew that was because of me. I pulled a jumper out of the bag. It had a V-neck with flowers on. Next I pulled out a handbag. It was brown suede, with a little brass clasp.

"I won't have to put my bus fare down my bra now. Thank you."

Mrs Roth said she would have to go home. Auntie Doris walked with her down the hall. I could hear them whispering. It was difficult to hear what they were saying. I was so tired I fell into bed and slept till the morning.

One evening after work, I found a shilling on the pavement. I decided to buy myself some chocolate. I walked across the road to the sweet shop. The shop was crammed full of shelves and there were so many large jars of sweets and bars of chocolate I didn't know which to choose. As I came out of the shop I caught sight of a familiar figure, standing outside the Temple billiard hall. It was my dad. My stomach churned and I wanted to run back in the shop. I held my stomach, to stop it from hurting. I tried hard to comfort it. I moved to the side of the shop so he wouldn't see me. He was taking a packet of cigarettes from his pocket. As soon as he disappeared from view, I left the shop and ran to Auntie Doris's. I managed to get my key in the lock, my hands were trembling. "Auntie Doris, I've just seen my Dad." My body was still shaking.

"Did he say anything?"

"No, he was walking down the road."

"He's got the right idea." I looked at her.

"How would you like to go to Israel, to work on a *Kibbutz*? It's the opportunity of a lifetime."

"Don't know." I smiled, if only I could cuddle her.

"Well, I think it would be a good idea, Mrs Roth thinks it's a good idea. You've had the brochures. Mrs Roth has arranged it. Get your tea, then bed."

"Yes, Auntie Doris. I love you." I waited. There was no reply.

I was finding it very hard to concentrate on my work. The supervisor told me I would have to try harder.

It was pay day. I clocked off, making my way to the bus stop. Checking in my handbag to make sure my wage packet was safe and secure, I waited patiently for the bus, checking my pulse now and again. I held onto the bus stop so I wouldn't faint.

"Have you got any money for a sandwich?" I turned around, there was a woman standing behind me. She was big. I looked at her from head to foot. She looked very much like my mum. "Have you got any money?" I opened my handbag and pulled out my wage packet, I handed it to her. She looked at me, grabbed it from my hand, and walked off quickly into the distance. The bus arrived. I had one sixpence for the bus fare, soon I was back at Auntie Doris's. The chopped liver was already laid out on the table along with slices of black bread. I walked through to the kitchen. Auntie Doris was dishing out the chicken soup. I watched as she checked the *Helzel* in the oven.

"Hello, Auntie Doris."

"Take this soup into the living-room." She handed me one bowl at a time. Soon it was time for the main course. I ate it quickly.

"Where's your wage packet?"

"I gave it to a lady in town. She had no money."

She looked at me her face distorted. "She hasn't got any money! Who do you think I am. The Baron de Rothschild?"

"No, Auntie Doris." She moved away from the table, and stood looking at the fire. I watched her, wondering what she was going to do. She turned to me.

"Are you joking about this?"

"No, Auntie Doris. Sorry."

She lunged towards me. For a moment it seemed to be in slow motion. She grabbed my jumper and pulled my head back.

"I'll kill you. In *dread*." She hit me across the face. I heard the gristle in my nose crunch.

"Come on." She pulled me towards the front door.

"Sorry."

"Sorry, *shmorry*, get out of this house and don't come back till you've got your wage packet."

I found myself on the pavement outside the house. I

walked around, wishing the money was back in my handbag, so I could give it to her. I walked past Melanie and Andrea. They were outside their house talking.

"Jane," Melanie shouted. I didn't hear at first. She ran after me. I told her what had happened and that I didn't know what to do. She took me back to her house. I could hear voices but couldn't concentrate on what was being said. "You must try to come for your tea."

"Thank you." I went back to Auntie Doris's, letting myself in. I went upstairs and was pleased to fall asleep.

My first few months at Marshall Wards passed quickly. Each Friday I would give Auntie Doris my wages. In return she handed me my bus fare plus two shillings spending money, which I spent at Bookbinder's kosher bakery. I couldn't concentrate on the billing section and was moved to a desk where all I had to do was put invoices into envelopes. Sometimes it was too difficult for me to stay awake. I would have to go into the toilets and sleep. After the first six weeks I was given a prize for good timekeeping. A few weeks later the supervisor told me that my behaviour wasn't satisfactory. I was sacked.

CHAPTER 24

On my last day of work I got the bus back to the house.

"What's for tea Auntie Doris? I'm starving. I'll wash up after tea." She didn't answer. I went into the kitchen, almost falling over a large box of clothes. Auntie Doris was cooking.

"Look at me." She said dancing about. "Look what I've got: a fox stole, three quarter fawn kid evening gloves and handmade shoes made by Miss Rayne the Queen's shoe maker." She wiped her hands on her apron. "Mrs Roth's mother died. She brought me some of her clothes." She seemed very happy. Dancing about, she handed me my meal. I ate it quickly.

"Please can I have some bread, Auntie Doris, and the crusts? I'm very hungry."

"Yes, after you've given me your wage packet."

"Auntie Doris, I'll get up early tomorrow and do all the shopping for you. Sunday I'll get up and do the housework. Then I'll go to the laundry. I'll do my best, anything you want"

"What have you done? Come on, out with it." She looked angry.

"I've got the sack, Auntie Doris." I sat on the end of the couch.

"Ring Mrs Roth. Tell her. She went to a lot of trouble to get you that job. You're stupid. You'll have to ring her on Sunday. After *Shabbas* is over. What do you think she's going to say? I know what I'd say. Miss Grateful for Nothing." I went to bed and slept.

Saturday morning I got up. Eric had gone away. Auntie Doris was sitting at the table still wearing her fox stole and kid gloves.

"Auntie Doris, can I have Eric's breakfast? I'm hungry."

"Hungry *shmungry*. Do you really think I'm going to waste food on you?" On Sunday morning ring Mrs Roth to tell her you've been sacked. It's the *Kibbutz* for you. In *dread*."

On Sunday morning I listened in my room to see if she was awake. I straightened the clothes I had slept in and crept down the stairs. She wouldn't notice if I had some extra toast. The living-room door was slightly open, it was still dark. All I could think about was the extra toast.

"What are you doing?" I almost jumped out of my skin. She was lying on the couch. I stayed very still. She fell asleep again. Walking past her, my foot hit something. I bent down. It was a bottle of tablets. Some had fallen out of the bottle and they were scattered on the floor. I turned the living-room light on. The capsules were red and brown like Duraphet tablets. I picked up the bottle and read the label. They were the same tablets that mum had taken. I threw them down.

"Auntie Doris, wake up, please!" I was sobbing, shaking her. She opened her eyes and looked at me.

"What are you doing? Get off me. *Meshugginah*," She pushed me back towards the floor. I got up.

"Please don't take them," I begged, shaking her arm.

"Get off. Do you think I'd be taking them if you weren't here, It's you that's done this to me. Mrs Roth's coming next week. You're definitely going to Israel."

"OK, Auntie Doris. Can I make some toast?" She didn't answer. I went into the kitchen.

"Don't burn it, or else!" My heart was pounding and I

knew this time if it stopped, it wouldn't start again.

"Get upstairs, to bed." She pointed towards the stairs. I stayed in bed waiting for her to call me. I was so hungry I soon fell asleep. Her footsteps on the stairs woke me. I could tell it was afternoon, I could smell food. I opened the door, my heart banging. She had left my meal outside the bedroom door. I wondered if she would give me Eric's tea. I stayed in the room, she didn't call me. I was warm and comfortable with all my clothes on. I put my arms around myself. "Go to *shloff*, Hikey, I love you," I whispered. Later there was knocking on my bedroom door. "Israel's the best place for you. We're all agreed on that. You can take the laundry tomorrow morning as you've ruined today for me."

"OK, Auntie Doris." I got out of bed and walked around the room for what seemed a long time, looking at my photos and holding the wall. I loved the wall so much, almost as much as my school uniform. I knew they cared about me too. I opened the door and leaned over the banister.

"Auntie Doris." Eric was coming through the front door.

"What do you want?" Eric said.

"Will you ask Auntie Doris if I can go and see Melanie and Andrea?"

"Yes," he shouted. I ran down the stairs and closed the door behind me. I hurried to their house before my heart stopped. I banged on the door.

"What on earth is the matter?

"Mrs Levy. I'll never see any of you again."

"Calm down, come in."

"I've got to go and live in Israel. Auntie Doris and Mrs Roth said. I went to Mamlock House the lady said I was British, not English. She gave me lots of brochures. I'll earn

half a crown a week. I'll never be able to come home for as
long as I live."

"Jane, calm down. When are you going?"

"I got the sack for sleeping in the toilet. They said I should
take off my coat."

"Who, when, what are you talking about? You're not
making sense."

"I've got to go now. Auntie Doris needs me."

"Would you like a piece of cake and a biscuit?"

"Yes, please." I looked up, they were all looking at me.

"Would you like a cup of tea?"

"Yes, please." I ate my cake and drank my tea. I could hear
Mr and Mrs Levy talking.

"Jane, what exactly did your auntie say?"

"I can't remember. I'm never going to hold down a job.
I'm stupid."

"Did they say you were going to work on a *Kibbutz*?"

"Yes. No. I don't know. When I filled in the form there
were pictures everywhere."

"Why don't you have your tea here one night next week?"

"I'll ask Auntie Doris." I thought for a moment. Perhaps I
could have my tea at Auntie Doris's first, then come here.

"I'll go now and ask."

"Wait for me. I'll come with you." Melanie said.

"Auntie Doris, can I have tea at Melanie's house next week?
Can I have my tea here first, then go to Melanie's."

"Are you doing this to me on purpose? Haven't I suffered
enough?"

"Sorry, Auntie Doris. Is it my bedtime now?"

"Yes."

"Melanie, I can come next week. I'll have my tea here first."

I closed the front door and went upstairs. Auntie Doris had left some money in my bedroom for sanitary towels. I looked at it knowing I was going to buy a bilberry plate pie from Bookbinder's bakery instead. I got into bed desperate to sleep.

I was back in Johnson Street, in the attic. There was a baby on the floor, dead. I had murdered it. I was panicking. I managed to get the bricks out of the wall with my bare hands, leaving a large hole. I put the baby behind the wall and brick by brick I closed the hole. No-one would know what I had done. I heard banging on the front door. I ran downstairs to the bedroom and looked out of the window. Two policemen were standing there.

"*Mummy, what have I done?*" *She wasn't there.*

I went downstairs and looked on the couch in the living-room for her.

"*Open up.*" *The banging on the front door was getting louder.*

"*Mummy, where are you?*" *I started trembling, not knowing where she could have gone.*

"*I mustn't tell anyone what I've done.*"

The policeman started breaking the door. The banging got louder. I tried to run. I couldn't. My legs were stuck in the floorboards, my legs bleeding badly. "*They mustn't know what I've done.*"

My whole body was shaking. "Wake up!" Auntie Doris was shouting.

"I didn't do it Auntie Doris. I wouldn't do that. I didn't do it." She carried on shaking me.

"What are you doing on the floor? Why are all the bedclothes scattered all over?" She looked very angry. She leaned over to where I had been lying and looked very carefully.

"You've pissed yourself, haven't you?

"Sorry, Auntie Doris." I smiled, relieved to be awake.

"Sorry! *Don't* bother saying that."

She walked out of the bedroom muttering. I looked around the room. The dreams felt so real. I was still surrounded by the atmosphere. "You'll suffer for this," she said as she walked past my room and headed downstairs.

As morning arrived I listened at my door to see if she was awake. The landing light was on. My heart was thumping. It meant she had stayed downstairs on the couch. She got very angry when I disturbed her sleep. "Auntie Doris, don't forget I'm going to Melanie's next week for my tea." There was no reply.

One evening Mrs Roth came to see Auntie Doris. I was upstairs. She took her into the front living-room and closed the door. I couldn't hear what they were saying. I waited behind my door. The living-room door opened.

"Ask her if she's got the brochures upstairs. Really, I think the best thing is for her to go back to Mamlock House and get the paperwork finished. In the meantime I'm going to see a friend about a job for her. She's looking for an office junior."

Mrs Roth had arranged a second interview for me at the Jewish Agency. As I approached the building my heart was pounding. I felt light headed. It smelt like the Benevolent Society. She had also arranged a new job for me as an office junior at G.A Nicholas Ltd. Electrical Wholesalers, to start the following week. I was called into the same office as before. I sat down. "Am I going to Israel to work on a *Kibbutz*?"

"Take a seat." She pulled out a pile of brochures. "Have you got these?"

"Yes."

"Let me find the form you filled in." She sat looking at it. "You need to go to the library. Find some books on Israel, the food, the language. Can you speak Hebrew?"

"I know some Hebrew words. I can read it a little."

"Can you translate?"

"I don't think so."

"As I was saying, you need all the information you can get. Tell your mother."

"Thank you." I stood up to leave.

"Miss Levene, here, you need this. It's a list of clothes you will need."

"Thank you."

I started walking back to the house. Half way down Cheetham Hill Road I stopped at the library. I walked through the front doors and felt all the smells, noises, and atmosphere of school, the Benevolent Society, the children's homes and my father's flat. I stopped dead. If I don't go in, Auntie Doris and Mrs Roth will kill me. I could see all the books on shelves. I felt sick. Looking at the children made me feel very sad. I wasn't one of them. I must keep my head down. I couldn't open a book. I couldn't read a book. It was too painful. I ran out of the building and made my way to Auntie Doris's. When I turned off the main road I bumped into Mr Levy.

"I'm going to live in Israel. I'll never see anyone again."

"Come over later and see the girls."

"Alright."

I told Auntie Doris that I was going to see Melanie and Andrea. After tea I left the house. I could hear Mr and Mrs Levy talking to Melanie and Andrea. I could see their lips moving. Their voices seemed very distant and low.

"I don't want to live in Israel," I mumbled.

"Would you like to live with us? We haven't got much room. There are only the two bedrooms. It means you girls would have to share," Mrs Levy said.

"Yes please. Does that mean I don't have to go to Israel?"

"Yes. Go and tell your auntie. Mrs Roth will also have to know. You can pay me for your board and keep the rest of the money for yourself." I looked at her.

Mrs Roth visited Mr and Mrs Levy to make arrangements for me to move in.

"I haven't got a suitcase to put my clothes in," I told Mrs Roth.

"I thought that might be the case. I have a small one in the car." I packed my clothes, then the candlesticks that I had brought from the Jewish Board of Guardians for my mum, as well as the photographs of her."

"I love you, Auntie Doris." She was sitting on the couch. She looked away.

"Let them have the *storris*. I've done my best."

I walked down the street with my little brown suitcase and my suede handbag and knocked on the door of the house that was to be my new home.

CHAPTER 25

"Hello, Jane." Mrs Levy greeted me at the front door. "Take your suitcase upstairs. Are you hungry?"

"I'm starving and cold." I should have had something to eat at Auntie Doris's, I thought to myself. Melanie showed me the bedroom.

"This is our room, that's your bed, mine is next to yours and Andrea's is in the corner." I pushed the case under my bed.

"Come on, Mum's got some bagels," Melanie told me. I opened my case and pulled the photographs out. I put them under my pillow. Not having to worry now, in case Auntie Doris found them. I thought for a minute. I put one of the photographs down my blouse in case there was a fire. I would have one safe.

"Come on, Jane," Melanie shouted from the bottom of the stairs. The house was similar to Auntie Doris's, but smaller. I knew I would have to be good or they might ask me to leave. Mrs Levy handed me a plate with two bagels and some chopped liver. I sat on the couch rigid and ate them. I looked around, Mrs Levy had disappeared.

"Jane," she shouted from upstairs. My heart was pounding as I walked up the stairs. I didn't know what I had done wrong.

"Unpack your case. This is your drawer." She opened it, taking out a piece of old newspaper.

"I don't want to. Please can I leave my clothes in the case?" She closed the drawer.

"Take your coat off. Put it on the hook on the back of the door."

"Please can I leave it on. I'm very cold?"

"Well fine. Get your toothbrush and toothpaste and I'll show you where the bathroom is."

"I haven't got any."

"What, not even an old one? Did you leave them at your auntie's? What did you clean your teeth with at her house?"

"Nothing, no, I've never had any." I looked at her, wondering if she was going to be like Auntie Doris. "Can I go to bed now? I'm very tired. I need to *shloff*." My head felt very heavy. I wanted to close my eyes.

"You'll have to buy a toothbrush and toothpaste when you get your wages."

"Alright, I'll go to bed now." Mrs Levy left the room. I opened the door a little in case a fire broke out. I noticed their bedroom across the landing. I didn't want to look at it. I was pleased the door was closed so I wouldn't smell Mr Levy's body.

Morning arrived. "Wake up girls." Mr Levy was standing beside Melanie's bed holding a tray with three mugs of tea. "Where's your nightdress and slippers? Have you got a dressing gown? Did you sleep in your clothes?"

I looked over, Melanie and Andrea were both wearing nightdresses. I could see their dressing gowns on the end of the bed and slippers on the floor. I didn't like them. I only liked my clothes. I couldn't answer. My heart was pounding.

"Mrs Roth came to see us last night. You're starting your new job this morning. She's also arranged for you to have English and Maths lessons on Tuesday evenings. She's left directions for your new job and lessons." I went downstairs.

"Will I get my tea when I have to go for the lessons?"

"Of course, I'll put it in the oven for you."

"Thank you." My mind wandered. My case would stay under the bed with all my clothes in it. I knew I wouldn't be able to unpack, or change my clothes. I didn't want a nightdress or dressing gown or slippers; they were for children in Delamere and the Sarah Laski Home. Nobody would ever make me wear them. They were false and unreal. Children wore things like that so they could pretend to be nice and clean, and good. I could see through them.

"Jane, it's time for you to leave for work. Would you like to take these onion buns with for your lunch?"

"Yes, please. Good morning."

"Good morning to you too. A bit late, but never mind." They all laughed.

I found the offices of G.A. Nicholas Ltd. It was in town. I was desperately hungry. Mrs Levy had given me some money, which was to be paid back out of my first wage packet. I bought two Mars bars and two packets of crisps and ate them before I entered the building. It was near the canal. I found the office. The office manageress Mrs Brown greeted me. "I'll take you to your desk." I looked at the desk where there was a pile of invoices and a typewriter.

"I want you to copy these invoices. As you do, make a neat pile here on your desk." I was worried in case it involved tables or fractions. There were women typing, some on comptometer machines. Their fingers were working so quickly it was difficult to see them. "OK, Mrs Brown." I looked at the people around me. What does she mean? I didn't understand what she was saying. Mr Nicholas's office was in the corner of the room. It had glass panels around it. I was placed well away from it, I was pleased. I didn't want to smell him.

It was lunchtime. Mrs Brown came to my desk. "You haven't done much. Do you know what you are supposed to do? Look at all the mistakes on the invoices. I can't use these."

"I'm sorry."

"You have to go to the Sovereign café to get lunch. Here's a list and the money." I went to the café and ordered the food. I still had some money. I bought myself a meat and potato pie. I had my onion buns too. All I needed now was to sleep.

Tuesday evening after work, I made my way to have the English lessons. I managed to find the house. It was like the doctor's surgery on Victoria Avenue and the Sarah Laski Home. All the smells haunted me. I knew I didn't like it straight away. My stomach churned badly. I wanted to eat and sleep. Nothing else mattered. I pressed the doorbell and a young woman opened the door.

"Jane Levene?"

"Yes."

"Come in." She led me through the hall, into a strange room. It was half kitchen, half living-room. She was smiling at me. I lowered my head. "That's my Mother." She pointed to someone walking past the window. I half smiled, pleased she had a mother. She told me to sit at a large round table, and passed me two books. I felt myself shaking. I gasped for air. I felt faint. She opened the book. "Write that paragraph and fill in the missing words." I looked at the book. I could see the words but nothing meant anything to me. I hated them. They made my stomach ache, my head felt empty and I was even more cold and hungry than usual. I thought I was going to be sick. She passed me a writing pad, and opened another text book. The words made me feel ill. I was trying to make the pains in my stomach go away, it was too difficult.

"Would you like a sandwich?"

"Yes, please. I'm starving."

"I'll leave them on the table, for when you've finished your lesson." She brought them over. I looked at them. I could hear the young woman's voice as she said something about adjectives and verbs and sentence construction. I didn't know what she was talking about. I couldn't make sense of any of it. The lesson was over. I was allowed to eat my sandwiches. I was so hungry I couldn't wait to get back to the Levy's for tea. Perhaps I could stop at Auntie Doris's first for a meal.

"I've finished my sandwiches. I'm going now."

"See you next week." She showed me to the front door. She was only pretending to be polite. I knew she didn't like me.

Mrs Levy passed me my dinner. She had kept it in the oven to keep warm. She put it on the kitchen table with a piece of cake. It was wonderful to feel so full, my body felt warm inside and out. I wished the feeling would last forever. My English and Maths lessons lasted a few weeks. I couldn't bear the text books anywhere near me. I didn't understand the numbers. The house made me feel ill. I knew the teacher hated me and made fun of me as soon as I left the house. On the way home I would buy two Mars bars and two packets of crisps.

At work I was taken off the copy typing because of the mistakes I was making. Now I was ripping invoices along their perforated lines as they came out of the computerised machine. I was put in a corner to do the job. I enjoyed being away from the other people in the office. At times when I couldn't keep my eyes open I would have to go into the toilets to sleep. I always kept my coat on.

Each week I would give Mrs Levy my wages. She would take out the money for my board and give me the rest. Each day when I went for the lunches I had enough money to buy two or three meat and potato pies and two or three rolls. I knew I would feel full inside even if it didn't last very long. When I arrived at the office one morning, the office manager told me I would have to go on a week's training course to learn how to use a punch card machine. They were short of punch card operators. My heart missed a beat. It started pounding. I was very worried that it would involve numbers or tables. Nine o'clock the following morning, I arrived at the training centre and was taken to an office on the second floor. The room was lined with tables. Each table had a punch card machine. I found a desk at the back of the room and waited. The room soon filled with young women and I watched as they started punching in the information from their invoices.

"What's your name?"

"Jane Levene." I felt a terrible sense of dread. I hoped she wouldn't give me an invoice to punch.

"Learn this sequence of numbers; it's very easy." She walked away. I looked at the numbers, then the keyboard. There were nine numbers. I looked again but I couldn't take it in. My head was aching. I stamped my foot to keep me alive. She walked over to me.

"Look, numbers one and four make the letter 'A.' It's easy." She smiled.

"Yes," I smiled. The course finished. I hoped that I could keep my job ripping the invoices back at work.

I arrived at work on Monday morning, sitting at my desk,

waiting for the invoices to come out of the machine so I could separate them. Hopefully they'd forgotten about the punch card machines. Mrs Brown walked over to me and beckoned me to follow her into the computer room. There was a huge computer in the room. At the end was another very large machine.

"This is a verifying machine. This young lady punches all the cards you have punched to make sure they're correct. If there happens to be a mistake, the red light will come on, and you'll hear a buzzing noise." She sat me at a desk with a punch card machine in the middle and a bundle of invoices on the side.

"Thank you," I mumbled. She left the room. I wanted to go to the toilet and sleep. I desperately wanted to get the work done correctly and started looking at the invoices, then the machines. Soon I had finished my first pile of invoices. I watched as Mrs Brown lifted the pile of invoices taking them over to the verifying machine. I was feeling very pleased with myself as I had finished sooner than I imagined I would.

Mrs Brown passed them over to the young woman on the verifying machine. I started work on my next pile. From the corner of my eye I saw the flashing red light and heard the buzzer. Both were continuous. My head was banging, my stomach aching. "Please don't give me the sack," I whispered. At lunchtime I was sent to the café as usual to collect the pies and sandwiches. When I arrived back at the office the punch card machine had been removed from my desk.

"After lunch, you can go back on folding the invoices," Mrs Brown said.

When work finished I waited at the bus stop, feeling desperate, wishing I had been able to understand what I had been taught at the punch card classes. My tea was ready when I arrived back at the Levys' house. I asked if I could go to bed because I was so tired. When I pulled my suitcase out from under the bed I could see it had been opened. I had a few clothes in it and a bag of used sanitary towels that I couldn't part with. I closed the case and pushed it back under the bed. I got into bed with all my clothes on and pulled the blankets over me. I closed my eyes, after a while I could feel I had something in my eye it was itching and very painful. I rubbed it, I could hardly open it. My heart was thumping. I hurried to the nearest mirror. It was in Mrs Levy's bedroom. My eye was swollen and bloodshot; it looked as though it was falling out. I could smell Mr Levy's socks. I couldn't feel my heart beating, my pulse had stopped. I tried to get it going again, by stamping my foot on the floor. It didn't work this time. My heart had stopped. I felt faint and could feel myself dying.

"Help me!" I shouted. I heard the living-room door open. "Please ring an ambulance, my eyes falling out. I'm dying. I'm dying."

Mrs Levy ran up the stairs, I could see her out of one eye. "What's the matter? What's going on?" She looked as white as a sheet.

"I'm dying, my eye's falling out. Please ring the fire brigade and an ambulance." I sat on the floor, gasping for air, feeling my pulse. There was nothing.

"Come on, get off the floor. You're alright." She helped me get up. "You're alright. Look you've frightened them all downstairs."

My eye wasn't so swollen now. As I looked in the mirror I could see a lash stuck in the corner. "If I was going to die, would I be dead by now?" I asked her, still gasping for air.

"I think so," Mrs Levy said. She looked very angry.

"I'll go back to bed now. You don't have to ring the fire brigade or ambulance."

I stayed in bed because I was so desperate to sleep. I knew if I went downstairs it would cause trouble, Melanie was getting very jealous when I spoke to Andrea. I dared not go near her mother or Melanie would attack me.

At work I was still separating the invoices. One morning when I arrived for work, the boss Mr Nicholas was already in his office. He walked over to me and my heart started racing. Please don't hit me, I thought to myself, cowering away so I wouldn't smell his body.

"There are no typists working today. You will have to sit at this desk, so you can answer the phone." I watched as he walked to another desk and brought the typewriter over, placing it next to the switchboard. He picked up the punch card machine from a desk at the other side of the room. I desperately wanted to be in the corner separating the invoices along the perforations. "I'll leave you to it." He walked back to his office. A light on the switch-board started flashing, my head felt like lead. I had no idea what to do. I flicked one of the switches.

"Mother, Mother! What's happened? I was talking to my Mother. I've been cut off," Mr Nicholas shouted from his office. I could see him rushing towards me.

"Did you cut me off?" His face was blood red.

"No, Mr Nicholas." I watched as he walked back to his office. "My Mother's deaf you know." He closed his office door. I felt relieved, only needing to stamp my foot once on the floor. Five minutes later he came back, this time waving a piece of paper. "Type this up for me. I need it straight away. Make three copies." He looked at me. "Why are you wearing your coat in the middle of summer?" I didn't answer him and started typing. I couldn't read his writing and there were no commas or full stops. I didn't know what to do. The phone rang. It was the manager from the Tipton office. It was difficult to say, "Good morning, this is G.A. Nicholas Limited, Electrical Wholesalers" when you have a stutter.

"Take this dictation over the phone," he said. I found a pen in the drawer and started to write down what he was saying. Mr Nicholas beckoned for me to pass him the letter I had just typed.

"Get my Mother on the phone." He pulled the letter off me. "She's deaf so you'll have to talk loudly. Her telephone number is in the book on your desk." I found the small brown book. Her number was on the first page. I started dialling. Mr Nicholas brought the letter back to me. "You haven't punctuated the letter. Where are the capital letters? There are words here I didn't write down." He put it down beside me and stormed off. My heart was pounding.

"Your mother's on the phone," I shouted after him. I looked towards his office, he picked up the phone.

"Mother, is that you?" He shouted very loudly into the mouthpiece. "Mother, is that you? You're not my Mother." I heard him shout.

I looked around as he slammed the phone down. He rushed over to me, he looked very angry.

"Sorry, Mr Nicholas." He didn't reply. He put a pile of invoices that had just come off the computer in the corner of the office and pulled the large table over.

"*I'll* man the switchboard, you separate the invoices," he said.

I felt sick with worry. What if he sacked me? How would

I pay Mrs Levy for my board? I knew I wouldn't be here for long. On the way home from work, I noticed a raincoat manufacturing factory; they were advertising for trainee coat machinists. Once home, I ate my tea and went to bed. Later on I heard a knock at the front door. I heard Mrs Roth's voice. I stood near the door so I could hear what was being said. They were standing in the hall.

"She won't unpack her suitcase or throw her used sanitary towels away. She won't change her clothes or have a wash. She has nightmares and wakes up screaming in the night. I don't know what to do for her. It's wearing us all down. She thinks she's dying. She wants us to call ambulances, the fire brigade."

"I had a telephone call from Mrs Brown. She's out of work from the end of next week. They don't want to keep her. Will you tell her in the morning?" I pushed the door to and got back into bed. I curled up and put my arms around myself.

"Don't worry, Hikey. I'll take care of you." I whispered.

The following day after work I stopped at the sewing machine factory to see if they had any vacancies for trainee machinists. The smell of the factory was familiar to me and the whirring noise of the sewing machines in action caused me so much pain I had to hold my tummy. It was difficult for me to keep my mind on what the supervisor was saying.

"I've always wanted to work on a sewing machine, my Mum was a machinist." The words poured out of my mouth.

"You can start a week on Monday."

"Thank you very much."

When I arrived at the office I was told to work a week's notice. I looked over to a young blonde woman sitting at her desk by the window. She was a comptometer operator, surrounded by complicated sets of machines with numbers on them. I wished I was as clever as her. Then I watched the young woman who walked over to the reception desk, each time the office door opened. "May I help you?" she would ask whoever had walked in. She was slim and nicely dressed, she never stuttered. I knew they were false, pretending to be nice and clean. I knew what they were doing with their fathers to get money for pretty clothes and makeup. I was glad I didn't have to do that anymore.

"You're a good girl, Hikey," I whispered.

At the end of the week I was handed my last wage packet, along with some holiday money. I looked in the envelope to see how much extra I had. I wished I could buy a carrier bag full of food to take home to my mum. I walked towards the bus stop.

"I'll write to Jeffery soon and tell him I was almost a punch card operator." I held the wall. I walked past a boutique. When I looked in the window I saw a midi coat and a pair of very baggy trousers, they were both very large. I knew they would hide me more than the clothes I was wearing. I didn't want people to notice me at the factory. That way I wouldn't get the sack. I wouldn't part with my duffle coat. That could stay in my suitcase.

I went into the shop and bought them with my holiday money. When I arrived home Melanie and Andrea had invited a friend around, called Beverly. She was Andrea's friend and studying fashion design at Salford Technical College. I showed them what I had bought. They were going to a disco nearby and asked me to go with them. First, I had to put the clothes I was wearing in my suitcase. I wouldn't part with them. Soon after we arrived at the disco I started feeling very tired and went home to bed.

The following morning I decided to go to the chemist to

buy myself some makeup. I wanted to be like them. The chemist was at the top of the road. My heart sank as I approached it. The chemist appeared from the back of the shop. I looked at him, smiling. I knew he was selling tablets to someone else's mum who needed them. I kept smiling at him so he would know how kind and helpful it was. He didn't smile back. "Can I help you?" He didn't look very much like the other chemist. I lowered my head.

"I would like some face makeup please."

He walked over to another counter, picking up three or four tubs of makeup off the shelf. "These are Leichner; they're very good. What shade would you like to try?"

"The dark brown one please"

"It's very dark, take a little and rub it on the back of your hand to see if you like the colour." I put a little on my finger and rubbed it on the back of my hand, until it had almost disappeared.

"If you rub it on your face like that, it won't last long and you'll damage your face. Do it very gently." I lowered my head again.

"I'll have that one." It was called 'Blend of Coffee'. I put it in my brown suede handbag. I felt very grown up. Once out of the shop, I checked my money to make sure I hadn't overspent. The sweet shop was just over the road. I was desperately hungry so I decided to go and buy as much chocolate as I could afford. I had paid Mrs Levy my board money. I was so tired and cold I couldn't wait to get back to the house, to have my tea and go to bed. After tea Mrs Levy was very quiet. She was sweeping. She carried on without lifting her head. I got frightened. I went to the bedroom. I pulled my suitcase out. I could see it had been moved. I had left it in the middle of floor under the bed. My heart started racing. I looked in it, my duffle coat had gone. My sanitary towels were nowhere to be seen. I looked around the room, they had disappeared. They were mine, no-one else's. I cried at the thought of losing them. I got into bed and ate all my chocolate. I heard the stairs creaking. I felt faint. My heart stopped.

"What are you doing, Jane?"

"Having a *shloff.*"

"I hope you haven't got any food in the bed." I pushed the blankets back off my face.

"I'm very hungry. Please don't hit me."

"Have I hit you in the past?"

"No."

"Well then. Go downstairs. It's not healthy to be in bed all the time. You need to wash your face.

"I'm very hungry and tired." I went downstairs to the kitchen and closed the door behind me. They were all quiet. I knew they didn't like me. I noticed a bag of bagels. I pulled one out of the bag and stuffed it in my mouth. If only the terrible hunger would go away. I knew nothing would make it better; only sleeping. Mrs Levy banged on the door.

"What are you doing?"

"I'm having a wash." I could hear them talking. It was muffled. Melanie was shouting and crying. I knew it was because of me. I washed my face, then went into the living-room and sat on the couch.

"Mrs Roth brought this for you." Mrs Levy handed me a paper bag. I opened it and took out a housecoat. I looked at Melanie and Andrea. I sat rigid.

"It's very nice."

"It's horrible," Melanie said. She looked at her mother.

"Don't talk to her," she shouted. Mrs Levy looked at me and smiled.

"You can wear it on Sunday morning when the girls wear theirs."

"Shut up Mum," Melanie shouted. I went upstairs.

Monday morning arrived. I had to be at the factory early to start my new job. When I arrived I was taken upstairs to the sewing machine section. The supervisor took me to her office. It was in the far corner of the room. I was taken away by all the smells and noises. I loved them. I wanted to cry.

"Are you listening to what I'm saying?" I hadn't heard a word. "I'll only be sewing won't I?"

"Yes," she pointed to the machines. Rows of them, all manned by people, their heads lowered over their machines in concentration as they worked. "This is your machine. I'll show you how to thread it. This is where you keep the oil. The machine has to be oiled regularly. This is the box where your bundles of material will be put." She carried on explaining what I had to do. I hardly heard a word. I felt comfortable with the surroundings. She passed me a bag of material, to practice on and she watched as I put two pieces of material together and started sewing in a straight line.

"That's very good, and you haven't pressed down to hard on the treadle. You have a light touch."

"My Mum was a machinist." I carried on sewing. I knew the machine would go out of control if I pressed down too hard. Mum had told me.

"You can practice all day today." I carried on until lunchtime.

The supervisor told me I was to go to the nearby café to collect the lunches. "You should take your coat off. You'll feel the cold when you go out." She handed me the list and money. The shop was across the road from the factory. I waited in the queue and handed my list in as soon as it was my turn. I realised my lunch hadn't been added to the list. I asked him to add one meat pie, two meat and potato pies, a bun and a Mars bar. That would fill me up. By the end of the week I had I had made my first coat backs and sleeves. I loved being near the machine. In the mornings I couldn't wait to go to work to be near it and my heart broke in the evenings each time I had to leave it.

Soon I was on piece work. Weeks had passed and Melanie was getting more and more jealous. Mrs Levy called Mrs Roth, complaining about my behaviour. Beverly called round to see if Melanie wanted to go out to a disco. She didn't feel like it. She asked Andrea and I to go, Melanie was very angry when I said yes. Mrs Levy said we should be home by 10pm. They didn't mind that I walked near to the wall and gasped for breath. At eight o'clock I was getting very tired. The desire to sleep was too great. I walked home. I put my key in the lock. I noticed my suitcase on the step. There was shouting coming from the house.

I looked at the case and ran. Mrs Levy opened the front door and shouted to me. I ran and ran, crying. I didn't know where to go. I ran towards the Sarah Laski Home. I was banging on the front door. A woman opened it.

"My name's Jane Levene. Please can I come in? I haven't got anywhere to go?"

"You'll have to go to the Matron's office."

"Matron, can I stay here? Can I have something to eat? I'm very tired."

"Yes, you can stay. I'll have to ring Mrs Roth." I stayed in the room while she rang her.

"Mrs Roth will come and see you tomorrow evening."

"Please can I have something to eat?"

"Yes, you must have a bath after you've eaten."

"I will." I headed for the kitchen. I opened the fridge door. There was so much food, I couldn't believe it. I took six eggs and grated some cheese, then put them in the frying pan to cook. I couldn't wait and had a cheese sandwich while the omelette was cooking. My heart was racing. I found some food to hide up my sleeve so I would have some to take to bed. The Matron came into the kitchen. "Have you any nightclothes?"

"No."

"You can sleep in the large bedroom. I'll bring you some nightclothes." I went upstairs to bed. "Here, I've got you some things."

"I'm alright. I need to sleep. Please don't close the door in case a fire breaks out."

"I have to close the door. It's a fire door." She left the room and I fell asleep.

CHAPTER 26

My body was shaking. I opened my eyes. One of the night staff was leaning over the bed. I was sweating, my heart pounding.

"You're having a nightmare. It's time to get up. You have a job don't you?"

"Yes, I'm learning to be a sewing machinist. Like my Mum." I wiped the sleep from my eyes. "I'll do the washing up."

Sitting down to eat as many bowls of cornflakes as possible, I still felt the lingering feeling of horror from the dream. I wanted to sleep again to see if I could see my mother's face.

"Mrs Roth will bring your case later," the Matron told me. I waited till everyone had finished eating, and started to clear the pots off the table. I could see plenty of leftovers. I couldn't wait to get into the kitchen to eat them.

"I'm going to work now, Matron. You won't forget I'm coming back after work, will you?" She looked at me.

"No."

I left the home and hurried to the bus stop. "I shouldn't have been nice to her because she hates me," I mumbled to myself. I knew they were all talking about me, saying how stupid I was. She won't trick me into being nice again.

My work was ready waiting for me when I arrived. "I'm putting you on backs and sleeves today." The supervisor leaned over my machine. "I'll show you how to sew the stand into the collar. This is the stand. She showed me the small piece of material. They're used to strengthen the collar. She explained very carefully, and left me to finish my work. It was difficult to concentrate on what I was doing. It took me a long time to finish. The supervisor walked over to me. "You'll have to hurry, this is a rush order. I want you to do me a favour. Go to the cutting room upstairs and ask for a long stand."

The cutting room was very quiet, only a few people worked on that section. "Can I have a long stand, please?" I asked the man directing the band knife through the material.

"Yes, of course." He carried on working. I waited for about five minutes.

"Please can I have a long stand?" I repeated.

"You've had one, what do you want already, to take root." There was a roar of laughter.

"Here take this to the supervisor, tell her it's the tartan cotton she asked for."

"OK." I went back downstairs and handed the cotton to the supervisor.

"It's the tartan cotton you asked for." She smiled.

I sat at my machine trying very hard to make as many belts and collars as possible, so I could buy plenty of food for myself. Mrs Roth was waiting for me when I arrived back at the Sarah Laski Home. She was sitting in the Matron's office.

"We're going to have to work something out. You're fifteen so you are too old to stay here."

"Yes, Mrs Roth."

"Mrs Levy told me you kept your used sanitary towels in your suitcase. Is that correct?"

"I don't know. I'm going to have something to eat now.

I'm starving." One of the staff walked into the office.

"Your tea's ready. It's in the kitchen. You can have a bath then watch the television."

"I'll go to bed after my tea." I walked into the kitchen. I could see a plate with two sandwiches on. My heart sank.

"That will never fill me up," I whispered. I rushed back to the office. "Please can I have the crusts as well, with some cheese?"

"Yes. Don't forget to wash up after yourself, and have a bath."

Mrs Roth didn't appear again for a few weeks. She left a message to say she would call on Sunday. I awoke Sunday morning and wondered what Mrs Roth wanted to see me about. I went downstairs for my breakfast. I was very hungry. I had some money and decided to go to the nearest delicatessen for some food. I walked towards Cheetham Hill Road, passing King David School. I looked away. I couldn't bear to look at it. Levy's was the nearest delicatessen. As I walked through the shop door the different smells brought memories flooding back, I wanted to cry and huddle in a corner tightly, to stop myself remembering. I bought some herring and chopped liver. I pushed them into my pocket and went to the bakers to buy some bagels and onion buns. I pushed them all down in my pockets. I started walking back towards the Home. I realised I didn't belong anywhere, or to anyone. "Don't worry, Hikey, I'll take care of you."

Arriving back at the Home, I went back to my room. After lunch Mrs Roth arrived. I was called to the Matron's office. Mrs Roth was waiting for me.

"We've got to find you somewhere to live."

"Yes."

"I've been in touch with a woman who is advertising in the Jewish papers for a lodger. She's divorced with twin daughters. They're a few years younger than you. She will cook for you. You'll have your own room. We'll go now and see her."

I breathed a sigh of relief. If she was divorced there would be no man in the house. Mrs Roth's car was parked outside the home and we were heading towards Cheetham Hill Road.

"It isn't far." My mind wandered. I hoped I wouldn't get the sack from the sewing factory.

The house was off Cheetham Hill Road. It was a street away from Auntie Doris's house. Mrs Roth pushed the gate open. I followed her to the front door. "This is Jane." I didn't lift my head. I wondered if she had any cake in the house.

"Jane, this is Sybil. Say hello."

"Hello," I said, half smiling. We went into the living-room.

"Look, Mrs Roth. I want a lodger. I'm a single working mother. I haven't got time to devote to another child."

"If you foster Jane you'll get more money." Sybil and Mrs Roth carried on talking for a while. "Fine then, Jane will move in as soon as possible," Mrs Roth said.

As I looked around I knew they didn't like me. I wasn't like them.

"Would you like to see your bedroom?" Sybil asked.

"Yes, please."

"You can call me Sybil." I followed her upstairs. The house was modern and nicely furnished. I wished my mother could live here. She showed me the bathroom. I frowned to myself. I didn't like it. It was like them, false and unreal. "This is your bedroom." It was a very small bedroom, decorated in blue, like the rest of the house.

"Would you like a cup of tea and a biscuit?"

"Yes, please."

We went downstairs to the living-room. Mrs Roth was talking to the twins. I could see she liked them. They were nice Jewish girls. She could see how nice and clean they were. They knew how to speak English properly. I sat on the edge of the couch. Sybil had gone to get the tea and biscuits. I counted the seconds till she reappeared. The twins took one biscuit each. There was one left for me. It wasn't enough.

"Where are you working?" Sybil asked.

"In a sewing factory. I make backs and sleeves, like my Mum." She took the cups and plates away. I looked at the twins.

How could they survive on one biscuit I thought to myself?

"You can move in tomorrow. Come here after work."

"Can I stay at the Sarah Laski Home?"

"No," Mrs Roth replied. She turned to Sybil. "She'll move in tomorrow." Mrs Roth took me back to the Home. I went to bed. I could hear footsteps on the landing.

"Where are you, Jane," It was the Matron.

"In bed," She put her head around the door.

"What's that smell?"

"Chopped herring,"

"It's all over your face. Go and wash it off."

"Is supper ready? I'm coming back to collect my suitcase tomorrow. Can I have my tea here?"

"No. Mrs Roth's taking it to your new home." It was very difficult to sleep that night. I didn't need to ask for a bag so I could put things in it for my mum. I looked at the wardrobe. It was the one I had found the white cardigan in with flowers on when I had visited my mother in hospital. I got out of bed. I looked at the vests and knickers. They wouldn't fit me anymore. I laid them on the floor and fell asleep on them. I didn't want to have any nightmares. I didn't want to feel the pain of having to leave the Home again. The Matron woke me and told me to put all the clothes back in the wardrobe.

It was time for me to leave for work. I had eaten as much as my tummy could hold. The Matron was in her office. I asked if I could take a sandwich for my lunch. She was sitting at her desk. I wanted to lift my skirt to show her where it hurt, I wanted her to put a bandage and some cream on to take away the pain. I said nothing.

"Get yourself a sandwich. Good luck with your new home."

I hardly noticed the day pass. My huge bundle of backs and sleeves were finished: neatly stacked at the side of my machine. I walked out of the factory and headed towards the bus stop, wondering about my new bed. I was desperate to sleep. I hoped that Sybil would make a big tea for me. I felt dazed as to where I belonged. The bus stopped. I listened to my heart. "Best get it going before I go into Sybil's," I whispered.

Bookbinder's bakery was in sight, I promised myself one of their large bilberry pies, but they were closed.

I knocked on Sybil's door. "Your case is upstairs. Mrs Roth dropped it off for you. Wash your hands. Sit down with the girls. Tea's ready." My heart sank, it was like the children's homes. We all sat at the table. There were four small plates on the table each had a small amount of chopped liver and a piece of *Matzo* on. My heart sank. I knew that would never fill me up.

"Take your coat off before you eat." Sybil told me. I took no notice and carried on eating. "Go and take your coat off." I took it off and she showed me where to hang it. I felt extremely cold, hungry and insecure without it. I didn't like her for making me part with it. I wished the food was hot so it would warm my body.

I looked at the twins. They were still eating. I couldn't understand how they could survive on such small portions. I knew they were pretending to eat nicely. Chewing every little bit of their food. I knew they really wanted to stuff it all down their throats as quickly as possible. Sybil left her seat and took one of the twins into the kitchen with her.

"Pickled meat and chips; do you like this?"

"Yes, please." I hoped my plate would be full of food. She handed me the plate. It wasn't the portion I had hoped for. I watched as they put their knives and forks down on the plate while they rested for a minute. I didn't do that. I ate mine quickly. "Can I wash the plates?" There were no leftovers. I wished for morning to arrive so I could have breakfast.

"Go and watch the television," I got my coat off the hanger, put it on. I sat on the couch in the corner. The twins were playing a game on the floor. It was false to play games like nice little girls. I wanted to be on my own in bed asleep.

"I'm going to bed now. I'm very tired." I pulled the blanket off the bed and wrapped it around myself. I woke up in the middle of a nightmare. Trembling, I felt very cold and hungry. My door was slightly open as usual. I couldn't hear anyone. I couldn't bear the hunger any longer and decided to creep down the stairs to the kitchen. It was difficult to open the fridge doors without making a noise. I noticed a small plate with some chopped liver on. My heart was pounding. I was desperate to eat. Very carefully I ate half the amount, remoulding the rest on the plate so she wouldn't notice. Next I opened the cupboard door and found a biscuit tin. I eased the lid off very gently and sat on the floor with the tin open on my knee. I ate the biscuits, sobbing at the relief of feeling the food in my mouth. I crammed them in one after another, leaving me enough time to take a breath between mouthfuls. Most of the biscuits had been eaten, as well as the crumbs lying at the bottom of the tin. I noticed jars of jam and honey in the cupboard. I grabbed them, eating as much as possible.

I crept back to the bedroom. Wrapping the blanket around myself, I slept till morning.

I was woken by the sound of the bathroom door banging.

"You can use the bathroom now. Don't have a bath, there isn't enough water."

"OK, Sybil." I filled the sink with water, splashing my hands in it.

"Breakfast is ready." I sat at the table eating my bowl of cornflakes and toast.

I'm going to have to do a lot more work at the factory, so I will have more money for food. I thought. "Can I have some crusts, Sybil?"

"Yes. Did you come downstairs last night?"

"No."

I arrived at work and rushed to the supervisor's office.

"Please can you give me some more work?"

"You need to improve quality and speed. Then you'll be on full piecework. Some of these girls make a lot of money."

On the way home from work, I counted my money. I had more than usual as the Matron hadn't taken any board off me.

All my clothes were getting too small because I had put on a lot of weight. I got off the bus at Heath Street. There was a small material shop. I bought two patterns; one for a large midi coat, the other for a pair of baggy trousers. I chose black material. That would hide me. I couldn't wait to get to work in the morning to start making them. "I'm making them for you, Hikey."

I noticed that Bookbinders was still open. They had large plate bilberry pies in the window. I bought one and some bagels. My tea was ready on the table when I arrived at Sybil's. First I put the pies and bagels in my bedroom ready for later. I hid the food under the pillow. After tea I went to my room. I pulled the blanket off the bed and wrapped myself in it. The photographs of mum were on the bed where I could see them. The food was beside me on the floor. I opened the door slightly in case of fire. I ate all the food as quickly as possible. Soon my tummy was full and I felt drowsy. The papers from the food were beside me on the floor. I felt comforted.

Sunday morning arrived. Sybil woke early. She wanted me to collect my dirty washing so she could show me how to use the washing machine. My old clothes were in my suitcase, in case I had to move house again. Sybil noticed a piece of bilberry pie on the sheet. It was stained. She was very angry. I could tell by the way she stormed up and down the stairs.

I had found David's address in the telephone book. "Can I go and see David?" I started trembling at the thought of Anita.

"You don't have to ask me. Tidy your room before you go. You will have to take more care with my property."

"Yes Sybil. Sorry."

The 81 bus stopped around the corner on Greenhill Road.

On the way there I made sure I had all the air in my lungs that I needed so my heart wouldn't stop. I practiced saying their names so I would get them right. I knocked on the door of the house. Anita opened it.

"Can I speak to David, please?" I looked through the window. I could see him sitting on the couch looking down at the floor. He was wearing clean socks and new clothes. He looked around at me. He stayed on the couch and I sat on an easy chair. Anita sat next to Morris. "His teeth were green when we got him. We had to take him to the dentist. That cost plenty. He had *no* manners. I'm having to teach him everything. We're his family now!"

Her voice was making my head ache. I wanted to cry.

"Your mother shouldn't have let you eat food that wasn't kosher: we're having to spend a lot more on food now. Kosher food is more expensive than *traif*. David told me your mother used to get second-hand clothes for you all and sell them for money for cigarettes, Morris smokes, that's OK we have the money to buy them."

I watched her mouth. Her words penetrated me like a knife. I looked at David. He tried to raise a smile.

"Morris, tell her about yesterday. We paid a lot of money for good shoes for him. What did he do? He walked in a puddle; it was raining. He knows no better. I knew your mother. She let your father make her pregnant so he would have to stay with her. She told everyone she had a bad case of wind. She knew she was pregnant. We wanted to adopt him when he was a baby. She wouldn't let us. A good job she made of it. I don't think so. We've bought David a dog. We're his family now. Me, Morris and 'Pepsi'. You make a life for yourself."

She kept talking, my ears closed to her words.

"We've got to go to the *B'selem* now. We do things right in this household. We're good Jews. The rabbi said." She opened the door for me. "David has plenty of family now. Uncles: one's a solicitor in Israel. Nice cousins. That's all he needs."

I said goodbye to David and mimed that I loved him. He seemed too frightened to respond.

CHAPTER 27

I had been living with Sybil for some time. Mrs Roth called at the house to tell me she had arranged a holiday for me in Southport. An elderly Jewish woman had agreed to let me stay with her for a week. I asked the supervisor at the sewing factory if I could have a week's holiday. It was all arranged.

The day of my holiday arrived. I didn't need to pack my case. I got the bus to the train station in town. I was told that the woman would meet me at the station in Southport. I boarded the train. "What if this isn't the right train?" My heart was banging. "Excuse me. Is this train going to Southport?" I asked two women sitting nearby.

"Yes, we hope so; that's where we're going." I looked at them. They didn't seem sure. I felt faint. The train on the opposite platform started to move. Perhaps that's the train I need to be on? I felt a terrible sense of dread in case I got lost. I would never see David again. Standing up, I ran to the door and opened it. A couple were getting on the train.

"I don't think this is the train for Southport." They turned around and asked the porter.

"Yes, it is. It'll be pulling out in a few minutes, the whistle's blowing now." I sat down, not sure about anything. I decided to sit near the door in case the train crashed. I knew mum, Jeffery and David needed me. I didn't want to leave them on their own. The train jolted and started moving forward.

"*Shama Yisroel*, please God," I whispered to myself. Each

time the train stopped at a station, I waited, looking out of the window, perched on my seat with my suitcase on my lap, double checking in case I missed the stop. The train started to slow down again. I couldn't see the name of the station, it was too far away. People started collecting their luggage. I could see the sign; it read Southport.

"*God sei dank*," I whispered out loud, banging my foot on the ground. I followed all the other people to the exit, handing my ticket to the guard. What if the woman forgot about me. Where would I sleep tonight? I was tired and needed to go to bed.

"Are you Jane Levene?"

"Yes." I half smiled.

"There's a lady waiting for you."

A grey haired lady was walking towards me. She looked nice and clean. I wanted to cry, I knew I didn't belong to her. I wished I was back in Manchester in my bedroom. "My car's in front of the station." I followed her, hoping she had plenty of cakes and biscuits at home. I sat in the back of the car. I wasn't sure where I was going. It felt as if I was being taken to the children's home. "We're almost there." I looked out of the window. All the houses were very large. My heart sank. They had large gardens full of flowers. "We're here. Bring your suitcase." I followed her to the front door, my head bowed, waiting for her to tell me what to do. "Bring your case upstairs. I'll show you where you will sleep." I knew I didn't belong here. "Unpack and leave your case under the bed, I'll go and make us a cup of tea. Would you like a piece of cake?

"Yes, please. I'm starving. I haven't eaten for ages."

"Fine." She smiled. I looked around the room. It was huge. I frowned.

"Here we are." She placed the tea tray on a small coffee table and sat down.

"Have you been to Southport before?" She handed me a piece of cake.

"No." I watched the plate, wondering if she was going to eat what was left.

"Would you like some biscuits?"

"Yes please. I'm starving." She went into the kitchen and brought some more cake and biscuits.

"Mrs Roth tells me you're a sewing machinist."

"Yes, I make backs and sleeves."

"Would you like to go for a walk, when you've finished eating?"

"No, thank you. Can I stay here with you?"

"Do you have a boyfriend?" I lowered my head.

"No. Are you going to make me have one?" I put my plate down on the table and waited for her to reply.

"No, dear, finish your tea."

"Can I go to bed please, I'm very tired."

"Yes. What would you like for your evening meal?"

"Anything."

I stayed in bed sleeping. In the evening she knocked on my door. Tea was ready. Walking down the stairs I could smell the food. The table was set in the kitchen. My heart raced, not knowing if I should speak to her or not.

"I've made meatballs. Do you like them?"

"Yes, thank you. Have you got any crusts?"

I heard the sound of a fire engine siren outside. I ran upstairs, got my suitcase from under the bed and ran downstairs. I hid under the table, crouching, praying that I wouldn't burn to death.

"What on earth are you doing under there?" she said, lifting the table cloth. "It was only the sound of a fire engine."

"Is the house on fire?" The sweat was pouring off my body.

"No. However, your meal's going cold." I crawled out from under the table. "Take your case upstairs." The meatballs and potato *kuggle* were delicious. She gave me two crusts. A big bowl of Danish Apple turnover with custard followed.

"You've got a healthy appetite, haven't you?"

"Yes, I'm always starving hungry." After we had eaten I asked if I could ring David. I wanted to tell him I was on holiday in Southport.

"Hello, Anita speaking."

"Hello Anita. Can I speak to David?"

"No." The phone slammed down.

"Have a bath. I'll bring you some fresh towels. Are you going to put some clean clothes on?"

I didn't answer. After filling the bath I sat on the floor looking around. The heat from the bath made the room feel warm and comfortable. The bathroom cabinet door was slightly open. I sat wondering what was inside it. I decided to take a look. There were bandages, all sorts of tablets and a packet of razor blades. I took one out of the packet and pressed it gently on my finger tip to see how sharp it was. I sat back on the floor and loosened my trousers. "Jane Levene the smelly baked bean," I whispered. The razor blade was still held firmly in my hand and I grabbed a handful of pubic hair with my other hand. My heart was racing, my head felt so heavy I could hardly keep my eyes open. I slashed the blade across the hair. I laid them in a pile beside me. I could see some blood. My heart was racing even faster. I looked at my body. I was my mother. In my head I smelt my father: I didn't know who I was. Soon, there was a pile of hair on the floor beside me. I couldn't bear to throw it away and stuffed it into one of my pockets. I held the razor blade and started prodding myself with the corner of it. The flesh between my legs was soon swollen out of all proportion and I could see more blood. I went to bed and slept. When I awoke, it was dark. My heart was racing and pounding. I could smell fire. I was back in Delamere. I got out of bed, stamping my foot to restart my heart.

"What are you doing?" she shouted up the stairs.

"Nothing." I wrapped myself in some blankets, took my photos out of the case and curled up behind my open door. Soon I fell asleep.

The following morning I could hear the woman talking on the phone. I wondered if she was talking to Auntie Doris or Mrs Roth. I didn't know what I had done wrong. I waited for my punishment. I heard the stairs creaking. I waited expectantly.

"Get up dear. Have a bath. Would you like to go into town later? There's a nice department store. They do lovely afternoon tea. Would you like that?"

"Yes, please."

She had her handbag and was looking for her car keys.

"Did you have a nice relaxing bath?"

"Yes, thank you. Look I'm nice and clean. Honestly."

"Come on. We'll go for a drive."

It was time to visit the department store. We had a look around. She took me into a large seating area. I could see tables full of sandwiches and cakes.

"Sit down"

"We'll have afternoon tea for two." The waitress brought over a large three tiered cake plate full of sandwiches and cream cakes. "I'll pour the tea. Take some sandwiches."

I piled my plate with different sorts of sandwiches. Eating them, not noticing anyone else, I was in a world of my own.

"Have a cake."

"Thank you, how many?"

She laughed. "Take as many as you like."

I ate and ate. Soon I wanted to sleep. "What are we having for breakfast in the morning?"

"Boiled eggs and toast,"

I didn't reply, it was still difficult to pronounce 'egg.' "That sounds good."

"We'll go to the delicatessen mid-morning. Get some bagels? Would you like that?"

"Yes, please. That would be nice."

Sunday morning, she knocked on my bedroom door.

"Come on, breakfast is ready. Then we'll go to the delicatessen."

The familiar smells hit me as soon as I opened the shop door and walked in. I looked around the shop recognising the young man behind the counter.

"Are you Sidney?" He looked at me.

"Yes."

"Did you used to work for Levy's on Cheetham Hill Road?"

"Yes."

"Did you know my Mum, Annie Levene?"

"Yes."

"She's dead now."

"I know. I remember when you were a little girl. Mrs Levy would give you bits of meat that had fallen off the slicing machine and smoked salmon skins."

"I remember that."

"Mrs Levy went to school with your mum."

"I didn't know."

I looked to see what the woman was buying. I noticed she had ordered plenty of food.

"How many bagels am I allowed?"

"Three." We put the food in the car and drove back to the house.

"Set the table. Make sure you use the *fleishik* cutlery, I'll take you to the train station after lunch. "Come on. We'll go for a drive before the train's due."

I sat in the car on the back seat, looking out of the window, wondering where I was and what part of me belonged to the woman who was driving the car.

CHAPTER 28

It was good to be back in Manchester. It was late afternoon. I waited for the bus to take me up Cheetham Hill Road. I checked in my suitcase to make sure I had the three bars of rock that I had bought for Sybil and the twins. It was a struggle to get the key in the lock, my hands shaking in case Sybil had cause to be angry with me. One of the twins was behind the door. She had heard me struggling and opened the door. Sybil was in the kitchen.

"Hello Jane," Sybil shouted from the kitchen.

"Hello Sybil. I bought you all some rock from Southport." She kept looking me up and down. I didn't know what I had done wrong.

"You've put on so much weight. I've never in my life known someone double in size. You've only been gone a week. What have you been eating?" I lowered my head.

"Do you think you should go on a diet? Your clothes hardly fit you."

I looked at her my whole body went into a state of shock.

"I'm very, very hungry. What's for tea? It smells good."

"Take your suitcase upstairs and get washed."

I started back at work the following day. I was now working on PVC and 'Borge' fur lined coats and sleeves. I had finished my first bundle. The supervisor collected them and left me another one.

"The PVC's really catching on. All the orders coming in are for PVC trench coats. Did you enjoy your holiday?"

"Yes, thank you." I carried on sewing, wondering what I would be having for tea.

"Jane, *look* at this." My heart started racing. "I've explained to you time and time again about this overstitching. That's nothing. Look at these sleeves; they're OK till you get to the cuff, then they flare out. Do you know how much this material costs? These will have to be binned. Don't you listen when I explain things? You've got cloth ears. I've got to tell you this. Some of the girls have complained about your personal hygiene."

"I need to go to the toilet." My head was heavy and I needed to sleep.

"Don't be long. What do you do in there, for God's sake?"

When I got home there was a letter for me. It was an invitation to David's *Bar Mitzvah*. It was to be held at the Holmes Kosher functions establishment. I thought of all the people who would be going. I didn't like the thought of it. I wanted to stay in bed. The telephone rang.

"Jane, Mrs Roth is on the phone," Sybil shouted.

"Hello, Mrs Roth."

"Did you enjoy your holiday?"

"Yes."

"Is something wrong?" she asked.

"I've got an invitation to David's *Bar Mitzvah*."

"You'll enjoy that, won't you?"

"No. I don't think so."

"Have you got a dress to wear, some nice shoes?"

"No. I don't know what I'll wear, but I hope there's plenty of food there"

"Meet me at the boutique on Bury Old Road after work tomorrow evening. I can get you a good discount."

After work I made my way to the boutique. Mrs Roth was inside talking to the assistant. I walked in and felt very uncomfortable. I liked the clothes I was wearing. The black trousers and midi coat were part of me now. I didn't like the place, the dresses or the assistant. I wanted to curl up and die. Mrs Roth was browsing along the rails. "Have a look, see what you like. Look, they have shoes, over by the wall. Go on, pick yourself a pair." After a while she handed me two dresses. One was black, a high neck, with gold buttons. The other was beige with a small collar. "Try these. I'll choose some shoes."

"Alright, Mrs Roth."

"Go into the changing rooms. Try them on." I didn't want to take my clothes off. I looked at myself in the mirror. All I could see was my mother. How would these dresses fit me? They seemed too small. I sat in the changing room, looking at the dresses. They were someone else's dresses, not mine.

"Are you ready, have you tried one on yet? It's getting late."

"I won't be a minute." I took off my midi coat. That was all. I looked at the beige dress. I didn't like the colour. It wouldn't hide me. I put the black one on over my jumper and trousers. I walked out of the cubicle. "I like this one."

"It looks very smart. You'll have to wear it on its own for the *Bar Mitzvah*. Do you hear?" I frowned.

"Yes," I replied. The assistant folded it and put it in a bag. I paid for it and headed for the nearest bus stop, glad the ordeal was over.

The day of the *Bar Mitzvah* arrived. I woke up in the morning with all the same atmospheres I felt during *shiva*: not wanting to hear the praying and chanting; wanting to stay in bed and sleep. It was time to go to the reception. I was in the grounds of the Holmes, at the main doors. People were milling about everywhere. "*Mazel Tov*," was being said every two seconds. David was standing in the corner with Anita and Morris. I felt lost. I didn't belong here. David looked stunned. I wanted to grab him and take him home. He was my brother. I should be looking after him. The sound of the *Mazel Tovs* brought me back to reality once more. Auntie Doris and Eric walked into the big hall. I could see them talking to Anita and Morris. I watched as all the people were being ushered into the dining hall. I was one of the last to go in. Everyone was seated. I noticed the top table, covered with a brilliant white table cloth. Anita, Morris and David were sitting together. Auntie Doris and Eric were sitting beside them. I started walking towards the top table.

"What's your name?" A young woman asked me.

"Jane Levene," I replied. "Your table is over there." She checked her list and pointed to a small table for two in the corner of the room, near to the exit. There were two place names on the table settings. Jane Levene and Jeffery Levene. I desperately wanted to be at home in my bedroom asleep. I watched very carefully as the waitresses walked in, laden with plates. I watched them walk out of the room and return with silver platters full of food. The waitress came to my table, and lowered her platter beside me. She started to pile the food onto my plate. "Can I have some more please? I'm very hungry." My throat ached for food. My head felt so heavy with all the dark feelings I had ever known.

"Well you'll have to make sure you've room; there are four more courses." She smiled and walked away.

"I'll manage them," I whispered. I didn't take any notice

of what was happening around me. My plate was full to brimming. It would make the pain disappear for a short while. I stopped eating. I thought the food had caused a blockage in my intestines. My heart stopped and I couldn't breathe. I stamped my foot on the floor, it made no difference. My life was ebbing away. I looked to the exit doors and ran out of the big hall. I saw a sign leading to the toilets. I looked in the mirror. I knew I was nobody. If only I could get all the food out of my intestines I would live. Then it dawned on me that I would feel better if I could get more food into my stomach. I could feel full for longer. I stood in the cubicle pushing my fingers down my throat till I could feel myself heaving, my fingernail scratching the back of my throat. My eyes and nose were watering. "That'll teach you, Jane Levene the smelly baked bean." The darkness in my head lifted. I rushed back to the table. There was plenty more room for the next three courses and supper at Sybil's. I looked over to David's table. They were all laughing and joking. I ate the last scrap of food and decided to leave. I wanted to sleep.

Sybil was watching the television when I arrived home. I managed to get some biscuits and a piece of cheese without disturbing her. I was looking forward to being near the sewing machine at work.

After work I rushed to get the bus. Jumping off the bus I noticed Bookbinders was still open. "Please can I have a piece of cheesecake, a bilberry pie and an apple pie?" Rushing to my bedroom, my heart pounding, I wrapped the blanket around myself and stuffed all the food down my throat, relishing the short peace of mind which followed. The crumbs from the cheesecake were scattered on the floor I picked them up one by one, making sure nothing was left uneaten. It wasn't enough. My tummy desperately needed more food. I looked through my pockets and found some change. I rushed out of the house to the nearest shop. It wasn't a kosher shop. I bought a tin of Heinz chicken soup, a sliced loaf and a packet of chocolate biscuits. Back at Sybil's I found the tin opener and put the soup on to heat, eating the biscuits at the same time. I touched my breast. "Don't worry, Hikey, I love you. I know Mummy." Soon the soup was boiling hot and I poured it into a bowl. I looked through the fridge and cupboard, to see if there were any bits of food, but Sybil hadn't done the shopping, there was very little. I looked through the waste bin, to see if there were any scraps. It was spotlessly clean. Sybil had tidied up. Rushing upstairs with all my food, I huddled behind the door. The bowl of soup was on my legs. Ripping up most of the bread I put the bowl near to my mouth, starting to eat as quickly as possible. I finished my last mouthful of soup. My trousers were unfastened so I could cram everything in. I lay down. The front door slammed. I knew it was Sybil. I stayed very still for a moment in case she came upstairs.

"Jane, I know you're in, get down here quick." I hurried downstairs, my heart banging, my head feeling like razor blades were slicing through it.

"What's the matter, Sybil? What's wrong?"

"What's wrong?" She shouted "I'll tell you what's wrong. I have *never* cooked anything in this house that isn't kosher! I'll have to throw this pan away!" She lifted the pan from the draining board and threw it out the back door. "My house isn't kosher anymore, because of you. Do you hear? I'll have to ring the synagogue and ask the rabbi what to do. He'll probably have to come and kosher the house again!"

I ran out the front door, wondering where I could go.

There was nowhere. Then I remembered Beverly. She lived off Waterloo Road in Salford. It wasn't far. Running all the way and checking my heart, I found the house. Her sister was playing outside. "Is Beverly in?" I was trembling.

"Yes."

"Please can I speak to her?" Beverly came to the door.

"I can't stay at Sybil's anymore. I've un-koshered the house."

"Sit down I'll make you a cup of tea," Beverly's mother said. "There's a Polish lady not far from here. She takes in lodgers, on Cluney Street." Beverly and I walked around the corner and knocked on the door.

The Polish woman told me the attic room had just become vacant and offered to show it me. I followed her upstairs, to the top of the house. She opened the attic room door, it was very small, over the bed hung a picture of Jesus. I looked at it, hoping he wouldn't realise I was Jewish. "You can cook on this." She was leaning over, turning the dials on a small 'Baby Belling' oven. "I will change the bed for you once a week. The rent is thirty shillings. Do you want it?"

"Yes, please."

"Do you work?"

"Yes, I'm a machinist. I make backs and sleeves."

"In the evening you can come and watch TV with me and my husband." I shuddered at the thought.

"That's OK. I get very tired. I'll stay in bed."

"When would you like to move in? tomorrow?"

"That would be very nice. Thank you."

We went back to Beverly's house. They couldn't afford a television and went to bed early. I slept on the sofa. Beverly's mother brought me a cushion and coat to cover myself with.

She tucked me in and kissed me on the forehead. "Night night," she whispered, turning off the light. I pulled the coat over my head and wrapped my arms around myself. A few hours later I woke up. Beverly's mother had put the light on.

"Are you OK? You were having a nightmare." I looked at her, trying hard to focus. She was wearing wellingtons. "I've got to wear these because of the cockroaches scurrying on the floor." She switched off the light and I pulled the coat over my head once more. I could hear them moving around the floor. I left the house early the following morning to go to work. I waited at the bus stop. Perhaps Mum's still alive? I hadn't been back to the flat to check.

After work I made my way to Upper Park Road to visit the flat. Stepping off the bus, I could hear singing and chanting. Four *Yeshivah Bochers,* were walking by the side of the school, going towards the *Yeshivah,* it was raining and two of them had Tesco carrier bags pulled over their huge black hats. '*Doved Melech Yisroel*,' they were singing. I watched them till they disappeared into the distance. It took my mind back to when some of the children from King David School dressed up a dummy as a rabbi for bonfire night. They sat it next to the wall of the *Yeshivah,* it was wearing a *Tallis, Teffilin* and a *Yamulkeh.* Around its neck hung a cardboard sign: *A penny for the goy* was printed in large black letters.

The rain brought me back to reality. I was very hungry and tired, it was difficult to keep myself upright. I decided not to visit the flat. I walked back towards my lodgings. All the houses were the same: little, old and decrepit Victorian terraces. Some of the streets were being demolished. Walking down one of the streets I noticed a narrow black line a few feet in front of me. As I approached I could see it was a line of cockroaches going from one of the demolished houses, they were all crossing the road to another house. I watched them; they must all have been members of the same family, moving house. I was pleased they had each other. I waited till they had all passed. Walking around the corner, I could see the house. The front door was slightly open. I knocked on the door and the Polish woman appeared. "Go, your room is ready." She handed me my key. Her living-room door was open, the smell of her husband's body made me freeze. "Go. Everything is ready for you. Come down, watch TV with us."

I walked up the flights of stairs, past the bathroom, until I reached the small attic door. I put my key in the lock and pushed the door open. The picture of Jesus still hung over the bed. I looked away from him quickly in case he came to life. I closed the door and went over to the small cupboard under the Baby Belling to see if there was any food in it. It was completely empty. I had two bars of chocolate in my handbag. My stomach was hurting me. I pulled my trousers down. I could feel blood. I looked at it and felt comforted.

I awoke early the following morning. It was difficult to get myself out of bed. I straightened my clothes. Before lunch the supervisor came over. "A lady brought this and asked me to give it to you." She placed my suitcase from Sybil's down on the floor. It was difficult to get through all the work the supervisor had given me. I looked around and noticed all the girls were talking and looking my way. I could see the supervisor approaching. "I want to talk to you. Some of the women have complained about your personal hygiene. Do you use a deodorant?"

"No."

"Well, I think you should."

"OK." I carried on with my work. When I was nearly home I bought some meat and potato pies and chocolate. I went upstairs and put them under my pillow. I got into bed and curled up. I started pulling at the pies, frenziedly eating them. I looked at the picture of Jesus to see if his eyes moved or he had turned into a monster. I was going to say the *Shama* but I didn't think he would like it.

Weeks passed. I was still at the flat on Cluny Street. At work the supervisor approached me. "You must do something with yourself." She looked stern, walking off.

"Yes."

I passed a job agency on my way home. Looking in the window I noticed a job vacancy for a live in chambermaid, in the Lake District. I thought about it for a few moments and went in. I was interviewed by a young man.

"What's your name?"

"Jane Levene. I'm not Jewish. I'm British not English."

"Right, um, well. I'll ring the hotel in Bowness."

"You can start as soon as possible. Is that suitable for you?"

"Yes. Thank you." I replied.

GLOSSARY

B'selem: In this instance, cemetery.

Drek: Dirt.

Fleishick: Meat.

Frum: Orthodox.

Gaygazunterheit: Go in good health. Spoken with irony.

Grobbo tochos: Large posterior.

In dread: In death. Said with irony.

Ipish: Stink.

Loch in Kop: Hole in the head: something definitely not needed.

Mazel Tov: Good luck.

Meshugginah: A mad person.

Mezuzah: A passage from the Torah, placed inside a wooden or metal case that is attached to the doorpost of a Jewish house. Thought to protect from evil.

Nebach: In this instance: poor little thing, said with irony.

Nisht gut: Not well.

Oitskimatted: Exhausted.

Ribizon: Cheese grater.

Sheitle: Wig worn by Orthodox women.

Shiksah: Non-Jewish woman.

Shnorrer: One who habitually takes advantage of the generosity of others.

Shul: Synagogue.

Tallis: Prayer shawl.

Tefilin: Two small leather, leather boxes with straps. Used at prayers.
Traif: The opposite of kosher.
Tsorris: Suffering, woes.
Yeshiva: Institute of learning where students study sacred text.
Yeshivah bocher: Student.